Biblical Lionesses
Protectors of the Covenant

Biblical Lionesses
ஐ *Protectors of the Covenant* ೞ

By Diana Webb

Copyright 2014 Diana Webb
All Rights Reserved

ISBN: 9781611660845

Edited by Josh Leavitt
Cover design by Kent Minson, Y Mountain Press

Preface	1
Introduction – *Pass It On*	7
Chapter 1 – *Sarai, Wife of Abram*	13
Chapter 2 – *Ordeal in Egypt*	20
Chapter 3 – *Fateful Decision*	31
Chapter 4 – *Mother of Nations*	39
Chapter 5 – *The Birth of Laughter*	51
Chapter 6 – *Sarah's Legacy*	63
Chapter 7 – *Seeking Rebekah*	73
Chapter 8 – *Wooing Rebekah*	81
Chapter 9 – *The Revelation*	90
Chapter 10 – *The Blessing*	96
Chapter 11 – *Jacob's Quest*	108
Chapter 12 – *Rachel and Leah: The Agony and the Ecstasy*	118
Chapter 13 – *The Baby Derby*	128
Chapter 14 – *Rachel's Legacy*	137
Chapter 15 – *In the Beginning*	150
Chapter 16 – *Making Sense of the Rib Story*	161
Chapter 17 – *The Two Trees*	170
Chapter 18 – *The Consequences of Mortality*	180
Chapter 19 – *Conclusion*	187
Glossary	193

Preface

Several years ago, I attended BYU Women's Conference. I was a member of one of the service committees, and we stayed in the dorms—I even slept in a bunk bed. Although I spent most of my time overseeing the distribution of crochet-edge flannel blanket kits, I was able to catch a few of the speakers that were broadcast in the Martin Building. The very first talk I heard was the keynote address offered by Relief Society General President Julie Beck, entitled "Choose Ye This Day." She talked about Rebekah and her impact on the house of Israel.

I have been a different person since I heard that talk. It was an answer to prayer. The women of the Old Testament have fascinated me for many years. Twenty years ago, I wrote a master's thesis called *Portrayal of the Matriarchs in the Old Testament Pseudepigrapha*. (How's that for a soporific title?) The thesis explored the way matriarchs like Eve, Sarah, Rebekah, Rachel, and Aseneth—the wife of Joseph of Egypt—were portrayed in stories outside the Bible. And that, I thought, was that.

And it was, until 2009 when I got an unexpected phone call. The man on the other end of the line was Jeff Marsh, a BYU religion professor who had helped me with my thesis fifteen years before. He was working for a publishing house that wanted to put out a book about the women of the Old Testament, and he wondered if I would be interested in publishing my thesis as a book. In the end, the publishers decided that they were more interested in the relatively unknown women like Aseneth. They weren't interested in the matriarchs at that time, only the "forgotten" women. So, I found twenty other lesser-known women and gathered stories from Jewish tradition. *Forgotten Women of God* came out in 2010. It was a great idea for a book, and I really felt that those stories held a message for women everywhere. I thought, however, that the stories about the other women needed to be told, as well. Especially Rebekah. She was my favorite.

Once that project was finished, I turned my attention to writing a family history for my husband's family, the Webbs. I had previously written a book for my family, the Bartons, and thought it would be nice to do the same for my husband's family. But it was not going well. A spiritually sensitive friend asked me, "Have you prayed about it? Are you sure you are supposed to be doing this book right now?"

Her question took me aback. I answered that in fact, I hadn't prayed about it, because I thought it was a "no brainer." Didn't the Lord want us all to write our family histories? "Not necessarily," she said. "Timing is everything. You should pray about it." So I did. When I was writing the book about my parents and their ancestors, the Barton family, amazing things fell out of the sky at my feet almost daily. My father's wife brought me five orange boxes full of slides from my Barton grandparents; an old mimeographed program from the Sixth/Seventh Ward where my dad was listed as the deacon's quorum president, with Thomas S. Monson as secretary; and my father's handwritten life story from when he was a teenager. My second cousin "accidentally" found a web site on the Jeppeson line when she searched for my Grandpa Peterson on Google. (I had already tried that the month before with no results. My newfound "cousin" had just posted it that week.)

There was no question in my mind that I was supposed to write that book. I felt a power beyond myself propelling me forward.

That very week, I went to BYU Women's Conference and heard Sister Beck's talk. Right off the bat she talked about Rebekah, and how she had been studying about her in the Old Testament for months. I immediately heard bells go off in my brain because I had been thinking so much about her as well. Sister Beck talked about Rebekah being one of the women at the head of the house of Israel. This meant a lot to Sister Beck because her father had passed away just ten days before, and he had shared some important thoughts with her during the last week he was alive. He asked her to think about what her mission was as a member of the house of Israel, and why we are here on Earth. He was very impressed that one of the greatest reasons we are on Earth is that we are to pass on the blessings of the house of Israel, the blessings of the fullness of the gospel. He saw this responsibility as a "panorama" in which the passing of the torch of faith and covenant to our posterity is our purpose before the Lord.

Sister Beck said that Rebekah was one of the most pivotal and important people in the history of mankind, and certainly in the house of Israel. She emphasized that without Rebekah—a woman worthy to receive revelation and capable of recognizing it for what it was—the house of Israel would not have been brought forth. Rebekah knew her responsibilities and acted accordingly.

The lesson Sister Beck said she learned from all this study was that each and every woman in our day is as important to the current generation of our families as Rebekah was to hers. Each of us is pivotally important to our families, and we each need to understand our place in the house of Israel and our mission on the earth. Sister Beck stated emphatically, "The success of the house of Israel is now dependent on millions of Rebekahs who understand their place and mission on the earth."[1]

As I sat there, I thought, "Here I am with fifteen thousand active, faithful, scripture-reading women at this conference, and I bet that it is the minority who even know what Sister Beck is talking about. It is time for Rebekah's story to be told." If every woman needs to be a Rebekah to her family, she should know what that means.

Rebekah was a powerful woman because she listened to the spirit of revelation. *She recognized God's will for her family, and she acted upon it.* Having the spirit means *knowing God's will and doing it.* It is the potency of personal revelation. Sister Beck has said, "The ability to qualify for, receive, and act on personal revelation is the single most important ability that can be acquired in this life."[2] With the Lord's spirit, every woman—no matter her circumstances—can know what to do. No matter her social status. No matter her level of education. No matter her intellectual abilities. Sister Beck said that when women have the Spirit of the Lord upon them, they become powerful women. They can discern God's will and solve major problems in their lives. "Education is wonderful," she told us, "but being able to feel the Lord's power and Spirit upon us is the highest education we can achieve."[3]

Perhaps her speech's most arresting image is that women are like lionesses at the gate of the home. I thought, "Wow! If that doesn't describe Rebekah protecting the son she knows is supposed to carry on the covenant, I don't know what does." Sister Beck said that the things that matter to the lioness at the gate of that home matter to that family. The lioness at the gate ensures that the covenant will be carried forth within the walls of that home. If the lioness at the gate is aware of the mission of the house of Israel, then that mission will go forward. It is very difficult to get a lion cub away from a lioness unless she believes wholeheartedly that the cause that draws her cub away is for the benefit of the house of Israel and for the continuation of the everlasting covenant. That's how important the lioness is.

Sister Beck told each woman at the conference that she was like the lioness at the gate. Each woman wields power and influence that she cannot even imagine. This means that she needs to make sure she is giving top priority to the absolutely essential things for her family. And how does she know what these top priorities should be? *Revelation*.

Rebekah must have had a direct connection with her God. She went straight to the Lord about the future of the twins struggling within her. She found out that the elder would serve the younger. She *knew* this before they were even born. The Lord confided in her the future of his covenant line. She never wavered in her determination to make it happen. If Rebekah had failed in any part of her responsibility, the house of Israel would never have come forth. Sister Beck emphasized that Rebekah knew and understood the importance of her mission, even though she never lived to see the outcome of her commitment. The blessings she brought to pass are only now unfolding after all these thousands of generations. Sister Beck said, "The house of Israel is being gathered up, the temples being built. This is what she invested her life for."[4]

It is our privilege today to be part of the house of Israel. We need to be lionesses. We need to be Rebekahs. I would like to present to you a few lionesses of the Old Testament who show how to live righteously, with a fierce commitment to follow the Lord's will. If you are a member of the house of Israel—in spirit, if not in blood—these women are your great-grandmothers.

The biblical text that records the lives of these amazing matriarchs of the covenant is very sparse. The author of the record found in the book of Genesis has measured his words carefully. We have limited instances of dialogue between these women and those around them. What *is* recorded is minimal, and we readers are left on our own to flesh out these sometimes bare-bones accounts. In attempting to convey the personalities of these noble women, I have studied the words of many scholars and rabbinical sources. (A glossary listing these sources can be found at the end of this book.) I realize that these are the ideas of men, and not prophets. However, I believe that truth can be discovered in many places, and if there is anything "true" or "praiseworthy," we should "seek after these things."[5] We have been given the gift of the Holy Ghost that we may discern truth from non-truth. We encourage investigators of our doctrine to pray and ask God to "manifest the truth" unto them by the power of the Holy Ghost.[6]

When Joseph Smith inquired of the Lord whether he should include the Apocrypha in his translation of the Bible, the Lord answered that it was not necessary. "There are many things contained therein that are true, and it is mostly translated correctly; There are many things contained therein that are not true, which are interpolations by the hands of men" (D&C 91:1–2). Those who read the material with the Spirit would be able to discern the truth themselves, and did not need a prophet to translate it for them. "Therefore, whoso readeth it, let him understand, for the Spirit manifesteth truth; And whoso is enlightened by the Spirit shall obtain benefit therefrom; And whoso receiveth not by the Spirit, cannot be benefited" (D&C 91:4–6). Those who read the scriptures with the Spirit do not need to be spoon-fed. That is the purpose of the Gift of the Holy Ghost. Joseph Smith writes that there are many things therein that are the "interpolations" of men, but that "there are many things contained therein that are true." It is up to the reader to read these things with the Spirit to discern truth, and thereby receive the "benefit therefrom."[7] The prophet Joseph recognized that there is benefit to be gleaned from a study of these apocryphal writings, but that we will miss obtaining these benefits if we do not invest time in reading them with the Spirit.

During my graduate studies at Brigham Young University, one of my favorite classes was "Apocrypha and the Latter-day Saints," taught by Stephen Robinson. Dr. Robinson made this scripture from D&C 91 the theme for the class. There was much truth to be gained from these extra-canonical books, but it was not easy to recognize without the Spirit. We had to be miners, carefully examining every nugget to see if it contained any gold. We students were under obligation to seek those golden nuggets of truth and to place them in their proper place in the grand repository of truth we had already received in the restored gospel. If we did so, we could be "benefitted therefrom."

Elder Boyd K. Packer includes a poem in his book *Teach Ye Diligently* that emphasizes this principle.

> We scholars toil on with the zeal of a miner
> For nuggets and nuggets and one nugget more,
> But scholars are needed to study the uses

> Of all the great mass of data and lore.
> And truly our tireless and endless researches
> Need yoking with man's daily problems and strife,
> For truth and beauty and virtue have value
> Confirmed by their uses in practical life.[8]

We do not study just to become great scholars. We do so in order to enrich our lives, the lives of our families, and the lives of those we serve. I have included the ideas of these rabbinic scholars and others because I want to increase my understanding of the great matriarchs I look up to and love. These scholars were seeking to understand the scriptures they possessed. There was no living prophet around to fill in the whys and wherefores of the biblical narratives. These individuals used their ingenuities and imaginations to explain why certain things happened the way they did. We will not know whether they were correct unless we read what they have to say with the Spirit of truth. When I encounter truth, I find I don't have to choke it down. It slides right down and fits in with what I already know to be true.

---

[1] Julie B. Beck, "Choose Ye This Day," Keynote speech at BYU Women's Conference, April 29, 2010.

[2] Julie B. Beck, "And Upon the Handmaids in Those Days Will I Pour My Spirit," *Ensign*, May 2010.

[3] Julie B. Beck, "Choose Ye This Day," Keynote speech at BYU Women's Conference, April 29, 2010.

[4] Ibid.

[5] See Article of Faith 13 in the *Pearl of Great Price*.

[6] See Moroni 10:4-5. "And when ye shall receive these things, I would exhort you that ye would ask God, the Eternal Father, in the name of Christ, if these things are not true; and if ye shall ask with a sincere heart, with real intent, having faith in Christ, he will manifest the truth of it unto you, by the power of the Holy Ghost. And by the power of the Holy Ghost ye may know the truth of all things."

[7] See again Doctrine and Covenants 91:5.

[8] Boyd K. Packer, *Teach Ye Diligently*, (Deseret Book: Salt Lake City, Utah, 1979), 271.

Introduction
Pass It On

Much of the story of the Old Testament deals with the bestowal of the covenant between God and man. It begins in the Garden with Adam and Eve. There were problems, obviously. The children of Adam would not live the covenant, and God had to raise up a new heir who *was* worthy of it. We see the covenant pass down through Enoch, who so inspired his people to righteous living that they created a Zion society. This society was taken from the earth—it was too *righteous* to live any longer on the earth. Noah's society was at the other end of the spectrum—it was too *wicked* to remain on the earth any longer. Samuel Dresner expresses this point eloquently when he writes

> After nineteen generations of disappointment, God found a righteous man and entered into an eternal covenant with him. The covenant with Abraham is a narrowing to a single person what was meant from the very first for all humankind. From Abraham it was to reach, in succession, one family, one people, one land, and, in the end of days, all lands and all peoples.[1]

Abraham is placed where he is in the chronology of the history of mankind that he might sustain all those generations who will follow after him. It is quite a sobering thought to consider—that the Almighty God would enter into an everlasting covenant with a frail human being. Moreover, that this God would have unwavering faith that this precious endowment would survive to be passed on to the rest of his children. Will Abraham find a way to hand down this newly formed covenant with his God to the next generation? Or will this new bond be short-lived, ending in the same generation as it begins?[2]

The essence of the patriarchal story of the Old Testament is the struggle to successfully pass on this vital covenant to the next generation—to ensure that the recipient of this legacy is fit, strong, and fervent in his or her commitment to continue the transmission of the covenant to the next generation. That is the whole story of the Old Testament—the success or failure of the children of God to receive his covenant, live it, and pass it on. This is the purpose of the plan of eternal families today. To impart to them the covenant of the gospel, teach them to live it, and to pass it on to their own children, who will in turn pass it on to their children. Julie Beck has repeatedly emphasized the necessity of passing on the legacy of the gospel covenant in her addresses to members of the Church of Jesus Christ of Latter-day Saints.

> We know that we cannot achieve eternal life without the ordinances and covenants of the restored gospel of Jesus Christ. We find other teachings about living the commandments, serving, and giving away all we have to the Lord, but all of those things are based on the covenants we make. Without those covenants, we cannot achieve eternal life. That's why we share the gospel and prepare missionaries because Heavenly Father says, "All my children need to be taught and given an opportunity to make the covenants that will save them." That's why we build temples because Heavenly Father says, "All my children need an opportunity to make these covenants." So we do vicarious work for those who have died. Heavenly Father wants every one of His children to have an opportunity. That's why we teach the gospel to our youth, so they will understand and make and keep the covenants that they need to receive eternal life.[3]

In ancient times, it was customary for the eldest son to inherit the birthright from his father, the firstborn son enjoying special privileges. However, the transmission of the covenant in the Old Testament was so important that even the time-honored law of primogeniture sometimes had to be broken, so that the priceless covenant would be received by a righteous beneficiary. Neither Isaac nor Jacob is the firstborn; Ishmael and Esau enjoy the rights of primogeniture. Yet both younger sons receive the birthright and the covenant from their fathers. Although the law is clear, neither one of these firstborn sons is deemed qualified to be entrusted with the mission of receiving the covenant and handing it down. The patriarchs and their righteous wives had to face the challenge of circumventing the custom of the birthright going to the firstborn son, if that son was not worthy to receive such a blessing.

This is the mission given to the patriarchs and their wives—to ensure that the covenant survives. This will only happen if it is *received* and then *transmitted* to the next generation. The key to the continuity of the covenant is to establish this pattern: receiving, and then handing down. It seems simple enough, but as parents of the rising generation can attest, it is not as easy as it sounds. What the patriarchs receive *must* be passed on, or the covenant will not survive. God would have to find another people and another way to make it happen. Talk about pressure on a patriarch or matriarch! The scripture about "the world being wasted at his coming" comes to mind.

As we reconsider the stories of the patriarchs and matriarchs in the Old Testament in light of this absolute necessity to preserve and pass on the covenant, the intrigues and shenanigans that baffle us take on new meaning. The stories of Abraham and Sarah, Isaac and Rebecca, and Jacob and the sister-wives Rachel and Leah can only be truly understood if we realize that they all have one special mission—they are to accept and transmit the covenant with God.[4]

Sarah, the first of the matriarchs, is seen in the biblical narrative as a woman as noble as her husband, Abraham. Like Abraham, she leaves her home and family to journey to a new land. She joins her husband in bringing comfort to travelers, speaking with angelic messengers, and bringing souls to the true faith. Jewish tradition recounts that Sarah is the ultimate sister missionary, teaching the women of Haran about the one true God. She is entrusted with the responsibility of making sure the covenant is passed to the son designated by the Lord as the heir. According to scripture, Abraham is satisfied to have the covenant go to Ishmael, his eldest son, but Sarah believes the Lord when he says that the covenant will be with Isaac through her (see Genesis 17:21). She does what she feels is necessary to bring that about, and to Abraham's sorrow, she has Hagar and Ishmael removed from the family circle.

Isaac must endure, unimpeded, as the heir of the covenant. Living in Canaan as he did, taking a wife from among such an idolatrous people would endanger the crucial process of receiving the covenant and handing it down. Marriage to a pagan woman could not be tolerated. Therefore, the chapters of Genesis record the elaborate search for the perfect wife for Isaac. The scriptures carefully record the considerable lengths Abraham and his servant go to in ensuring that a union with a local Canaanite woman does not take place.

Where could a faithful wife—one who would not only embrace the sacred covenant, but also pass it on to her children—be found? Abraham and Sarah conclude that such a wife could only be found in a place removed from the corruption surrounding the land of Canaan. They decide to send their trusted servant Eliezer back to Sarah's family in Haran. There, he discovers Rebekah, a woman with all the strength, courage, and kindness necessary to carry on the covenant, and be fit for a man such as Isaac.

Abraham receives the covenant directly from the mouth of God, and it is sealed in a dramatic fashion in Genesis 15:17, when God passes through the middle of the divided sacrificial animals in a flame of fire, sealing his end of the covenant. Yet Isaac endures his own brand of drama in being bound to the covenant. Abraham is commanded to sacrifice his miracle son on Mount Moriah as a test of his faithfulness. But he is an old man, Isaac a young adult. Isaac could have easily overcome his father if he so desired, but seeing the knife in his father's hand and being bound upon the altar, he tacitly acquiesces to his father's will in the matter. It is inconceivable to imagine that a man over a hundred years old had the strength to bind a young man in his prime. For Christians, this incident has become a powerful metaphor, symbolizing the willingness of the Savior to be sacrificed on Calvary. Isaac was not a passive participant in the ordeal on Mount Moriah. He, too, struggled to find faith in Abraham's God. His faith had to be strong enough that he was willing to face death for the sake of the covenant. No, it was not just a test for Abraham; Isaac too had his mettle tested.[5]

Even with the help of Isaac's righteous wife Rebekah, only one of their twin sons is worthy to bear the responsibility of the covenant. The successful passing of the covenant to Jacob is due largely to Rebekah's insightfulness and initiative. She and Isaac watch in grief as Esau takes Canaanite women as wives, heedless of his responsibility to the covenant. Rebekah ensures that the covenant does not go to the firstborn, who despises his birthright and is unfit for it. She takes action to guarantee that the birthright is transferred to Jacob—who, although he is the younger son, is worthy and faithful.

After Jacob has obtained his father's blessing and the birthright, Rebekah becomes concerned for his present safety and future prosperity. She speaks to Isaac about her concerns that Jacob would make a marriage with the world, as Esau had. Consequently, Isaac encourages his son to travel to Padan-aram and take a wife from Rebekah's family. Besides the first blessing Jacob receives from his father (Genesis 27:28–30), he also receives the "blessing of Abraham," which was given from God (Genesis 26:3–5). Isaac promises him *land* in addition to the blessings of *posterity* (Genesis 28:1–4). The Abrahamic blessing joins the inheriting of land to the mandate to be a blessing to all the nations. This can only be accomplished by marrying a wife who also accepts the covenant, so no marriage with a pagan wife can be tolerated. Thus, the promise of land is made conditional: "You shall not take a wife from amongst the Canaanite women (Genesis 27:46, 28:6)."[6]

Thus we see that the bestowal of the covenant and the transmission of that covenant to the next generation is so crucial to the establishment of a holy people that it occupies over half the pages in the book of Genesis. The patriarchs—Abraham, Isaac, and Jacob—received the covenant, but the difficult task of passing it on required the presence of a righteous woman. Sarah, Rebekah, Rachel, and Leah play major roles in the successful transmission of the indispensable covenant.

Sarah emerges from the pages of Genesis as a noble pillar of strength, not one whit behind her husband in spreading the doctrine of the one true God and in nurturing all who cross her path. Isaiah invites straying Israel to hearken back to her parents, Abraham and Sarah.

> Listen to me, you who pursue justice, you who seek the Lord.
> Look to the quarry you were dug from, look back to Abraham your father and to Sarah who brought you forth (Isaiah 51:1–2).

Sarah joins Abraham in fostering the covenant in Isaac, and in making sure that he is given a righteous companion to advance the cause of transmitting the covenant.

Rebekah is no less pivotal in passing the covenant forward. She has the vision and the resolve to ensure that the birthright goes to Jacob and not to her eldest son. She converses with God personally—not relying alone on the prayers of her husband—to find out what the events in her life signify. She acts on her firsthand revelation from God regarding the destiny of her family. She influences her husband to bless Jacob and send him to a land where he can find a righteous wife who will pass the covenant on to the next generation.

Rachel, too, is obsessed with the concept of succession, "for the matriarchs play as important a role in accepting and handing down the covenant as do the patriarchs."[7] The continuity of the covenant hangs on the birth and loyalty of each individual child. Rachel's love story in the book of Genesis is unparalleled in biblical history, indeed in much of world literature. But even possessing the love of an adoring husband cannot fill her emptiness without a child. The focus of her life is evident in the name she chooses for her firstborn son: Joseph, which means "he will add." She still desires that God will yet "add another" son to her posterity.

Tammi Schneider comments, "The primary role of women in Genesis is to determine who will inherit the promise from the Israelite Deity."[8] Throughout the chapters of this book, we will explore the stories of these matriarchs who so valiantly labored to pass on the covenant. Besides the Bible, other non-canonical sources will be cited to round out the sparse stories of Genesis, and to more fully flesh-out the women who were responsible, in large part, for the transmission of the covenant. They are the grandmothers of the entire house of Israel.

I pray that you may have the Spirit with you as you read about these valiant matriarchs: Sarah, Rebekah, Rachel, and Leah. I have also included Eve in this collection because, although not a matriarch *per se*, she is the archetype of all womankind. She is *the* matriarch. I saved Eve's story for the end, however, because I wanted the messages learned from Eden to linger and be fodder for much pondering.

---

[1] Samuel H. Dresner, *Rachel*, (Minneapolis: Fortress Press, 1994), 4.

[2] See Dresner (1994), 4–5.

[3] See Julie Beck, "Teaching the Doctrine of the Family," *Seminaries and Institutes of Religion Satellite Broadcast*, August 4, 2009.

[4] See Dresner (1994), 6.

[5] See Dresner (1994), 9–10.

[6] See Dresner (1994), 13.

[7] Dresner (1994), 16.

[8] Tammi J. Schneider, *Mothers of Promise: Women in the Book of Genesis*, (Grand Rapids, Michigan: Baker Academic, 2008), 16.

Chapter 1
Sarai, Wife of Abram

The matriarch Sarah is first introduced in the Bible in Genesis 11:29 after a long line of "begats."

> And Abram and Nahor took them wives: the name of Abram's wife was Sarai; and the name of Nahor's wife, Milcah, the daughter[s][1] of Haran, the father of Milcah, and the father of Iscah.

Not much of an introduction for the future mother of nations, but commentators are quick to flesh out the bare bones of Sarai's genealogy. Because Haran died leaving behind two unmarried daughters—Milcah and Yiscah (Sarai)—Abram and his brother Nahor each marry one of their orphaned nieces in order to preserve Haran's memory. Solomon Ben Isaac, the famous Rashi—the eleventh-century commentator from Troyes, France—goes on to say that Sarai's alternate name, Yiscah, is from the Hebrew root *sacho*, which has several meanings: "to foresee, to view, or to possess royal bearing." He comments that all three highlight Sarai's qualities: Sarai can "*see* into the future with Divine inspiration," "the people *viewed* her beauty," and that she had a "*royal bearing.*"[2] This is a great deal to derive from just a name, but thanks to Rashi we now expect the mother of nations to be prescient, exquisite, and elegant.

The next verse adds an astonishing pronouncement. "But Sarai was barren; she had no child" (Genesis 11:30). We readers are not prepared to hear so soon that this great matriarch is unable to bear children, a woman's greatest dread in the ancient world.

Abram and Sarai leave their home in Ur of the Chaldees and settle in Haran, along with his father, Terah, and his nephew Lot. As the story continues in the next chapter of Genesis, we see that Sarai's barrenness is no barrier to her effectiveness as Abram's wife. Rather than wallowing in self-pity at her childlessness, she becomes actively involved in her husband's activities, losing herself in reaching out to those in need. She is able to surmount the stigma of barrenness and find a useful place in her husband's work.

In Haran, God speaks to Abram and makes grandiose promises to him.

> Now the Lord had said unto Abram, Get thee out of thy country, and from thy kindred, and from thy father's house, unto a land that

I will shew thee: And I will make of thee a great nation, and I will bless thee, and make thy name great; and thou shalt be a blessing: And I will bless them that bless thee, and curse him that curseth thee: and in thee shall all families of the earth be blessed. So Abram departed, as the Lord had spoken unto him; and Lot went with him: and Abram was seventy and five years old when he departed out of Haran. And Abram took Sarai his wife, and Lot his brother's son, and all their substance that they had gathered, and the souls that they had gotten in Haran; and they went forth to go into the land of Canaan; and into the land of Canaan they came. (Genesis 12:1–5)

Few details are disclosed in the biblical text concerning Abram's and Sarai's activities while in Haran, but tradition from many sources fills in the blanks. Pirke de Rabbi Eliezer relates that "[Abraham] made for himself a house opposite to Haran and he received everyone who entered into or went out from Haran, and he gave him to eat and to drink. He said to them: Say ye, The God of Abraham is the only one in the universe."[3] Abram provided not only prodigious hospitality, but also profound preaching.

Accounts of the magnitude of Abram's hospitality are abundant.[4] Angelo Rappoport writes that Abram is a master of hospitality, feeding hungry wanderers as they journeyed. He builds a "sumptuous palace" where he plants a garden with fig and other fruit-bearing trees, and offers of his abundance to all. Hungry and thirsty travelers are offered food and drink as they pass by, and they are invited to rest their weary bodies upon one of the couches. Beneath his shady trees, weary travelers can always find rest and protection from the "burning sun of the east."[5]

Not only does Abram reach out to weary wayfarers with life-sustaining sustenance and nourishment, he offers them spiritual succor, as well. Rappoport describes how Abram would greet a guest who worshipped idols. After offering them refreshment, he would say, "Eat and drink, my friend, and bless the Lord who feeds the needy." He would wait upon each guest as a servant waits upon his master, and speak to him about the "loving kindness of the Lord, of Him who had created Heaven and earth, and all its creatures." Rappoport emphasizes that Abram would never leave a man who worshipped idols until the man had "opened his eyes and begun to understand the power and love of the Lord of the Universe."[6]

In all this ministering labor, Sarai is not one whit behind Abram. Rabbi Adin Steinsaltz states, "[Abram] and [Sarai] were not just a 'married couple' but a team, two people working in harmony."[7] Commenting upon the meaning of the phrase "the souls that they had gotten in Haran" in Genesis 12:5, he asserts that this does not refer to slaves, but rather to those they have converted, those who have acquired their faith through Abram's and Sarai's ministering efforts, Abram converting the men and Sarai the women. They work as partners, laboring together for the same goals, "walking together along the same path, united in thought, word, and deed." Rabbi Steinsaltz observes that "this is the kind of relationship that was common only in a much later age, perhaps only in modern times, and was certainly extremely rare in ancient times."[8] *Midrash Rabbah* corroborates the tradition that "Abraham converted the men and Sarah the women."[9]

The legend of this noble couple's good works was widespread in the ancient Near East. Rappoport notes that as Abram's fame spread far and wide, "all the lowly and oppressed, the needy and the miserable, the suffering and the downtrodden, the hungry and the naked, came to him to seek solace and help." These he received with open arms, feeding and clothing them, comforting and consoling them, and tenderly wiping away their tears. Sarai was ever present in "sharing the charitable work of her aged husband." She worked tirelessly day and night assisting Abram, waiting upon travelers and offering them food and drink. She spent her nights diligently "weaving, with her own hands, garments to cover the naked." She "sought wool and flax and worked willingly with her hands," although she was aged and wealthy by the standards of the day. "Her candle never went out at night, from Saturday to Saturday."

The more these two labored for the benefit of the poor and needy, the miserable and the afflicted, the greater their fame grew. "The "Lord blessed their work, and they became a blessing." When Abram's guests would kiss his hand and thank him for his consolation, he would reply, "The Master, mine and yours, my friends, is the Lord of the Universe."[10]

Although his wife is "barren," Abram has become the "father" to many souls in Haran, and childless Sarai has become their mother. God calls Abram and his wife to leave all the success and wealth they have known and depart for an undisclosed location, promising them spectacular blessings. What does this all mean to Abram? This is an astonishing request made to an aging man with a barren wife, and the command is made even more profound by the fact that Abram doesn't even know where he is going.

Bruce Feiler provides some knowing insights into the reactions of Abram to God's words. Who does Abram think is making this promise? Later generations conclude that Abraham understands that the voice belongs to God, specifically the one and only God. However, "[Abram], far from the complete monotheist of Moses, still retains echoes of the polytheism of his ancestors. He is a transitional figure, with a foot in both worlds. If anything, this position makes his trusting Yahweh even more remarkable." Rooted in a polytheistic society—a world where "gods had form and physicality and were identified with tangible facets of daily life, like rocks and trees—he is prepared to put his trust in an … indiscernible, unprovable god." In essence God is saying, "I want you to have total trust in me, [Abram.] You're not going to know where your next meal is coming from. You're not going to know where your next home is. If you're going to be in covenant with me, you have to trust me with every cell in your body. And if you do that, I will bless you."[11]

These stories about Abram are important in Sarai's narrative because they express the sacred nature of the world of these two amazing people. As Abram's wife, Sarai's life is totally involved in the things of God—his work, his voice, and his promises. She and Abram are a team. Abram is devoted to her. *Midrash Rabbah* notes that Abraham "acted lovingly toward Sarah."[12] The Stone Edition of Genesis states, "Abraham always honored his wife by pitching her tent before his own."[13]

James Strahan describes the kind of wife Sarai was to Abram. She always "called her husband 'Adoni'—my lord (see Genesis 18:12). … [The] word is weighted with all the love of a lifetime." When Abram ventures forth in faith, leaving his homeland to live the life of a nomad, enduring trials and afflictions, Sarai is "always by his side, lightening the way he traveled, doubling his joys and dividing his sorrows, ordering the peace and comfort of his house, cheering him to face all hardships with constancy of mind, and sometimes in hours of temptation and danger putting him to shame by her quiet-hearted heroism." Sarai has the courage of a true and noble woman. She is a regal princess, "in name and in nature. She understood her husband's divine vocation, shared his religious aspiration, and never ceased to be his true helpmate."[14]

Abram and Sarai's journey to the promised land is long and difficult. En route, Abram receives a visit from the Lord, who promises the land to him for an inheritance.

> And Abram passed through the land unto the place of Sichem, unto the plain [(Hebrew) oak] of Moreh. And the Canaanite was then in the land. And the Lord appeared unto Abram, and said, Unto thy seed will I give this land: and there builded he an altar unto the Lord, who appeared unto him. And he removed from thence unto a mountain on the east of Beth-el, and pitched his tent, having Beth-el on the west, and Hai on the east: and there he builded an altar unto the LORD, and called upon the name of the Lord. And Abram journeyed, going on still toward the south. (Genesis 12:6–9)

Later, the Lord tells Abram, "Arise, walk through the land in the length of it and in the breadth of it; for I will give it unto thee" (Genesis 13:17). Here, the Lord tells Abram to walk around the land, for it is to be his inheritance from God. The modern mind does not understand the ramifications of such an ancient rite, but Anne Roiphe offers insights as to the purpose of this practice:

> Walking about the perimeter of property was a common legal ritual in the ancient Near East for taking final possession. The conveyance of property was expressed in this manner in Ugaritic texts composed in the fourteenth and thirteen centuries B.C.E.[15]

A severe famine strikes the land, and Abram and Sarai decide to journey to Egypt, where food is plentiful. This seems like a logical solution, but the trip to Egypt develops into a character-testing trial for them both.

---

[1] Kent P. Jackson, *The Restored Gospel and the Book of Genesis*, (Salt Lake City, Utah: Deseret Book, 2001),151 fn 3. Jackson notes that in the first printing of the book of Abraham text in 1842, Sarai and Milcah were identified as "the daughters of Haran," making Sarai Abram's niece. See *Times and Seasons*, 1 March 1842, 705.

Tuchman and Rapoport in *The Passions of the Matriarchs* also render this verse as "daughter[s]." See Shera Aranoff Tuchman and Sandra E. Rapoport, *The Passions of the Matriarchs*, (Jersey City, New Jersey: KTAV Publishing House, 2004), 3–4.

[2] Shera Aranoff Tuchman and Sandra E. Rapoport, *The Passions of the Matriarchs*, (Jersey City, New Jersey: KTAV Publishing House, 2004), 3–4.

[3] Gerald Friedlander, *Pirke de Rabbi Eliezer: The Chapters of Rabbi Eliezer the Great According to the Text of the Manuscript Belonging to Abraham Epstein of Vienna*, (New York: Hermon Press, 1965), 184.

[4] S. Baring-Gould, *Legends of the Patriarchs and Prophets and Other Old Testament Characters From Various Sources*, (New York: John B. Alden, 1885), 214.

"Abraham planted a grove in Beer-sheba, one hundred ells long and one hundred ells broad, (an ell equals 45 inches) and he planted it with vines and figs, pomegranates and other fruit trees; and he built a guest-house adjoining this garden, and he made in it four doors, one towards each quarter of the heavens; and when a hungry man came by, Abraham gave him food; if there came a man who was thirsty, he gave him to drink; if one who was naked, he clothed him; if one who was sick, he took him in and nursed him; and he gave to every man who passed by what he most needed for his journey.

"He would receive neither thanks nor payment; and when any one thanked him, he said hastily, 'Give thanks, not to me the servant but to the Master of this house, who openeth His hand, and filleth all things living with plenteousness.' Thus Abraham instructed those whom he relieved. And if a traveller asked further, how he was to worship the great God, Abraham answered, 'Say only these words, Praised be the Eternal One who reigns over heaven and earth! Praised be the Lord of the whole world, who filleth all things living with plenteousness.' And no traveller went on his way without thanking God. Thus that guest-house was a great school, in which men were taught the true religion, and gratitude to the Almighty God."

[5] Angelo S. Rappoport, *Myth and Legend of Ancient Israel*, Volume 1, (The Gresham Publishing Company: London, 1928), 276. Original spelling preserved.

[6] Ibid.

[7] Adin Steinsaltz, *Biblical Images: Men and Women of the Book*, (Basic Books: USA, 1984), 21.

[8] Steinsaltz (1984), 24.

[9] H. Freedman, *Midrah Rabbah: Genesis, Volume One*, (New York: The Sconcino Press, 1983), 324. See also S. Baring-Gould, *Legends of the Patriarchs and Prophets and Other Old Testament Characters From Various Sources*, (New York: John B. Alden, 1885), 186.

[10] Rappoport (1928), 276–277.

[11] Bruce Feiler, *Abraham: A Journey to the Heart of Three Faiths*, (New York: William Morrow, 2002), 40, 41, 48, 49.

[12] H. Freedman, *Midrash Rabbah: Genesis, Volume Two*, (New York: The Sconcino Press, 1983), 518.

[13] As quoted in Anne Roiphe, *Water from the Well: Sarah, Rebekah, Rachel, and Leah*, (New York: William Morrow, 2006), 24.

[14] James Strahan, *Hebrew Ideals: A Study of Genesis from Chapter 11 to 50*, (Edinburgh: T. & T. Clark, 1915), 111.

[15] Roiphe (2006), 51.

Chapter 2
Ordeal in Egypt

Abram and Sarai are living in the land of Canaan, the land of promise where the Lord has commanded them to go, when a brutal famine strikes. Suddenly, the land of promise doesn't look so promising. Abram decides to take respite in Egypt, where food is plentiful. Up to this point, nothing seems unusual about the story. Abram has proven a compassionate, caring, loyal, selfless servant of the Lord, and seemingly joined-at-the-hip with his adoring wife, Sarai. They are a team. From the text and from tradition, he appears to be totally devoted to her.

But as we continue reading the narrative in Genesis, red flags start going up everywhere. In the text, Abram tells Sarai to say that she is his sister in order to protect his life. It seems that Abram fears the Egyptian men will desire Sarai because of her great beauty, and the presence of a husband will complicate matters. He might prove an impediment to the enjoyment of her loveliness, and his life might be perceived as dispensable. Can this really be Abram? The hero we have grown to love, now seemingly a man solely concerned with self-preservation? What is going on here?

> And it came to pass, when he [Abram] was come near to enter into Egypt, that he said unto Sarai his wife, Behold now, I know that thou art a fair woman to look upon: Therefore it shall come to pass, when the Egyptians shall see thee, that they shall say, This is his wife: and they will kill me, but they will save thee alive. Say, I pray thee, thou art my sister: that it may be well with me for thy sake; and my soul shall live because of thee. (Genesis 12:11–13)

Biblical commentators, convinced of Abram's integrity and loyalty to his wife, have conceived various explanations as to why Abram acted as he did. The story has been embroidered upon in countless patterns that are fascinating to observe.

The Zohar, also incredulous that Abram would place Sarai in a life-threatening situation to save himself, asks: "Can we believe that a God-fearing man like Abram should speak thus to his wife in order that he might be well treated?!" The commentator resolves this issue by explaining that Abram sees a guardian angel at the gates of Egypt, accompanying Sarai.[1] The Zohar's depiction of Sarai is so exalted that *her own merit* calls up a guardian angel to watch over her in Egypt. Shera Tuchman and Sandra Rapoport conclude that "faced with the text's grim fact that Abram has placed his wife's life in jeopardy, the commentaries justify his behavior by explaining Abram's expectation that Sarai's guardian angel would save her from harm." The Zohar thus concludes, "The truth is, that Abram relied on his wife's merit, and not his own merit to warrant Divine intervention forestalling Pharaoh's evil intention. Abram expected God to intervene on *her* behalf, acknowledging that Sarai's merit was greater than his own."[2]

As we investigate further, we find that the praise of Sarai just keeps mushrooming. Another creative account portraying Abram's devotion to Sarai is found in *Genesis Rabbah* in a commentary on Genesis 12:14, "And it came to pass, that when Abram was come into Egypt, the Egyptians beheld …" The commentators ask why only Abram is mentioned as having come into Egypt. Where is Sarai? They surmise, "Abram put her in a box and locked her in it so that the Egyptians should not see her. When Abram reached the portals of Egypt, the customs people asked, 'What are you carrying in this box?' He replied, 'Barley.' Said they, 'You are carrying [something more valuable] wheat.' 'You are carrying pepper.' 'Charge me the duty on pepper.' 'You are carrying gold.' 'Charge me the duty on gold.' 'You are carrying silks.' 'Charge me the duty on silks.' 'You are carrying precious stones.' 'Charge me the duty on precious stones.' They figured: If he did not have something of extraordinary worth in his possession, he would not have agreed to whatever duty was asked of him. So they said to him, 'You will not stir from here until you open the box and show us what is inside.' When he opened the box, all of Egypt was illuminated by the radiance of Sarah's beauty."[3]

These are but a few examples of how commentators have struggled with Abram's reported actions for millennia. When I read the Old Testament and find something that is glaringly irrational, I ask myself, "What could make sense of this seemingly inconsistent behavior? Could something be left out here?" And indeed, that is exactly the case. The Book of Abraham in the *Pearl of Great Price*, first published in 1842, makes perfect sense of Abram's actions. The whole ruse is God's idea, not Abram's.

> And I, Abraham, journeyed, going on still towards the south; and there was a continuation of a famine in the land; and I,

> Abraham, concluded to go down into Egypt, to sojourn there, for the famine became very grievous. And it came to pass when I was come near to enter into Egypt, the Lord said unto me: Behold, Sarai, thy wife, is a very fair woman to look upon; Therefore it shall come to pass, when the Egyptians shall see her, they will say—She is his wife; and they will kill you, but they will save her alive; therefore see that ye do on this wise: Let her say unto the Egyptians, she is thy sister, and thy soul shall live. And it came to pass that I, Abraham, told Sarai, my wife, all that the Lord had said unto me—Therefore say unto them, I pray thee, thou art my sister, that it may be well with me for thy sake, and my soul shall live because of thee. (Abraham 2:21–25)

The conundrum is easily solved by the restoration of the complete text. But this document has only been available for about 170 years. The Genesis Apocryphon (1QapGen), which was discovered with the Dead Sea Scrolls, provides an explanation for Abram's actions that has much in common with the account in the book of Abraham. This is not Abram's idea; it is given to him in a dream, presumably from God.

> And on the night of our entry into Egypt, I, Abram, dreamt a dream; [and behold], I saw in my dream a cedar tree and a palm tree ... men came and they sought to cut down the cedar tree and to pull up its roots, leaving the palm tree (standing) alone. But the palm tree cried out saying, "Do not cut down this cedar tree, for cursed be he who shall fell [it]." And the cedar tree was spared because of the palm tree and [was] not felled.
>
> And during the night, I awoke from my dream, and I said to Sarai my wife, "I have dreamt a dream ... [and I am] fearful because of this dream." She said to me, "Tell me your dream that I may know it." So I began to tell her this dream ... [the interpretation] of the dream ... "that they will seek to kill me, but will spare you. ... [Say to them] of me, he is my brother, and because of you I shall live, and because of you my life shall be saved."[4]

The account continues with a description of Sarai, as viewed by men from among the princes of Egypt giving their report to the king. They describe the loveliness of her eyes down to the hairs of her head. The "radiance of her countenance" is lauded, along with her desirable nose, her fair breasts, and her exquisite whiteness. Her perfect hands and "fair palms" and long and slender fingers are praised, as are her "comely feet" and "perfect thighs." "No virgin or bride led into the marriage chamber is more beautiful than she; she is fairer than all other women. Truly, her beauty is greater than theirs. Yet together with all this grace she possesses abundant wisdom, so that whatever she does is perfect."[5] Quite the report!

Predictably, when the king hears the report from these three men, he greatly desires Sarai and sends one of his servants out to take her. Upon seeing her, "he was amazed by her beauty, and took her to wife, but [Abram] he sought to kill. Sarai said to the king, 'He is my brother,' ... and [Abram] was spared because of her and ... was not slain."[6]

> And it came to pass, that, when Abram was come into Egypt, the Egyptians beheld the woman that she was very fair. The princes also of Pharaoh saw her, and commended her before Pharaoh: and the woman was taken into Pharaoh's house. (Genesis 12:14–15)

The Bible is noted for its terseness, and yet the great beauty of Sarai is stressed here, for she is *very* beautiful. *Midrash Rabbah* teaches us that the Hebrew word *isha*, or *woman*, in verse 14 reminds us of Eve's beauty, since it was first used to describe Eve, the first woman in the Bible. The commentators conclude that because the text uses the word *meod*, meaning "much" or "very," it teaches that Sarai was much more beautiful than Eve.[7]

Also fascinating to consider is the timing of what is disclosed next in the narrative. At the same time we are informed that Sarai is being taken—against her will, we assume—to Pharaoh's palace, we are told that Abram was made rich by the king. "And he entreated Abram well for her sake: and he had sheep, and oxen, and he asses, and menservants, and maidservants,[8] and she asses, and camels" (Genesis 12:16). The word translated "entreated" is not correct. Today we use the word *entreat* to mean "to ask persuasively" or "to ask nicely," even "to ask urgently." But the Hebrew word translated as "entreated" comes from the root *yatav*, which in turn comes from the word *tov*, meaning "good." It is in the causative conjugation of the verb, which means that Pharaoh caused lots of good things to happen to Abram. (Pardon me for being a former junior high grammar teacher. Now, I teach Hebrew and feel compelled to bestow a little of that language's grammar upon you, so you will understand just how much the king valued his new acquisition.) Notice that Abram had "sheep, *and* oxen, *and* he asses, *and* menservants, *and* maidservants, *and* she asses, *and* camels" given to him. Any English grammar teacher would return such a composition covered with red pencil and the note, "Run-on sentence, use commas." But alas, bad English grammar is excellent Hebrew grammar. The continuous use of the word *and*—the letter *vav* in Hebrew—in such a long string of possessions hits the reader like a waterfall. We see just how much wealth Pharaoh is willing to give Abram in "payment" for his extremely beautiful "sister." The word *very* in verse 14 takes on new meaning. Abram receives "much" indeed in exchange for his "sister."

Verse 17 gives us a glimpse into the private chambers of the king, and it is not the romantic event that Pharaoh had anticipated. The King James text reads: "And the Lord plagued Pharaoh and his house with great plagues because of Sarai Abram's wife." In Hebrew, however, the text says "God plagued Pharaoh because of the *matter* of Sarai." The word in Hebrew translated in English as "because" is *davar*, which can mean "matter," "thing," "speech," or "word." In the English text, we miss the important noun *davar* and get only an insipid *because* in its place. Why am I telling you all this grammatical information? Because otherwise you will not understand why this verse is fodder for so many commentaries. Some commentators seek to explain exactly what it was that Sarai "said." Others try to determine exactly what the "matter" was that Pharaoh was being punished for.

The commentator Rashi identifies the "matter" as the plague which made sexual intimacy difficult, if not impossible.[9] Tuchman and Rapoport quote many commentaries that go to great lengths to explain why Pharaoh was so stricken. They ask, "Was the plague a miraculous measure that *prevented* Pharaoh from sexually approaching Sarai? Or was the plague a *punishment* for his abduction of her?"[10] Commentator Kli Yakar states that the matter of the king's ailment was directly attributable to the fact that Sarai was Abram's wife, not his sister, and was thus forbidden to Pharaoh or any man. The plague, therefore, was seen as both a punishment and as a preventive measure.[11]

Both *Midrash Rabbah* and Rashi support the second meaning of *davar*, that of "speech." The Biblical text does not record Sarai's words, but *Midrash Rabbah* gives her a voice. The commentary describes Sarai lying in a prone position in the chambers of Pharaoh. She cries out to her God saying, "Help me! My faith in You is greater even than that of my husband, Abram. For Abram left his homeland only after he received the word directly from You, while I went forth based on faith alone. I heard Your promise only from the mouth of my husband, for You did not speak directly to me."[12] Sarai argues that she left her homeland without assurances from her Creator that she would be rewarded, and she passionately hopes that God will reward her for her righteousness and deliver her from this desperate situation. The commentary relates that God speaks directly to Sarai, saying, "Whatever I do, I do for your sake."[13] In other words, Rashi asserts that Pharaoh's plagues are God's method of protecting Sarai.

The Genesis Apocryphon records another part of the story: Abram's reaction to Sarai's abduction. In this text, Abram weeps aloud that Sarai has been taken from him. He prays that night with tears running down his face, imploring the Most High God to raise his hand against Pharaoh, king of Egypt, who has taken away Abram's wife by force. He says, "Judge him for me that I may see Thy mighty hand raised against him and against all his household, and that he may not be able to defile my wife this night (separating her) from me, and that they may know Thee, my Lord, that Thou art Lord of all the kings of the earth." During that night, the Most High God sends a spirit to scourge Pharaoh and all his household, so that "he was unable to approach her, and although he was with her for two years, he knew her not."

At the end of those two years, the scourges and afflictions grow greater upon him and his household, so Pharaoh sends for all the sages and magicians and healers of Egypt, that they might heal him and all his household of this scourge. "But not one healer or magician or sage could stay to cure him, for the spirit scourged them all and they fled."

Then the officer of the king comes to Abram, beseeching him to go to the king and pray for him. He asks Abram to lay his hands upon Pharaoh and heal him. He requests all these things because "the king had dreamt a dream." But Lot says to the officer, "Abram my uncle cannot pray for the king while Sarai his wife is with him. Go, therefore, and tell the king to restore his wife to her husband; then he will pray for him and he shall live."

When the officer hears Lot's words, he goes to the king and says, "All these scourges and afflictions with which my lord the king is scourged and afflicted are because of Sarai the wife of

Abram. Let Sarai be restored to Abram her husband, and this scourge and the spirit of festering shall vanish from you."

The Pharaoh calls Abram to him and says, "What have you done to me with regards to [Sarai]? You said to me, She is my sister, whereas she is your wife; and I took her to be my wife. Behold your wife who is with me; depart and go hence from all the land of Egypt! And now pray for me and my house that this evil spirit may be expelled from it."

So Abram prays for Pharaoh and lays his hands upon his head. The scourge departs from him, the spirit is expelled from him, and he lives. The king swears an oath to Abram and gives Sarai much silver and gold, "and much raiment of fine linen and purple, and Hagar also." He appoints men to lead Abram out of the land of Egypt, and Abram leaves with great flocks and riches.[14]

And thus we see that according to the Genesis Apocryphon account, Sarai is protected by the spirit of the Lord, and her chastity is not compromised. Pharaoh's plague is God's means of protecting her. Lot is the one to tell the king that Sarai is Abram's wife, and Pharaoh is healed from his affliction through a blessing[15] from Abram, who then leaves Egypt with great wealth.

Midrash Rabbah also describes another private encounter between Sarai and the king. In this account, Sarai tells Pharaoh that she is forbidden to him because she is the wife of another man, but the king does not hear her pleas. God has positioned a guardian angel in Pharaoh's chambers, visible only to Sarai. When Pharaoh approaches her "with immoral intentions, coming close enough to touch her slipper," Sarai orders the angel to strike the king with his whip. The angel obeys her every order. When she orders him to strike, he strikes, and he desists when she orders it.[16] This account ascribes to Sarai the power to solicit and even to direct divine assistance. Imagine the power of this woman, having an angel at her beck and call.

Another version of this same story is given by Rashi. This account is very graphic, describing oozing sores and pus and how the scourge affects Pharaoh's sexual anatomy. After suffering great pain from the affliction, the king grabs Sarai's hand, only to have the angel hit him between his shoulder blades. He looks around his bedroom, seeing leprosy on the bedstead, on the beams, on the curtains, and on the pillars. Even his eunuchs waiting at the door suffer similar afflictions. When Pharaoh asks Sarai what has happened, she sits up in bed and replies, "My Lord, the one true God who is not made of wood or stone but stands above the worlds and holds us all in his regard, has sent this plague down upon you. Do not touch me." Pharaoh stands back aghast and asks, "Who are you?" Sarai is silent. "Answer me," he calls out, being a ruler and accustomed to obedience. Pharaoh attempts to step toward her, but the angel hits him hard right behind his knees. "Who are you?" he asks now in a small voice, almost a child's voice. Sarai answers, "I am the wife of the man you thought was my brother. My Lord has protected me."[17]

When I first pondered this tragic episode, I could not help but wonder what Sarai herself must have been thinking during this two-year nightmare. At that time, I wondered why such a powerful missionary, a loyal wife and partner, a champion of the one true God, and a nurturer of the weak and downtrodden should be rewarded with an ordeal in Pharaoh's palace that would test the mettle of the bravest and the best. I wondered what Sarai must have been thinking about her God. After having pondered this for months I have come to a conclusion: I believe Sarai trusted God just as Abram trusted God. Abram did not abandon Sarai to fend for herself in Pharaoh's palace; he trusted God implicitly. He believed that if God told him to ask Sarai to say that she was his sister, then he would provide a way for her to survive the ordeal with her honor intact.

I do not know if the musings of the rabbinic commentators have any truth to them. I do not know if an angel was sent to protect Sarai from Pharaoh's advances. These are mere speculations, invented to preserve the integrity of both Abram and Sarai in the minds of the faithful. However, God *has* sent angels to protect his children in the past—in dens of lions, fiery furnaces, and the like. If it were made known to me at some point that there was indeed an angel sent to protect Sarai in the palace of the king, I certainly would not be surprised.

We know from the text of Genesis that some sort of "scourge" was sent upon Pharaoh and his household. Just how "oozing" were the sores inflicted upon him, we do not know, but it does not tax my imagination to believe that a totally miserable Pharaoh would request a blessing from Abram. At this point in the Genesis narrative, we are not told what Abram is doing during the two years Sarai is in Pharaoh's palace, but we are told elsewhere that Abram sat on Pharaoh's throne and expounded the secrets of the cosmos to his wise men and sages.[18] All were greatly impressed with his vast knowledge of the unknowable. It would not have been a great leap for the court to surmise that Abram was not just an ordinary man, but a man of God who could aid them in their troubles. I would be more surprised if they did *not* seek a blessing at his hands.

Abram trusts God. Although he was raised in a polytheistic society, he has come to know the one true God. Sarai shares this firm testimony. Together they have shared these glad tidings with many "souls" in Haran. She, too, trusts this God unreservedly. Abram knows Sarai. He knows her very soul. They have shared the joy of seeing many souls accept the one true God. Abram knows that God will not abandon Sarai. This unshakeable faith in God is the reason he is able to comply with the shocking request to sacrifice his miracle son on Mount Moriah. Both Abram and Sarai know and trust the one true God. Whatever he commands *must* be right. He has the power to turn every seemingly hopeless situation to his advantage. After all, he *is* the one true God.

Any serious student of the Old Testament is aware of the many literary "types" used repeatedly in the biblical text. Trevor Denis proposes that Sarai's rescue from the palace is yet another literary "type." He asserts that as "God comes wielding great plagues to rescue Sarai from the pharaoh's embrace," so too will he in the early chapters of Exodus "arrive again in similar fashion to rescue his people. ... This little story at the start of the ancestral narratives will foreshadow the events that lie at the heart of the Old Testament's gospel. Sarai will 'play the part' of the trapped Israelites,"[19] and her being set free is a type of the exodus.

The Armenian Commentary on Genesis provides one idea that caused me to rethink God's motives here. Was this a test designed exclusively for Sarai? The text reads, "God allowed [this] so that [Sarai] might be examined and tested, just as [Abram] had been tested. ... And [God] handed [Sarai] over to this because it was her trial; [God] willed that she be examined and tested in a woman's task just as [Abram] had been in a man's task. And when she too had been examined and tested, she too did not grumble against God that because of this He had abandoned her."[20]

Joseph Smith had much to say about the reasons God tests his servants. John Taylor heard him teach, "God will feel after you, and he will wrench your very heartstrings. If you cannot stand it, you will not be fit for the kingdom of God."[21]

There is no doubt that God has his eyes on Sarai. He knows she is to be the ancestress of a great people. She will be yoked with his servant Abram throughout life and as an ancestor of the people of the one true God. He has to know what she is made of. Now he knows.

---

[1] The Zohar (Tazriya 52a), quoted in Shera Aranoff Tuchman and Sandra E. Rapoport, *The Passions of the Matriarchs*, (Berrien Springs, MI: KTAV Publishing House, Inc., 2004), 9.

[2] Ibid.

[3] Hayim Nahman Bialik and Yehoshua Hana Ravnitzky, eds., *The Book of Legends: Sefer Ha Aggadah - Legends from the Talmud and Midrash, Translated by William G. Braude*, (New York: Schocken Books: 1992), 34. See also S. Baring-Gould, *Legends of the Patriarchs and Prophets and Other Old Testament Characters From Various Sources*, (New York: John B. Aldin, 1885), 187.

[4] G. Vermes, *The Dead Sea Scrolls in English*, (London: Penguin Books, 1987), 253–254.

[5] Vernes (1987), 254.

[6] Ibid.

[7] *Midrash Rabbah* (40.5) quoted in Tuchman and Rapoport (2004), 10.

[8] *Midrash Rabbah* and other sources disclose that Hagar was among the maidservants given by Pharaoh, and in fact was his daughter. In the Targum on Genesis 16, we are told that according to the Midrash, Hagar had been given to Abram by her father, the Pharaoh of Egypt, who said, "My daughter had better be a slave in the house of Abram, than a mistress in any other."

J.W. Ethridge, *The Targums of Onkelos and Jonathan ben Uzziel on the Pentateuch, Genesis and Exodus*, (London: Longman, Green, Longman, and Roberts, 1862), 204.

[9] Rashi, quoted in Tuchman and Rapoport (2004), 10.

[10] Tuchman and Rapoport (2004), 10.

[11] Tuchman and Rapoport (2004), 10–11.

[12] *Midrash Rabbah* (41.2) quoted in Tuchman and Rapoport (2004), 11.

[13] Ibid.

[14] Vermes (1987), 254–256.

[15] This blessing is given by the laying on of hands, which is news to Christians who thought this practice originated with Jesus and his apostles.

[16] *Midrash Rabbah* (41.2) quoted in Tuchman and Rapoport (2004), 12.

[17] Anne Roiphe, *Water from the Well: Sarah, Rebekah, Rachel, and Leah*, (New York: William Morrow, 2006), 43–44.

[18] See Facsimile Number 3 in the *Pearl of Great Price*.

[19] Trevor Denis, Sarah Laughed, (Nashville, Abingdon Press, 1994), 38.

[20] _____, *The Armenian Commentary on Genesis Attributed to Ephrem the Syrian*, translated by Edward G. Mathews, Jr., (Louvain: Editions Peeters, 1998), 79.

[21] John Taylor, *Deseret News: Semi-Weekly*, Aug. 21, 1883, p. 1.

Chapter 3
Fateful Decision

Sarai and Abram return to Canaan bearing incomparable wealth. She is reunited with the man she loves, her marital integrity amazingly intact. She has survived the furnace of affliction. Everything seems picture perfect, right? Not quite.

In a previous chapter, we discussed the shocking impact of the second verse in the Bible to mention Sarai by name. "But Sarai was barren; she had no child" (Genesis 11:30). Many modern women who are unable to bear children have agonized about this vacuum in their lives. In the ancient world, it was even worse. Rashi comments, "For whosoever is childless is accounted as dead."[1] Another commentator went a step further and said, "It would be better to be dead than not to have a child."[2] Anne Roiphe explains, "The survival of the group depended on the fertility of its members. There were no effective medicines, so few second chances. If one fell ill or broke a bone or ate a poisonous fruit, death waited. The birth of children was essential for the survival of the community. No wonder it loomed so large in these our first stories. But even without this pressure to survive, most of us still wish to bear life, to hold a child of our own in our arms. The centuries have not replaced that need with another."[3]

Sarai realizes that the promises given to Abram about becoming a great nation and having a great posterity depend upon his having a child, and a male child at that, since inheritance was passed down through the male line in ancient Israel. Without this male heir and the children that would issue from him, of what use is a land of promise? What good is such a land if there are no children to inhabit it? Everything depends on Abram having a child.

Imagine the thoughts that must have passed through Sarai's mind. Unless the Lord heals her barrenness, she will not be the mother of the promised child, and Abram will have to find another wife. Sarai must have anguished over not being able to provide her beloved husband with this crucial child. Trevor Denis alleges that "God's promises represent ... his new initiative for the redemption of the world, his most important creative act since the creation itself."[4] Sarai must have felt like an obstruction to the fulfillment of God's plan for mankind.

She must have wondered if *she* had any part in these divine promises or if they were for Abram alone.

We have no way of knowing whether Sarai was aware of the then-prevalent belief about childlessness in marriage. "If a man marries a wife and she bears him no children for ten years, he must not refrain from propagating, but must divorce her and pay her dowry, for perhaps he is not destined to be built up [i.e. have children] by her."[5] Abram and Sarai had been married longer than ten years, but they had dwelt in the land of Canaan for ten years, and *still* had not produced the long-promised child. Louis Ginzberg makes this comment: "As long as Abraham and Sarah dwelt outside of the Holy Land, they looked upon their childlessness as a punishment for not abiding within it. But when ten years' sojourn in Palestine found her barren as before, Sarah perceived the fault lay with her."[6]

Sarai is driven by her desire to have a child and to see the Lord's promises fulfilled. This desire is so deep, and her faith in the divine promises so profound, that she considers a desperate alternative: sending a substitute wife to her husband's bed. For the first time in the biblical text, we hear Sarai's voice—desperate, pleading, seemingly convinced that she will never bear a child, and that this must be the will of God. "And Sarai said to Abram: Behold now, God has withheld children from me; come, please and take my handmaiden as a concubine; perhaps my family will be built up through her" (Genesis 16:2).[7]

Rashi says that Sarai's words teach us that "without children of her own, Sarai would effectively be annihilated. … She hopes that God will recognize her merit in bringing Hagar to Abram, and will reward her with a child from her own womb."[8] In other words, she hopes that God will recompense her magnanimous behavior in sacrificing her position as the "only wife" by giving her a biological child.

Ginzberg adds details to the story from Jewish tradition: "Without a trace of jealousy she [Sarai] was ready to give her slave Hagar to Abraham as wife, first making her a freed woman. For Hagar was Sarah's property, not her husband's. She had received her from Pharaoh, the father of Hagar. Taught and bred by Sarah, she walked in the same path of righteousness as her mistress, and thus was a suitable companion for Abraham, and, instructed by the holy spirit, he acceded to Sarah's proposal."[9] From this information, we learn that Hagar was given to Sarai by Pharaoh, who was Hagar's father. She walked in the ways of the one true God, as did Abram and Sarai. She belonged solely to Sarai—Abram had no jurisdiction over her. Also, Abram accepted Hagar as his wife only *after* receiving revelation from the holy spirit.

Apparently, Hagar has been a maid to Sarai ever since she and Abram left Egypt. According to this widespread legend, Pharaoh must have been so impressed by Sarai and her holy ways that he wanted his daughter to receive the benefits of being in Sarai's presence continually. According to Shera Tuchman and Sandra Rapoport, "Even in his frustrated and angered state, Pharaoh had realized that Sarai's salvation was due solely to a Divine intervention that far outweighed his own powers. He thought to himself: It is preferable that my daughter be a handmaiden in Sarai's home, than a mistress in her own home in Egypt."[10]

Genesis reports, "And Sarai Abram's wife took Hagar her maid the Egyptian ... and gave her to her husband Abram to be his wife" (Genesis 16:3). In her commentary on Genesis, modern Bible scholar Nehama Leibowitz indicates that Sarai's actions were in conformity with the customs of the times. In the Code of Hammurabi—which existed before the time of Abram—a barren woman had the right to give her husband a handmaiden to beget children for her.

> However, such customs are not the focus of the book of Genesis. Leibowitz cites Ramban, who reveals the character of both Abram and Sarai in his comments on Genesis 16:2, "Abram listened to Sarai," after her entreaty to take her handmaid Hagar. Ramban points out that the text does not state that Abraham "did so" but that "he listened to Sarai." This implies that although Abram deeply longed for children he did not take steps to achieve that goal without Sarai's permission. Furthermore, even at this stage he has no intention of being "builded up" through Hagar. He only intends to carry out Sarai's wishes to be "builded up" through her. His only concern is that Sarai should derive satisfaction from the children of her handmaid, thereby meriting children of her own. Additionally, the text states that "Sarai took," implying that Abram does not rush in and take Hagar. Instead, he waits until Sarai gives Hagar to him "to be his wife." By this action, Sarai indicates that although she has not given up hope of having children with Abraham, she also wishes Hagar to also have the status of wife and not merely a concubine.

"All this underlines Sarah's righteous character and the respect she showed her husband."[11]

At the conclusion of the commentary by Ramban, Leibowitz observes, "these two verses are thus studded with allusions to the peerless character of Abraham and Sarah, their unselfishness and respect for each other. Sarah introduces a rival into her home, making a supreme sacrifice to overcome the natural feelings of jealousy and egotism, whilst Abraham takes no initiative in realizing his ambitions for a son, but waits for his wife's agreement, suggestion, and action."[12] According to this commentator, both Abram and Sarai demonstrate sterling qualities throughout this emotional episode, each deferring to the interests of the other. Sarai brings Hagar into Abram's tent, and Abram only complies because it is Sarai's wish.

Sarai offers Hagar to Abram in the hope that she might be "built up" through her handmaiden. Trevor Denis says of Sarai's action: "Sarai, in her offer of Hagar, is not showing a lack of faith. She is simply being realistic. We might ask why she has not come up with the plan before this."[13] In fact, he further observes that the idea of adopting a surrogate was an established practice in the ancient Near East. He cites the actions of Rachel and Leah in Genesis 30, each of whom offers her maid to her husband, Jacob, in the hope of obtaining children. "The children of such unions were counted as the offspring not only of the husbands who fathered them, but of the original wives whose slaves the natural mothers were. So now, in this story, any child born to Hagar will count as Sarai's child. That is why she hopes she will 'be built up' through her. If Hagar has a child, Sarai will at last be able to shake off the status of the barren wife."[14]

Some Bible translations render "be built up through" as "obtain children through her," as in the King James version of Genesis 16:2. In many places where Hebrew scriptures are discussed, the term "build up" is used to indicate establishing a people. So when we hear the Hebrew words *build up*, we hear bells ring that indicate Sarai is thinking of more than just having a child. She has much larger purposes, even a cosmic mission. She wants to be an instrument in fulfilling God's promises for a covenant people.

Obedient to his wife's wishes, Abram takes Hagar unto himself as a wife. "And he went in unto Hagar, and she conceived: and when she saw that she had conceived, her mistress was despised in her eyes"

(Genesis 16:4). Hagar becomes pregnant almost immediately, and she uses this new status to make Sarai's life miserable. While Sarai herself is silent on the matter, Rashi gives voice to Hagar's words of contempt for Sarai: "My mistress, Sarai, cannot be as perfect as she appears. If she were truly righteous, her God would have certainly given her children by now. Yet he has not done so, and it is I who became pregnant even after my very first intimacy with Abram."[15] Although Hagar was thought to be a woman of righteousness and faith, she begins to "despise" her mistress and treat her with disdain.

Denis provides great insight into the situation. When Sarai gave Hagar to Abram as his secondary wife, "she gave her a status far higher than the one she enjoyed as her slave." Sarai assumes that her own status will be heightened by any child born to this union, but with Hagar pregnant, things turn out very differently. "The utterly powerless foreign slave has shown what female power there is to be found in fertility, and what degradation lies in barrenness." Hagar now views Sarai as far beneath her. "The Hebrew verb used to describe Sarai's loss of status, her becoming 'contemptible', is the same one as the poet of the Book of Job uses to describe Job's sense of smallness in the awesome presence of God (see Job 40:4). No wonder, then, that all the bitterness of her years of unfulfilled longing, all her sense of failure, and all her disappointment at the dashing of her new hope come spilling out in dark words of accusation."[16]

The text of Genesis 16:5 reads: "And Sarai said unto Abram, My wrong be upon thee: I have given my maid into thy bosom; and when she saw that she had conceived, I was despised in her eyes." Denis comments further on the word *hamas*, translated in the King James Version as "wrong." He translates this word as "violence," and expands the ramifications of Sarai's word choice. "We hear her [Sarai's] pain and it is now greater than before. ... Her feelings are summed up in the word 'violence.' My Hebrew dictionary explains, somewhat quaintly, that it often refers to the 'rude wickedness of men, their noisy wild ruthlessness.' It is the term used in Genesis 6:11 to describe the lamentable state of the earth before the Flood." Because of the world's "violence," God "decides to go within a hair's breadth of ending it all. Hagar may be the one who is pregnant, but by the use of the word 'violence' the narrator suggests it is Sarai who is left feeling as if she has been raped."[17]

These are powerful words indeed! Abram could not help but be moved by Sarai's expression of such fervent emotions. Genesis then reports the following words spoken by Sarai, "[Let] the Lord judge between me and thee" (Genesis 16:5). The English reader automatically assumes these are part of Sarai's words to Abram. If so, these antagonistic words color with anger and contention what she had previously said to Abram. Again, a closer reading of the Hebrew text shows that this is not the case. In his commentary of Genesis, Kasher explains, "*Benecha* (between thee) is dotted, indicating that she spoke to Hagar, not to Abraham."[18]

Douglas Clark finds support for this interpretation in the words of Rashi, Judaism's greatest grammarian and all-time Torah authority. The Hebrew word *between you* in this passage is written with a feminine indicator for the person being addressed, showing that "according to Rashi and other Jewish sources ... Sarah's statement about the Lord judging was addressed not to Abraham but to Hagar. Other Jewish sources agree that Sarah was invoking the Lord not against Abraham, but against anyone who would try to cause dissension between her and Abraham. Sarah's commitment to build Zion by being of one heart with her husband was of highest priority, even when she felt wronged."[19]

Abram's response to his wife is supportive. "Behold, thy maid is in thy hand; do to her as it pleaseth thee" (Genesis 16:6). Apparently, he gives her his approval for whatever actions she deems necessary. As the rest of this verse tells, "when Sarai dealt hardly with her, she [Hagar] fled from her face." We are not told exactly what Sarai did to Hagar, but the Hebrew word for *deal harshly* (*anah*) is the same one the narrator of Genesis uses just a few verses before this account, when he tells Abram of the oppression his descendants will suffer at the hands of the Egyptians (see Genesis 15:13). Hagar is an Egyptian, and she flees into the desert, exactly where the children of Israel will flee after crossing the Red Sea hundreds of years later. Just as God comes to the aid of the oppressed Israelites, he comes to the aid of Hagar. The Lord loves to tell history through the repetition of themes. When his children are oppressed, he will look after them.

Leibowitz strives to understand Sarai's actions. She argues that they are entirely reasonable. "After selflessly offering Hagar to her husband, she sees herself triumphed over by her handmaid." It is only a natural reaction. Who could condemn Sarai for such behavior?[20] Most Jewish commentators do not share Leibowitz's justification for Sarai's actions due to "extenuating psychological circumstances,"[21] but severely criticize her for her actions. In the end, it does not really matter how anyone chooses to interpret Sarai's action, because she is not condemned by the Lord, nor does he reverse her actions.

When Hagar flees to the wilderness, she is visited by a messenger from God. He greets her as "Hagar, Sarai's *maid*," and asks her what she is doing in the desert. "I flee from the face of my *mistress* Sarai," she replies. Following her admission, the angel exhorts Hagar to return to her *mistress*. By the threefold reference to Hagar's status as a slave, the narrator of Genesis—and apparently the Lord, also—supports Hagar and Sarai in returning to the relationship of servant and mistress. Tammi Schneider observes, "The Deity, while prepared to let Hagar suffer through Sarai's harsh treatment, is also prepared to offer her what other women do not usually receive, a blessing directly from the Deity and an increase of her offspring."[22] Hagar also bestows upon God her own private name, "The God Who Sees Me." God himself reveals to her the name of her son, a rare occurrence in scripture. Hagar could never say that she was abandoned by God.

We do not see Sarai again in this episode. Genesis tells us that "Hagar bare Abram a son: and Abram called his son's name, which Hagar bare, Ishmael" (Genesis 16:15). Abram is eighty-six years old when his son is born. Sarai's hopes for a child to "build up" her house have not been fulfilled in the way she has hoped. She had hoped that her own barrenness would be alleviated through the birth of this surrogate son. But she remains childless. As promised, God will remove Sarai's barrenness, but she will have to wait another fourteen years.

---

[1] Anne Roiphe, *Water From the Well: Sarah, Rebekah, Rachel, and Leah*, (New York: William Morrow, 2006), 30.

[2] Ibid.

[3] Ibid.

[4] Trevor Denis, *Sarah Laughed*, (Nashville: Abingdon Press, 1994), 37.

[5] Menahem M. Kasher, *Encyclopedia of Biblical Interpretation, Genesis: Volume II*, (New York: American Biblical Encyclopedia Society, 1955), 216.

[6] Louis Ginzberg, *The Legends of the Jews, Volume 1*, (Baltimore: The Johns Hopkins University Press, 1937), 237.

[7] Translation from Shera Aranoff Tuchman and Sandra E. Rapoport, *The Passions of the Matriarchs*, (Berrien Springs, MI: KTAV Publishing House, Inc., 2004), 13.

[8] Tuchman and Rapoport (2004), 14.

[9] Ginzberg (1937), 237.

[10] Tuchman and Rapoport (2004), 14.

[11] Nehama Leibowitz, *Studies in Bereshit (Genesis): In the Context of Ancient and Modern Jewish Bible Commentary*, (Jerusalem: Alpha Press, 1972), 154.

[12] Leibowitz (1972), 154–155.

[13] Denis (1994), 42.

[14] Denis (1994), 42–43.

[15] Tuchman and Rapoport (2004), 16.

[16] Denis (1994), 44.

[17] Ibid.

[18] Kasher (1955), 217.

[19] E. Douglas Clark, *The Blessings of Abraham: Becoming a Zion People*, (American Fork, Utah: Covenant Communications, 2005), 162–163.

[20] Leibowitz (1972), 156.

[21] Tuchman and Rapoport (2004), 19.

[22] Tammi J. Schneider, "Sarah: Mother of Nations," (New York: Continuum, 2004), 55.

Chapter 4
Mother of Nations

Thirteen years pass. Sarai, still childless, is eighty-nine years old. Abram is ninety-nine, but things have changed for him. Hagar has borne a son, giving him an heir. Sarai has suffered quietly, watching the child grow and become cherished by his father—the apple of his eye. She has gone through menopause, quenching the last hope of bearing Abram a child. It must have been a bitter disappointment after so many years of sustaining hope in God's promise.

Chapter 17 of Genesis begins with God's sudden appearance to the aged Abram: "And when Abram was ninety years old and nine, the Lord appeared to Abram, and said unto him, I am the Almighty God; walk before me, and be thou perfect. And I will make my covenant between me and thee, and will multiply thee exceedingly" (Genesis 17:1–2). Abram immediately prostrates himself before God and listens to the extraordinary covenants he makes, telling Abram that he will become a "father of many nations" (Genesis 17:4). Then God declares "Neither shall thy name any more be called Abram, but thy name shall be Abraham; for a father of many nations have I made thee. And I will make thee exceeding fruitful, and I will make nations of thee, and kings shall come out of thee" (Genesis 17:5–6).

Not only is this covenant between God and Abraham, but it also extends to Abraham's seed after him in their generations "for an everlasting covenant, to be a God unto thee, and to thy seed after thee" (Genesis 17:7). God promises Abraham the land of Canaan for an everlasting possession which will continue throughout the generations. As evidence of Abraham's acceptance of the covenant, he is commanded to circumcise all males in his household and all newborn males when they are eight days old. This commandment—the rite of circumcision—is the sign of God's everlasting covenant, and each ensuing generation must comply with it.

If Abraham is to be the *father of nations*, the implication is that his partner will be a *mother of nations*. Sarai is to be part of these marvelous promises at last! "As for Sarai thy wife, thou shalt not call her name Sarai, but Sarah shall her name be. And I will bless her, and [moreover] give thee a son also of her: yea, I will bless her, and she shall be a mother of nations; kings of people shall be of her" (Genesis 17:15–16).

These blessings are markedly similar to those promised to Abraham. In fact, the blessings are precisely parallel. The son that is born to Sarah will be the one we have been waiting for since the promise was first given to Abraham in Genesis 12. Since the first chapter of Genesis, the purpose of creation has been the reproduction of each species after its kind, and Sarah will at last be able to play the part she was created for.

For the first time, Abraham discovers that Sarah *will* have a son. His aged wife will actually conceive a biological son with her husband. Abraham is astonished at God's declaration. "Then Abraham fell upon his face, and laughed, and said in his heart, Shall a child be born unto him that is an hundred years old? and shall Sarah, that is ninety years old, bear?" (Genesis 17:7).

But instead of responding with unmitigated delight at the prospect of the long-barren Sarah bearing a son, Abraham wonders what will happen to the son he already has.[1] What place will Ishmael have in God's plan? "And Abraham said unto God, O that Ishmael might live before thee!" (Genesis 17:8). He pleads with God that *Ishmael* have a part in this covenant, but God must explain to him that there is no covenant without Sarah, and *her* son will be the covenant son. Ishmael will also be blessed, but in a different way. Patiently, God addresses both of Abraham's concerns—the first, that Sarah is too old to bear a child, and second, that Ishmael will be cast off.

> And God said, Sarah thy wife shall bear thee a son indeed; and thou shalt call his name Isaac: and *I will establish my covenant with him* for an everlasting covenant, and with his seed after him. And as for Ishmael, I have heard thee: Behold, I have blessed him, and will make him fruitful, and will multiply him exceedingly; twelve princes shall he beget, and I will make him a great nation. But *my covenant will I establish with Isaac*, which Sarah shall bear unto thee at this set time in the next year. (Genesis 17:19–21, emphasis added)

To Abraham's reservations about Sarah being able to conceive a child, God promises that Abraham will father a son with Sarah. In fact, he gives that son a name: Isaac, which means "laughter." Abraham need not fear for Ishmael, but God emphasizes the importance of the covenant which he will establish through Isaac, who will be a patriarch of God's chosen people. God makes it clear to Abraham that Ishmael is *not* the heir of this covenant. He will be blessed with a great posterity, even twelve princes, and will become the father of a great nation, but Isaac is to be the heir of God's covenant.

In Rabbi J. B. Soloveitchik's commentary on this conversation between God and Abraham, he makes note of how God emphasizes to Abraham that Sarah is to play a significant role in the transmission of the covenant. Abraham, despairing of having a child with Sarah, wonders whether God intends that the heritage be transmitted through Ishmael. "But [*aval*] your wife Sarah will bear you a son, and you shall call him Isaac, and I will keep My covenant with him as an everlasting treaty, for his descendants after him" (Genesis 17:18). The key emphasis is the word *aval*. "God is explaining that His covenant cannot be realized *without* Isaac. Why? Because Isaac is the son of Sarah. … Isaac will emerge out of both of you, but Ishmael is only derived from you. And there can be no covenant without Sarah."[2]

The word *aval* is an older Hebrew word with the force of *verily* or *of a truth*.[3] To me, this is a far cry from the insipid *but* of the King James translation. God here is telling Abraham, "Trust me, Abraham. Sarah *will* have a child, and that child will survive, and he will become the heir of the covenant. I know what I am doing."

Rabbi Adin Steinsaltz offers insight into the indispensable relationship between Abraham and Sarah. He points out that the nation of Israel is not descended from a single patriarch, Abraham. Abraham and Sarah together have a "special essence." This is why the nation of Israel has two parents: Abraham and Sarah together. "It is no accident that this relationship echoes that between Adam and Eve. Abraham and Sarah are the historical-ideological-spiritual fathers of the nation, just as Adam and Eve are its biological progenitors, the two fundamental elements of the human species." This is why "Abraham and Sarah saw themselves (and are thus seen by future generations) not as a couple raising a family, but as a people building a society, realizing an ideal: parents of a nation." To this day, converts to the Jewish faith are called "sons of Abraham," and the women among them "daughters of Sarah," because conceptually, "Abraham and Sarah are ideological ancestors of the Jewish nation, and all who join them are their children. Abraham and Sarah see themselves as leaders, forging a new road, a new worship of the Lord; as guides of a nation, diverse and yet united."[4]

Abraham's audience with the Lord is over. Let the circumcision begin. Immediately, Abraham circumcises himself, thirteen-year old Ishmael, and all the males of his household.[5] Abraham and his God have established an unbreakable affiliation. At this time in the ancient Near East, this type of indissoluble bond was always contracted by blood, usually the blood of a sacrificial animal.[6] But the blood of *this* covenant is to be Abraham's own, and that of every male that enters the covenant. Thomas Cahill offers his thoughts on why this is so. "It is impossible for any man to forget his penis, his own personal life force. By this covenant, the children of Avram will be virtually unable to forget the god who never forgets them."[7]

Carolyn Custis James expresses her own views about circumcision, which had long been a question in her mind. I need to offer a disclaimer here. This quote is very long, but I predict that you readers will understand why I chose to include it. It offers a woman's view of the rite of circumcision—which is unique in and of itself—but it offers many poignant insights as well.

> We [as women] want to know *why* the sign of God's covenant was so male? What is God trying to tell us? Was his covenant for men only? Are men more important in his covenant than women?
>
> Once again, God knew exactly what he was doing. The rite of circumcision is rich with symbolism intended to distinguish God's people from the rest of the world. Circumcision teaches us our need for soul surgery—the radical, costly, and bloody process of removing our sin that Jesus accomplished when he bled and died on the cross. It is a reminder of the painful battle against sin and the awful price of victory—for God and for his people. But there is much, much more to the sign of God's covenant.
>
> Circumcision takes us back to the beginning—back to God's great creation mandate to be fruitful and multiply. God was to reiterate the glorious creation mandate to "be fruitful and multiply and fill the earth" in a way that included, but went beyond, the call to reproduce physically. When he first called Abraham out of Ur of the Chaldeans, God promised to make a great nation from Abraham's descendants. Now God revisits the subject and reveals the kind of nation he plans to produce through Abraham: a nation of people who walk with God. The rite of circumcision came with the call to "walk before me and be blameless ... you and your descendants after you for generations to come."

> Circumcision cuts in a man's flesh a permanent reminder of his call to walk with God. Through circumcision, Abraham affirmed his personal intention to walk with God and do everything in his power to ensure that his children after them followed the same path. Far from excluding women, the rite of circumcision made women indispensable. Obviously no man can reproduce physically by himself. But Abraham's need for Sarah went well beyond sexual intimacy and the physical birth of a child. According to God's word in Genesis, "It is not good for the man to be alone." Abraham needed Sarah's help for the bigger and even more impossible job of reproducing spiritually.
>
> If God were trying to exalt men or show his preference for men over women, there were better, more visible ways of doing so. He could have made the sign of the covenant a symbol on the man's head—like a crown letting everyone know the man was chief, that he was supposed to do all the thinking, deciding, and leading. Or he could have marked a man's arm—symbolizing strength, power, and rule. Instead, God chose circumcision, not as a symbol of manhood, but of intimacy, vulnerability, and fruitfulness. Circumcision spoke of a man's intimate relationship with his wife and of their union in producing children, both physically and spiritually.
>
> Rather than being excluded, a woman could actually be represented twice by circumcision—first, as her father's descendant and one he guided to walk with God, and second, as a wife who united with her husband in fulfilling the call to raise up the next generation to follow God. By circumcising Abraham's household servants too, God's covenant broke the boundaries of biology, extending the Abrahamic covenant laterally to encompass Gentiles even at this early stage. Both Abraham and Sarah had responsibility to direct the hearts of their servants and their servants' children toward God. Circumcision isn't *male*-centered, but *descendant*-centered and *community*-centered. The sign of the covenant impressed upon the man his enormous spiritual responsibility to walk before God and be faithful and to influence others, especially those under his roof, to do the same. This burden was too great for any man to shoulder alone.[8]

Everything about God's covenant is descendant-centered. That is why Sarah's role in the covenant is so important. The prophet Isaiah invited all Israel to remember their origins. "Hearken to me, ye that follow after righteousness, ye that seek the Lord: look unto the rock whence ye are hewn, and to the hole of the pit whence ye are digged. Look unto Abraham your father, and unto Sarah that bare you" (Isaiah 51:1–2). Abraham and Sarah *together* are the parents of the covenant people. In his lifetime, Abraham will beget eight sons, Sarah only one. One hundred percent of Sarah's descendants are heirs to the covenant. The percentage of Abraham's covenant progeny is only twelve and a half.

As part of the establishment of the everlasting covenant, Abraham receives a new name. The matriarch of this covenant people was also to have a new name—Sarah instead of Sarai.

The Talmud explains the significance of these name changes. "The addition of the Hebrew letter *he* to Abram's name makes him a ruler not just over the land or Aram, but over all nations. Similarly, regarding Sarai, the Talmud elevates her to a princess over not merely her own nation, but over the entire world."[9]

Another important aspect of these name changes is the fact that both Abraham and Sarah are *theophoric* names, names that contain part of the name of God. The name of the Israelite God is spelled *yod he vav he* in Hebrew; YHVH in English. Douglas Clark observes, "The rabbis pointed out that the additional letter added to Abraham's name, the *he* (pronounced "hey") is one of the letters from the personal name of the God of Israel, Jehovah (*Yahweh*), a fact perhaps symbolizing that God was sharing part of His glory and divine nature with Abraham [and Sarah]."[10]

Rabbi Soloveitchik answers the question, When was Sarah's name changed? He notes that it occurred at the very moment Abraham's name was changed, because there was "an inherent interdependence between them both. The name change of both involved the addition of a letter from God's name, the Tetragrammaton, signifying that they will share a spiritual role which will reach out unto the nations of the world." He was to become "the father of a multitude of nations" (Genesis 17:4), she "a princess to the entire world." He could not do this with any other woman. Abraham could not be "a father of multitudes" if Sarah were not crowned as a "mother" of this multitude.[11]

Perhaps the most important perspective to consider here is the significance of names in the ancient Near East. According to Nahum Sarna in a commentary of Genesis, "A person's name was inextricably intertwined with his personality. … God carefully gives a name to the first things He created. … Conversely, anonymity is equivalent to non-being. Thus, to 'cut off the name' means to end existence, to annihilate. … Alternatively, posterity may be expressed in terms of the name."[12]

Because of the importance of name giving, it will be readily understood why the Bible invests the reception or changing of a name with such significance. Sarna continues, "Throughout the Near East, the inauguration of a new era or a new state policy would frequently be marked by assumption of a new name … on the part of the King. … The very fact of a new name distinguishes and even effectuates, to an extent, the transformation of destiny. … The patriarch [Abraham] is told that he will not only have an heir and be the progenitor of a nation but that he will even become the 'father of a multitude of nations.'" Abraham and Jacob each receive "names of destiny" from God himself. Isaac alone receives no change of name—though this is because God selects his name, making it "divinely ordained even before birth."[13]

Sarah's name will not be cut off. Her day has finally come. As Abraham is recuperating from his surgery in the door of his tent, hoping to find a refreshing breeze, he sees three men coming towards him in the distance. As was his custom, he rushes to greet them and offer them his hospitality. Abraham hurries into the tent to instruct Sarah to prepare special cakes for their guests, telling her to use the best flour, not the everyday stuff. He specifies that three measures be prepared, an *enormous* amount. (One measure, or *seah*, is equivalent to about thirty cups.) As a married woman, Sarah modestly remains inside the tent, out of sight, as dictated by custom. Abraham hurries off to have a calf prepared for their meal and to get curds and milk. The size of the meal is remarkable—a whole calf and endless cakes of superior quality for three visitors. The text of Genesis 18:1 says, "The Lord appeared to Abraham." Does Abraham know that he is entertaining the Lord? Suddenly, one of the visitors asks, "Where is your wife Sarah?" (Genesis 18:9). How do these strangers know that Abraham's wife is named Sarah? Abraham, not thinking to ask how they know says, "There, in the tent." Does he not think it unusual that these men would ask about his wife? No one has asked about her before. And how do they know her so-recently-changed name? Suddenly we readers realize that Sarah is not just a silent bystander in this drama. We ascertain that the visit of these messengers might have something to do with Sarah specifically. We recognize that Sarah is really at the *center* of the story, even though she remains unseen inside the tent.

To Abraham's curt answer, "In the tent," the messenger responds, "I will certainly return unto thee according to the time of life; and, lo, Sarah thy wife shall have a son" (Genesis 18:10a). It can only be the God who has been making promises to Abraham who now makes such a profound statement. The same God who covenanted with Abraham in the previous chapter of Genesis now brings the same message again. Abraham has heard it already, so this message is for someone else's benefit.

> And Sarah heard it in the tent door, which was behind him. Now Abraham and Sarah were old and well stricken in age; and it ceased to be with Sarah after the manner of women. Therefore Sarah laughed *within herself*, saying, After I am waxed old shall I have pleasure, my lord being old also? (Genesis 18:10b–12, emphasis added)

We learn several things from Sarah's words, only her third recorded speech since she first appears in Genesis 11. It looks as if Abraham has not told his wife about the phenomenal news he received in chapter 17, and we are left to guess at his motivation for withholding this information. Perhaps he has been instructed not to disclose it. Perhaps he fears raising her hopes, only to have them dashed once again. Or perhaps he is concerned for Isaac's future, or who-knows-what else. Obviously, Sarah is hearing this news for the first time, and from the lips of a seeming stranger. We also learn that Sarah has entered menopause, and there is no biological possibility that she could bear a child. Being a woman of faith, what must she be thinking? She believes in a God of miracles, but could this really be true? Sarah laughs "within herself," quietly considering the ramifications of such an announcement. The word *laugh* in Hebrew can also bear the connotation of "rejoice," which I am certain she does as soon as soon as she recovers from her initial shock. She uses the Hebrew word *ednah* (*pleasure*) in her statement, which has the sense of "delight," along with a possible sexual connotation.[14] Tammi Schneider argues that although Sarah believes that the promises given by the visitors will be fulfilled and bring her joy, she questions how "her delight will be with her husband, who is old." She notes that there is nothing in her statement that "demands reading the comment as one of disbelief that it will happen rather than pleased wonder at the news."[15]

Schneider goes on to propose a purpose for the messenger's visit. If Sarah is surprised that she will have "sexual pleasure" with her husband, it means, presumably, that she and Abraham are no longer having sexual relations. Schneider feels that "a reasonable purpose for the messengers being sent to Abraham and Sarah was to inform the couple that they needed to resume sexual relations." This is especially true since Abraham has not informed Sarah of God's announcement that she will become a mother.[16]

The next verse is the one that leads to the supposition that Sarah's laugh is cynical rather than the "pleased wonder" spoken of by Schneider. "And the Lord said unto Abraham, Wherefore did Sarah laugh, saying, Shall I of a surety bear a child, which am old? Is any thing too hard for the Lord?" (Genesis 18:13–14a). You will notice that the Lord did not repeat *exactly* what Sarah said in her original speech. Besides commenting on her own age, she said "my lord being old also." Tuchman and Rapoport note that God strategically omits her comment about Abraham's advanced age at the end of verse 12 in relaying to him Sarah's reaction to the news of her impending fertility. Rashi briefly explains God's strategy. "God did not wish to instill discord between husband and wife by reminding Abraham that Sarah was acutely aware of his advanced age." The Talmud agrees: "Peace between a husband and wife is so desirable that God Himself altered Sarah's words."[17]

The next verse, as translated, brings up several questions. "Then Sarah denied, saying, I laughed not; for she was afraid. And he said, Nay; but thou didst laugh" (Genesis 18:15). Did Sarah try to deceive the Lord? I don't think she would dare. The Hebrew word *cahash*, translated as "denied," can also mean "cringed."[18] This "cowering" response to the Lord's accusation is understable in light of Sarah's professed fear. She knows that she did not laugh *out loud* and denies doing so. The very fact that God knows something that happened inside Sarah's heart gives the game away for her. She knows that it is *the Lord* that has been conversing with her. Who wouldn't be afraid? As pointed out by a commentator, "The speaker knows that Sarah has laughed, though he has neither seen nor heard her."[19] Douglas Clark concludes, "The visitor's disclosure of what no mortal could have heard is thereby a disclosure of his own identity as a powerful messenger of God."[20] Now Sarah knows that the promise of a son to come a year hence has the force of divine authority.

The words "Is any thing too hard for the Lord?" in verse 14 have meaning beyond the miracle God has in mind for Abraham and Sarah. According to the Zohar, these words refer to "that future day when the Lord will miraculously bring to pass the resurrection of the dead, the great renewal."[21] Luke 1:37 includes an obvious reference to the Lord's words to Sarah when the angel Gabriel speaks to Mary about the upcoming birth of her divine child: "For with God, nothing shall be impossible." Indeed, nothing shall be impossible—not the prospect of a woman past menopause giving birth, not the reality of a virgin bearing a son, and not the certainty of the resurrection of the dead.

---

[1] In Abraham's defense, Jubilees' rendition of this account is "And Abraham fell on his face and he rejoiced and pondered in his heart whether a son would be born to one who was one hundred years old or (whether) Sarah, who was ninety years, would give birth."

Jubilees 15:17 in James H. Charlesworth, *The Old Testament Pseudepigrapha, Volume 2*, (Garden City, New York, 1985), 86.

[2] Abraham R. Besdin, *Man of Faith in the Modern World: Reflections of the Rav, Volume Two adapted from the lectures of Rabbi Joseph B. Soloveitchik* (Hoboken, New Jersey: KTAV Publishing House, Inc., 1984), 85.

[3] Francis Brown, *The New Brown-Driver-Briggs-Genesius Hebrew and English Lexicon*, (Peabody, Massachusetts: Hendrickson Publishers, 1979), 6a, entry 61.

[4] Adin Steinsaltz, *Biblical Images: Men and Women of the Book*, (New York: Basic Books, 1984), 26–27.

[5] Abram shows his great faith in God by his quick obedience and by his willingness to circumcise all the males in his household at the same time. Such action would leave him especially vulnerable to an attack by outsiders, as his entire military force would be recovering from surgery and in a weakened condition.

[6] Anne Roiphe gives her opinion of circumcision as part of the covenant of blood sacrifice:

"This circumcision was a far better blood-letting than the more common practice of human sacrifice. We have reports that the tribes around Abraham had offered their small children to their gods in hopes of evoking good fortune. Large graveyards have been found with the buried bones of tiny children assumed to have been sacrificed at the dawn of human history. Abraham's God only asked for a small piece of the foreskin as a token of loyalty."

Anne Roiphe, *Water from the Well: Sarah, Rebekah, Rachel, and Leah*, (New York: William Morrow, 2006), 66.

[7] Thomas Cahill, *The Gifts of the Jews: How a Tribe of Desert Nomads Changed the Way Everyone Thinks and Feels*, (New York: Nan A. Talese (Doubleday), 1998), 72.

[8] Carolyn Custis James, *Lost Women of the Bible*, (Grand Rapids, Michigan: Zondervan, 2005), 74-76 (emphasis in original).

[9] Brachot 13a of the Talmud as quoted in Shera Aranoff Tuchman and Sandra E. Rapoport, *The Passions of the Matriarchs*, (Berrien Springs, MI: KTAV Publishing House, Inc., 2004), 23.

[10] E. Douglas Clark, *The Blessings of Abraham: Becoming a Zion People*, (American Fork, Utah: Covenant Communications, 2005), 166.

[11] Besdin (1989), 86.

[12] Nahum M. Sarna, *Understanding Genesis*, (New York: McGraw-Hill Book Company, 1966), 130–131.

[13] Ibid.

[14] Tammi J. Schneider, *Sarah: Mother of Nations*, (New York: Continuum, 2004), 69.

[15] Ibid.

[16] Schneider (2004), 71.

[17] Rashi and Bava Metzia 87a of the Talmud are quoted in Tuchman and Rapoport (2004), 33–34.

[18] Francis Brown, *The New Brown-Driver-Briggs-Genesius Hebrew and English Lexicon*, (Peabody, Massachusetts: Hendrickson Publishers, 1979), 471, entry 3584, cahash; Tuchman and Rapoport (2004), 34.

[19] Skinner in Clark (2005), 177.

[20] Clark (2005), 177.

[21] Clark (2005), 178 quoting the Zohar from Kasher.

Chapter 5
The Birth of Laughter

Soon after the three messengers visit Abraham and Sarah, God annihilates Sodom and her inhabitants for their base immorality. Abraham flees from the destruction to the south country and comes to Gerar, where he sojourns for a time. Here, readers of the text begin to experience a sense of *déjà vu*. Of his wife Sarah, Abraham says, "She is my sister" (Genesis 20:2). "Wait a minute," we say. "Didn't this happen in Egypt, eight chapters ago?" It seems so. Although Abraham was driven to Egypt by a famine, no reason is given for his stay in Gerar.

Rashi argues that "Abraham, whose mission is to convert souls to monotheism, is seeking a more populous territory in which to pitch his tent."[1] Fair enough. Having seen the outcome for Sodom and Gomorrah, I can understand why Abraham would want to distance himself from the cities of the plain, especially if he can surround himself with people who haven't yet heard of the one true God. What I can't understand is why he repeats the same "sister act" upon entering Gerar twenty-three years later, knowing what happened to Sarah in Pharaoh's palace. The sages maintain that Sarah's body has been restored to its youthful state of fertility in preparation for the birth of her promised son. This sort of transformation would certainly explain why Abimelech, king of Gerar, would seize a ninety-year-old woman and bring her into his bedchamber. (We will hear more about this shortly.)

Abraham identifying Sarah as his sister instead of his wife baffles many, including me. Ramban tries his best to explain the motivation for Abraham's actions, and Shera Tuchman and Sandra Rapoport provide this explanation of Ramban's spin on the episode. Since Gerar was a more civilized place than Egypt—and Abimelech more "honorable" than Pharaoh—Abraham did not expect an abduction here. However, as a mere "itinerant tent-dweller", he is still somewhat cautious because of Abimelech's power and position. For this reason, a careful Abraham resorts again to the "sister stratagem."[2]

Anne Roiphe offers this defense: "A sage points out that while it is a sin to lie it is sometimes the only way that the powerless can survive in the face of the strength opposing them. He claims that lying is not always wrong if the purpose is to assure the survival of the nation."[3]

Because Sarah does not speak in the text throughout this entire episode, we can only guess at her thoughts. Does she trust Abraham so completely because of her faith in him as a man of God, meriting the Deity's protection? Or is her faith rooted in God, who has promised her a son in her old age? If God has the power to perform a mighty feat like that, maybe she is confident he will protect her from Abimelech. The commentator Alshich wonders why Abraham would again place Sarah in a situation where "only a miracle could extricate her." He postulates that Abraham was "relying on Sarah's special relationship with God to protect her again."[4] Netziv agrees with this supposition. "Whenever Abraham journeyed to a place that God had not told him specifically to visit—such as here in Gerar and formerly in Egypt—Abraham feared that God's protection would not follow him. In these situations, Abraham relied on God's continual protection for Sarah."[5]

The Bible text declares that "Abimelech king of Gerar sent, and took Sarah" (Genesis 20:2b), in much the same way that King David would later *send* for Bathsheba and *take* her to his palace. We have a problem here. Sarah will bear the promised son of the covenant during the next year. This is no time for a protracted, two-year sojourn in the king's palace as had happened in Egypt. The Lord must work quickly to protect Sarah's integrity. Therefore, the next verse does not surprise us. "God came to Abimelech in a dream by night, and said to him, Behold, thou art but a dead man, for the woman which thou hast taken; for she is a man's wife" (Genesis 20:3).

Abimelech defends his behavior before God. "But Abimelech had not come near her: and he said, Lord, wilt thou slay also a righteous nation? Said he not unto me, She is my sister? and she, even she herself said, He is my brother: in the integrity of my heart and innocency of my hands have I done this" (Genesis 20:4-5).

Even if Sarah's abduction had been done with the most proper intentions, it was still necessary for the Lord to intercede quickly to avoid Abimelech's sinning against God. He instructs Abimelech to return Sarah to her husband at once, and because Abraham is a prophet, he will *know* that Abimelech had honorable intentions and not seek vengeance on the people of Gerar. In fact, Abraham will use his godly powers to bless Abimelech and his house to escape the sentence of death that awaits his house if he does not comply with the Lord's instructions.

> And God said unto him in a dream, Yea, I know that thou didst this in the integrity of thy heart; for I also withheld thee from sinning against me: therefore suffered I thee not to touch her. Now therefore restore the man his wife; for he is a prophet, and he shall pray for thee, and thou shalt live: and if thou restore her not, know thou that thou shalt surely die, thou, and all that are thine. (Genesis 20:6–7)

Being held against her will in a king's chambers, Sarah must have thought she was having a recurring nightmare. *Midrash Rabbah* contends that Sarah was protected by God in Gerar, just as she was in Egypt. "Her guardian angel literally pushes [Abimelech's] hand away from her. It is thus clear from the text (verse six) and the commentaries that it was God—and not [Abimelech's] strength of character—who prevented [Abimelech] from 'taking' Abraham's wife."[6]

Roiphe details the pitiful state of Abimelech's household. "The sages tell us that as the night wore on a strange spell fell on all the people in his dwelling except for Abraham and Sarah. All their orifices were closed up. Their bodies could no longer lose their wastes. They could no longer smell, nor open their mouths except to moan. The wombs of the women were closed shut and the men's genitals became wrinkled and shriveled."[7]

In the morning, Abimelech sends Sarah back to her husband and calls Abraham to the palace to confront him with questions about his deceitful actions. Abraham tries to justify himself with two assertions. First, he thought the inhabitants of Gerar were not religious and were not above slaying an old man in order to get his gorgeous wife. Finally, he defends his use of the word "sister" when referring to Sarah— - who *is* his sister, as well as his wife. He goes on to explain that as a *kindness* to him, Sarah permitted him to introduce her as his sister as they journeyed from place to place.

> Then Abimelech called Abraham, and said unto him, What hast thou done unto us? and what have I offended thee, that thou hast brought on me and on my kingdom a great sin? thou hast done deeds unto me that ought not to be done. And Abimelech said unto Abraham, What sawest thou, that thou hast done this thing? And Abraham said, Because I thought, Surely the fear of God is not in this place; and they will slay me for my wife's sake. And yet indeed

she is my sister; she is the daughter of my father, but not the daughter of my mother; and she became my wife. And it came to pass, when God caused me to wander from my father's house, that I said unto her, This is thy kindness which thou shalt shew unto me; at every place whither we shall come, say of me, He is my brother. (Genesis 20:9–13)

Trevor Denis comments on the Hebrew word that is translated as "kindness," *hesed*. "It is often used in the Old Testament of relations between human beings, but it is also commonly applied to God. It is hard to translate, and it is impossible to convey all its nuances in a word or phrase. It speaks of mercy, kindness, love, fidelity, a love that will persist in the midst of great danger, and in the face of great provocation and rejection. It is often translated 'steadfast love', and when it is used of God it tells of his enduring commitment to his people more powerfully than any other word."[8]

Sarah and Abraham have an extraordinary relationship. Because they are both working toward the same goal and share the same vision, events that seem troublesome to us do not ruffle them. Apparently Sarah is supportive of the story that she is Abraham's sister. We marvel at this phenomenon, but Sarah takes these actions because of the fervent *hesed* she has for Abraham. Obviously, Sarah does not *want* to be taken to the king's palace, but she remains silent.

Adin Steinsaltz comments on her actions. He maintains that "this silence did not arise from passivity or surrender, nor from a wish to be taken by another man, nor because Sarah was a mere tool of her husband." He proposes that Sarah's amenability was obviously "prearranged" with Abraham, the beloved husband with whom she worked as a team. In Gerar, they had jointly decided, "despite the shame and humiliation involved, that it was preferable to preserve the wholeness of Abraham's camp—representing, as it did, the new ideal even at the cost of Sarah's honor." They felt it was better to take this course and endanger her happiness and well-being—with all that implies—because she and Abraham were "working together toward a specific common goal." Sarah's willingness to sacrifice her personal well-being for the common cause is "surely borne out by the fact Sarah never reproached Abraham for the injury done to her; nor, indeed, did she even mention it."[9]

Apparently mollified by Abraham's argument that "she really *is* my 'sister,'" Abimelech bestows great wealth upon Abraham in the form of livestock and servants. Abimelech also returns Sarah to him, and generously invites him to settle anywhere in Gerar under his protection. "And Abimelech took sheep, and oxen, and menservants, and women servants, and gave them unto Abraham, and restored him Sarah his wife. And Abimelech said, Behold, my land is before thee: dwell where it pleaseth thee" (Genesis 20:14–16). Then he turns to Sarah and says, "On your behalf I gave your brother Abraham one thousand pieces of silver. This sum will veil you and protect your reputation in the land" (Genesis 20:17).[10]

Rashi points out that "the king goes beyond what would have been expected in returning Sarah to her brother/husband. [He] says that Avimelech's announced gift, worth one thousand pieces of silver, is made specifically to appease and honor Sarah; such an immense gift will testify that Avimelech relinquished her against his will, and only because God miraculously appeared to him and instructed him to do so."[11] The commentaries base their views on the Hebrew word *nochachat*, which means "thou art set right, righted, justified."[12] Sforno writes, "[Abimelech's] tangible gift gave Sarah the ability to stand firm and to offer tangible proof of her worth against all slanderers of her reputation."[13]

Genesis 20 continues with the narrative. "So Abraham prayed unto God: and God healed Abimelech, and his wife, and his maidservants; and they bare children. For the LORD had fast closed up all the wombs of the house of Abimelech, because of Sarah Abraham's wife" (Genesis 20:17–18). Abraham prays that the infirmities besetting Abimelech and his household would be healed, and the plague that had closed off the bodily orifices is reversed. The pregnant women are now able to give birth, and all other bodily functions return to normal. Alshich implies "the reason the text enumerates specifically that Avimelech was healed, is so the reader clearly understands that when Sarah was alone in his presence, he was emphatically 'un-healed,' and it was therefore physically impossible for him to have impregnated her."[14] Ohr Hachayim states further that "the reason the text uses the double emphatic form of the verb 'closed' [up all the orifices], is to make it absolutely clear to any doubters that Sarah's future pregnancy was not to be credited to [Abimelech,] but to her husband, Abraham."[15]

Chapter 21 of Genesis begins with a simple announcement: "And the Lord visited Sarah as he had said, and the Lord did unto Sarah as he had spoken. For Sarah conceived, and bare Abraham a son in his old age, at the set time of which God had spoken to him" (Genesis 21:1–2). This verse refers to the parentage of Isaac twice. *Sarah* conceived and bore him, and he was the son of *Abraham*, in his old age. Rashi contends that the reason for this repetition is to remove any speculation that the child might have been sired by Abimelech, in whose palace Sarah had spent one day in Gerar. In addition, "the use of the Hebrew term 'son of his old age' seems to be a contraction of two other Hebrew words: *ziv ikunin*, meaning 'the precise image of Abraham.' This is an indication to us that the face of the infant Isaac was the image of Abraham, further confirming his parentage."[16]

Sarah has been through *so* much—it is wonderful so see her day of joy arrive at last. The Hebrew word *pakod* is also a tender word which means "paid attention to," "remembered," or "visited graciously."[17] Sarah is finally remembered by the Lord for all her good works. She and her husband Abraham have worked with fervor for decades preaching the doctrine of the one true God. She has been an equal partner with him in winning souls for God wherever they have dwelled. Her greatest desire has been to bear Abraham's son, the heir to God's covenant.

At this point we finally get to hear Sarah's voice: "And Sarah said, God hath made me to laugh, so that all that hear will laugh with me" (Genesis 21:6). Sarah is thrilled and filled with joy and rejoicing. No longer will anyone be able to scorn her for being unable to give birth. She glories in the miracle that God has wrought upon her. God himself has declared that Sarah's son would be named Isaac, and Sarah rejoices in that fact, for Isaac (*yitzhak*) means "rejoicing."

The Bible does not follow through with the account of the fulfilling of the promise made by the angel of the Lord to visit Abraham again. "At the time appointed I will return unto thee, according to the time of life, and Sarah shall have a son" (Genesis 18:14). Such a return *is* recorded in *Jubilees* 16:15–19 (circa 150 BC) in the Old Testament Pseudepigrapha, where the angels relate:

> We went forth to Abraham ... and we appeared to him [just as we said to Sarah that we would return to her. ... And we returned ... and we found Sarah pregnant before us] and we blessed him and we announced to him everything which was commanded for him—that he would not die until he begot six more sons and that he would see (them) before he died. And through Isaac, a name and seed would be named for him. ... From the sons of Isaac one would become a holy seed and he would not be counted among the nations (Gentiles) because he would become the portion of the Most High and all his seed would fall (by lot) into that which God will rule so that he might become a people (belonging) to the Lord, a (special) possession from all people and so that he might become a kingdom of priests and a holy people. And we went our way and we announced to Sarah everything which we had told him. And both of them rejoiced very greatly.[18]

Sarah's joyful musings continue. "And she said, Who would have said unto Abraham, that Sarah should have given children suck? for I have born him a son in his old age" (Genesis 21:7). It is as if Sarah is pouring out her heart in thanks to her God, who not only allows her to bear a child in her old age, but also to have the joy of nursing him herself. Abrabanel interprets the use of the Hebrew word *millel* in Sarah's speech to have the special meaning "to extol" in her praise of God. "This indicates that Sarah rightly senses God's even greater munificence: He did not stop at opening her womb; he allowed Sarah to experience the added satisfaction of nursing her own son until the time of his weaning arrived." It is as if God is rewarding Sarah for her faithfulness. "She was steadfast for ninety years, and now she will reap the full blessings of motherhood."[19]

Rabbi Nehemiah comments on this verse: "Old as Sarah was, she regained her youth. Her skin became soft, the wrinkles in her face disappeared, the warm tints of maidenly beauty returned, and in a short time she became pregnant."[20] Many commentaries extend the effect of God's merciful regeneration of Sarah to many women throughout the world at the same time. Rashi comments that "many other barren women (*'aqarot*) were remembered with Sarah and gave birth, many deaf gained their hearing, many blind had their eyes opened, many insane became sane, many sick became cured on the same day, many prayers were answered, and the world was filled with joyous laughter."[21]

Genesis 21:7 reads, "Sarah will nurse sons." *Sons*, plural. Commentators throughout the centuries have argued about this verse, asking, "Why does this verse say 'Sarah will nurse sons,' when we all know she only bears one son?" Rabbi Samson Raphael Hirsch responds that "Isaac and all subsequent generations originating from Isaac had their origins at Sarah's breast. It was Sarah, after all, who nourished the first covenant child. The text credits Sarah with this and is hinting to us that Isaac is the first of countless future 'sons of the covenant' who will issue from her."[22]

Louis Ginzberg offers a much more colorful explanation from Jewish tradition.

> That Abraham and Sarah were blessed with offspring only after they had attained so great an age, had an important reason. It was necessary that Abraham should bear the sign of the covenant upon his body before he bore the son who was appointed to be the father of Israel. And as Isaac was the first child born to Abraham after he was marked with the sign, he did not fail to celebrate his circumcision with much pomp and ceremony on the eighth day. ... They all were present ... all the great ones round about. On this occasion Abraham could at last put a stop to the talk of the people, who said, "Look at this old couple! They picked up a foundling on the highway, and they pretend he is their son, and to make their statement seem credible, they arrange a feast in his honor." Abraham had invited not only men to the celebration, but also the wives of the magistrates with their infants, and God permitted a miracle to be done. Sarah had enough milk in her breasts to suckle all the babies there.[23]

In Genesis 21:8, it reads, "And the child grew, and was weaned: and Abraham made a great feast the same day that Isaac was weaned." Trevor Denis helps us understand why a weaning day was the cause of such celebration in the ancient Near East. "Archaeological discoveries at burial sites in Israel have demonstrated what we might have guessed, that infant mortality rates could be appallingly high. Children were generally not weaned until they were in their third year, and so the feasting was chiefly to celebrate their surviving the most dangerous period of their lives."[24]

This event, which should have been such a joyous one for Sarah, soon disintegrates into disaster, although the details are not given. The text states, "Sarah saw the son of Hagar the Egyptian, which she had born unto Abraham, mocking" (Genesis 21:9). When this verse and the one prior to it are read aloud, we cannot help but be struck by the wordplay. Verse 8 ends in the Hebrew with Isaac's name, *yitzhaq*. Verse 9 ends with the word *metzaheq*. Denis comments on the ramifications of the use of these two words. "One commentator suggests we should translate *metzaheq* as 'Isaacing,' that is not playing *with* Isaac, but *playing Isaac*." This is Isaac's feast, *his* big moment. Apparently, Ishmael cannot help but attract the attention and the honor of the occasion for himself. After all, he is the elder brother and as such can consider himself the inheritor of the majority of Abraham's land and accompanying wealth. "No one has told *him* that he is not the heir that Abraham and Sarah and God have been waiting for." But we know. God and Abraham and Sarah know. "We can now more readily understand Sarah's reaction, and why it will meet with divine approval."[25]

Something Sarah sees makes her react violently. "Wherefore she said unto Abraham, Cast out this bondwoman and her son: for the son of this bondwoman shall not be heir with my son, even with Isaac" (Genesis 21:10). Sarah cannot even bring herself to call Hagar and Ishmael by name, but merely "this slave-woman and her son." Hagar is not even "my handmaid," as she was in Genesis 16. And yet in her expulsion of Hagar, Sarah assumes full authority as her mistress and commands Abraham to get rid of her. She has been living with Hagar and Ishmael—who is now a teenager—for many years without such a response. What is the difference now?

Tuchman and Rapoport offer some interesting insights. They observe that Sarah, "being fully aware of Ishmael's taunts as early as Isaac's birth," bided her time and refrained from complaining to Abraham. This she did because she knew of her husband's devotion to his "healthy, strapping son, Ishmael, over the precarious newborn Isaac. She was shrewd enough to wait until Isaac had matured physically and was safely past his weaning, because only then, to paraphrase Abrabanel, could Abraham appreciate the ripened fruit that was Isaac." Ibn Ezra characterizes Ishmael's behavior as "ordinary sibling rivalry between an older son accustomed to being the favored only child, and a young interloper." Although the rivalry was vexing to Sarah, it did not threaten Isaac's well-being, so she took no action at the outset. "It was only when the taunting evolved into behavior that actually endangered Isaac's moral, spiritual, and physical survival that Sarah intervened."[26]

I have always been mystified by Sarah's actions here. She has always been so cool, calm, and collected in other desperate situations. Something causes her to demand drastic action from Abraham. Other commentators have proposed interpretations of the word translated "playing." Tammi Schneider cites Friedman, who interprets the "playing" as "fooling around." She also quotes Robert Alter who says, "Some medieval Hebrew exegetes, trying to find a justification for Sarah's harsh response, construe the verb as a reference to homosexual advances."[27] Another refers to Ishmael showing Isaac how to play with his genitals.[28] Teubal maintains that the enigmatic term used to describe Ishmael's behavior can also be rendered as something like "sexual fondling."[29]

Another premise is proposed by *Midrash Rabbah*. In this commentary, Sarah one day watches Isaac and Ishmael together. On the pretext of showing Isaac their future inheritance, Ishmael lures the young boy out of Sarah's tent and into the fields. Once he is there, he sets Isaac up as a target and begins shooting arrows at him saying, "I am only making sport!"[30]

If *any* of these commentaries are true, it is easy to see why Sarah feels her son may be in jeopardy if Ishmael remains in close proximity. They don't even have to be true; just verging on possible truth is sufficient. She knows that she must maintain Isaac's safety if he is to grow to manhood and someday inherit the promised covenant. There is no clue in the text of Genesis that Sarah knows what God told Abraham in Genesis 17:20–21, that Ishmael would be blessed but God's covenant will be with Isaac. We do not know if Abraham has shared this information with his wife, but her actions articulate that she is aware, somehow. Schneider states that according to the rabbis, "Sarah is considered one of seven biblical prophetesses, and her prophetic powers have exceeded those of her husband, for she was able to discern the Deity's (Elohim's) will in expelling Hagar and Ishmael while Abraham resisted."[31]

---

[1] Shera Aranoff Tuchman and Sandra E. Rapoport, *The Passions of the Matriarchs*, (Berrien Springs, MI: KTAV Publishing House, Inc., 2004), 38.

[2] Tuchman and Rapoport (2004), 38–39.

[3] Anne Roiphe, *Water from the Well: Sarah, Rebekah, Rachel, and Leah*, (New York: William Morrow, 2006), 76.

[4] Tuchman and Rapoport (2004), 39.

[5] Ibid.

[6] *Midrash Rabbah* (52.13) quoted in Tuchman and Rapoport (2004), 42.

[7] Roiphe (2006), 77; see also Tuchman and Rapoport (2004), 44.

[8] Trevor Dennis, *Sarah Laughed*, (Nashville: Abingdon Press, 1994), 56.

[9] Adin Steinsatlz, *Biblical Images: Men and women of the Book*, (New York: Basic Books, 1984), 26.

[10] Translation from Tuchman and Rapoport (2004), 46.

[11] Tuchman and Rapoport (2004), 46.

[12] Francis Brown, *The New Brown-Driver-Briggs-Genesius Hebrew and English Lexicon*, (Peabody, Massachusetts: Hendrickson Publishers, 1979) 406–407, entry 3198.

[13] Tuchman and Rapoport (2004), 47.

[14] Tuchman and Rapoport (2004), 48.

[15] Tuchman and Rapoport (2004), 48–49.

[16] Tuchman and Rapoport (2004), 53.

[17] Brown (1979), 823, entry 6485.

[18] James H. Charlesworth, "Jubilees" in *The Old Testament Pseudepigrapha, Volume 2*, (Garden City New York: Doubleday and Company, Inc., 1985), 88.

[19] Tuchman and Rapoport (2004), 56.

[20] Gerard P. Luttikhuizen, *The Creation of Man and Woman: Interpretations of the Biblical Narratives in Jewish and Christian Traditions Vol. 3*, (Leiden: Brill, 2000), 135.

[21] Ibid. (See *Genesis Rabbah* 53,8) See also Louis Ginzberg, *The Legends of the Jews, Vol. 1*, (Baltimore: The Johns Hopkins University Press, 1937), 261–262.

[22] Tuchman and Rapoport (2004), 56.

[23] Ginzberg (1937), 262–263.

[24] Denis (1994), 58.

[25] Denis (1994), 58–59.

[26] Tuchman and Rapoport (2004), 59–60.

[27] Tammi J. Schneider, *Sarah: Mother of Nations*, (New York: Continuum, 2004), 94.

[28] Roiphe (2006), 84.

[29] Savina J. Teubal, *Sarah the Priestess: The First Matriarch of Genesis*, (Athens, Ohio: Swallow Press, 1984), 39.

[30] Tuchman and Rapoport (2004), 60.

[31] Schneider (2004), 95.

Chapter 6
Sarah's Legacy

For the first time in her life, Sarah dwells alone with Abraham and Isaac. The Chinese character for *peace* is the character for "woman" (just one) under the character for "roof." Sarah and her husband can raise Isaac to revere the one true God and follow his ways. Neither Sarah nor Isaac has to fear scorn, criticism, or resentment from any member of the household. These must have been idyllic years, filled with peace and contentment.

Sarah has been the target of criticism from commentators for demanding that Abraham expel Hagar and Ishmael from the camp, but God—for reasons never clearly articulated—has chosen *Sarah* as the mother of the chosen lineage. Abraham complies with Sarah's wishes for Ishmael's removal only *after* being commanded to heed the words of his wife in the matter, and he still experiences serious distress over the affair. Tammi Schneider states, "by telling Abraham to follow Sarah's plan, Elohim confirms that Sarah understands Elohim's plan better than Abraham does."[1]

But the halcyon existence of Abraham and Sarah's family comes to a grinding halt in Genesis 22. This is the heart-stopping story that everyone remembers in Genesis, the climax. Artists' depictions of the event fill museums, and philosophers have tried over the centuries to make sense of God's seemingly illogical injunction to Abraham. "Take now thy son, thine only son Isaac, whom thou lovest, and get thee into the land of Moriah; and offer him there for a burnt offering upon one of the mountains which I will tell thee of" (Genesis 22:2). The text includes nothing of Abraham revealing this astonishing command to his wife, let alone her reaction to it. This omission leaves a gaping hole in the story of Sarah's trials.

Anne Roiphe writes, "Sarah is most often ignored in these weighty discussions. And yet it is she who will lose the most if her son is sacrificed according to God's command to Abraham. She does not appear on the stage herself as this story unfolds, but the sages must have known that in ignoring her reactions we deny our own human perspective, which is both male and female, stemming from the love of the mother as well as the love of the father." Because of this, commentators have embellished the story, presenting it from Sarah's perspective. Until her perspective is considered, we only have half of the story. Roiphe concludes, "What happens to Isaac's mother is part of this tale of obedience to God's command because Abraham was willing not only to sacrifice his son for God but also to destroy the child his wife cherished beyond all else, which must have weighed on his soul heavily."[2]

Sarah's silence in the text is "thunderous," according to Shera Tuchman and Sandra Rapoport.[3] The text does not refer to Sarah again after the Lord commands Abraham to heed her voice and send away Hagar and Ishmael. In fact, it does not mention her again until her death. We do not know if she was even aware of God's command to slay her son. If she *did* know, what was her reaction? Did she rail against Abraham and God, or did she remain silent and supportive? The driving passion of her life had been to become the mother of the covenantal child. It is hard to imagine her remaining silent.

Many commentators have rushed to answer these questions. Sefer Tosfot Hashalem proposes, "Sarah knew of Abraham's plans. Abraham feared that had he disclosed to Sarah the true nature of his mission that day, she would have refused to let him go; had he absconded with Isaac without telling Sarah his whereabouts, she would have likely feared the worst, gone mad and killed herself. Therefore, Abraham told Sarah only that he was taking Isaac away in order to educate him."[4]

This same source goes on to describe the evening preceding the *Akedah*, "the binding." "Abraham approaches Sarah and proposes a feast. He tells Sarah, 'Prepare food and drink so that we might celebrate tonight.' Amidst her preparations, Sarah asks, 'Tell me, what is the special occasion that requires such a feast?' Abraham responds, 'God has commanded me to bring Isaac up to Mount Moriah, to educate him there in the ways of God's commandments. He has told me to bring Isaac to *that* mountain and no other.' Sarah yields to this, saying: 'Take him there in peace.'"[5]

In another commentary, Isaac tells his father as they approach the mountaintop, "When you tell mother that I am dead make sure she is not on a high place, not standing on a roof or high above a river, for she will throw herself down. She will not want to live anymore."[6] God's command to Abraham was wrenching on many fronts.

Other versions of this story relate that Satan visits Sarah and informs her that Abraham has bound Isaac on the altar and sacrificed him to his God. Hearing these words, Sarah assumes that her son is dead. Modern biblical scholar Aviva Zoren Gornberg continues the story. Sarah cries out with the same sound as that made by a shofar, "a wail, a complaint, a great broken sound." This pitiful cry contains all her rage at Abraham for following such a command. She asks, "What man would offer his own son as a sacrifice?" She cries again, "sounding like an animal bleating in pain." This cry contains "the fury she felt toward the Lord, whom she had served all her life." She has "done as the Lord has asked and moved when he asked her to move." She has tried valiantly to be worthy of his care and has believed in him even when surrounded by those who worship idols—"idols who would not have asked for the death of her child, her only child."[7]

The sages add that some of those who heard Sarah's wail went deaf. It was said that her cry caused a man to go blind and another man was never able to walk again. According to this legend, the terrible news of the death of her child caused Sarah to die instantly at the age of 127 at Kiriath-arba.[8]

Louis Ginzberg tells another version of the story of Sarah's death. In this account, Satan appears to Sarah in the form of an old man and tells her that her husband has built an altar, slaughtered Isaac, and offered him as a sacrifice upon it. Isaac cries and weeps before his father, but Abraham will neither look nor have compassion upon him. Hearing this, Sarah cries bitterly, saying, "O my son, Isaac, my son, O that I had this day died instead of thee. ... (echoing David's cry when he learns of the death of Absolom in 2 Samuel 18:33.) In my longing for a child, I cried and prayed, till I bore thee at ninety. Now thou hast served this day for the knife and the fire. But I console myself, it being the word of God, and thou didst perform the command of thy God. ... Thou art just, O Lord our God, for all Thy works are good and righteous, for I also rejoice with the word which Thou didst command, and while mine eye weepeth bitterly, my heart rejoiceth." Sarah goes about making inquiries after her son, but cannot find him. Satan again comes to Sarah in the form of an old man and says, "I spoke falsely unto thee, for Abraham did not kill his son, and he is not dead." When Sarah hears these words, her joy is so "violent" that "her soul went out through joy."[9]

It is fascinating to hear the divergent theories about how this noble lady passes from this world—was it from grief or from joy? In the end, we just don't know. I suppose we will all just have to wait until that great fireside in the sky when all our questions will be answered. I know I will be on the front row. In the meantime, the stories inspired by Sarah keep getting more and more captivating.

What we *do* know is that Sarah was ninety years old when she bore Isaac, and one hundred twenty-seven years old when she died. We do not know how old Isaac was at the time of the binding, but because her death is related immediately following the binding incident and was triggered, as many suggest, by news of the event, Isaac would have been thirty-seven.

Ginzberg reports that Sarah's death was cause for widespread mourning. "The death of Sarah was a loss not only for Abraham and his family, but for the whole country. So long as she was alive, all went well in the land. After her death, confusion ensued. The weeping, lamenting, and wailing over her going hence was universal, and Abraham, instead of receiving consolation, had to offer consolation to others."[10]

"And Sarah died in Kirjath-arba; the same is Hebron in the land of Canaan: and Abraham came to mourn for Sarah, and to weep for her" (Genesis 23:2). Netziv asks, "Why does the text say, 'And Abraham returned to eulogize Sarah, and to weep over her,' with the eulogy before the weeping?" Usually, one would expect the weeping to *precede* the eulogy. The commentator explains that the text's words are accurately placed and deliberate.

> When Abraham returned to Hebron after Sarah's death, he was greeted by throngs of people surrounding Sarah's house. As their communal leader, his first task was to eulogize Sarah. Abraham's private weeping and mourning for her came second. ... Abraham's grief was mitigated by the fact that Sarah had already fulfilled her life's goal of raising Isaac. It was Abraham's public eulogy of her—not his private tears—that was needed most by Sarah's followers. Abraham saw this and met that need.[11]

The Midrash Tanchuma relates that, although the exact words of Abraham's eulogy are not recorded in Genesis, they are kept elsewhere in Old Testament scripture. This commentary explains at length that Proverbs 31, which is known as *Eshet Chayil* ("Woman of Valor") is an anthem praising the matriarch Sarah. The psalm begins "Who can find a virtuous woman?" The word translated "virtuous" here, *chayil*, means "valor" and denotes inner strength and fortitude, rather than simply chastity.12

Abraham finds himself in a peculiar position. He needs to find a burial place for Sarah, but he is an alien in the land. As an immigrant, he needs to follow the legal traditions of the people in the land of Canaan. Although the Lord has promised him the entire land of Canaan for his inheritance, in the ultimate irony, he does not yet own a single square inch of property there. His settlement at that time was located in southern Canaan near the city of Hebron. In order to purchase a burial site for his wife, he has to go to Hebron and follow the legal procedures of the area for business, "all of which favored the settled community over the pastoral nomads," according to Victor H. Matthews.13

First, Abraham goes to the city gate (see Genesis 23:18), where most of the business of the city was conducted. There, he asks the elders of the city to be witnesses for him, as an alien, in his purchase of the property. He enters into legal bargaining with Ephron the Hittite, the owner of the cave in the field of Machpelah. They converse about the purchase price and the exact nature of the property being discussed. Abraham originally only desires to buy the cave, but in the end he is compelled to buy an adjacent field and its trees as well. The dialogue is amusing to the occidental (western) mind, but it is very typical of the ancient Near East, with great shows of courtesy and grandiose manners. Ephron first offers Abraham the cave as a gift. This maneuver was designed to force Abraham into being equally obliging by asking Ephron to set his own price. The sum Ephron names is an exorbitant one. The final step was the witnessing of the transaction by the elders at the city gate.

Thomas Cahill has an interesting, tongue-in-cheek interpretation of the goings-on in Hebron.

> Ephron would not dream of charging him, he can have "the choicest" site free of charge, even the cave of Makhpela, even though it is worth four hundred shekels. Avraham [b and v are the same letter in Hebrew] hears this and understands what is really being offered: a temporary burial site (with no assurances for the future) for free, or a permanent burial site for an outrageous sum.

> Through all the subsequent bargaining (interminable, full of ritualistic bowing, scraping, and profanations of sincerity, as is still typical of the Middle East), he keeps offering four hundred shekels until it is accepted by all. The amount, probably ten times the cave's actual value, is worth it to Avraham, for it gives him clear and irrevocable title to his wife's final resting place. One feels Avraham would have paid anything for this peace; and thus he shows ... his reverence for the matriarch.[14]

Savina Teubal points out that "Abram made no mention of seeking a family crypt when he negotiated for the purchase of the cave. He stated that the plot was for Sarah. It was for Sarah that Abraham carefully chose and contracted for the purchase of the burial ground, close to the sacred area in which the matriarch had spent the greater part of her life."[15]

Matthews notes that it was rather unusual for land to be sold outright in this manner. "Land was considered sacred, entrusted by the god/gods to the ruler, and he, in turn, entrusted it to individuals." The fact that Ephron was willing to make the sale here may be due to the fact that "Abraham specifically wished to use it for his wife's burial and not as a base of operations that could threaten the local people or their economy." An even more revealing explanation for the sale may be found in the title given to Abraham by the city elders, "a mighty prince among us."[16]

Another important aspect of this act of largesse on the part of Ephron was the implication in terms of what it meant in the ancient Near East. Matthews explains the significance of hospitality in the ancient Near East—the one prevailing legal custom among pastoral nomadic people. "Once it has been offered and accepted, no hostilities are possible until the parties separate and a mutually agreed upon period of time has passed. Thus, hospitality is not offered or accepted lightly, since it places obligations on both parties."[17] In light of this tradition, the purchase of the cave of Machpelah was, in essence, a *treaty* with the people of the land. Abraham and Sarah must have been held in high regard indeed.

As we reflect on Sarah's life, what do we remember? What kind of a legacy does she leave for those who follow? On Friday evenings in traditional Jewish homes, candles are lit and prayers are said. One line of this prayer reads, "God should establish you as He did Sarah,

Rebekah, Rachel, and Leah." Tuchman and Rapoport ask, "Considering the fraught saga of the life of Sarah the matriarch, we are naturally led to wonder: Do we really seek to bestow such a life upon our own daughters? ... We would hardly wish our daughters to experience dislocation, famine, abduction, infertility, the trauma of surrogacy, a sometime-indifferent husband, vexatious stepchildren, or the near-death of a long-awaited child."[18] I get fainthearted just reading that list! What exactly *can* we learn from Sarah's life? What about her do we want to emulate?

I love the answer given by Carolyn Custis James:

> Sarah's life was a long tortuous journey from "The Lord has kept me from having children" (Genesis 16:2) to the miracle birth of Isaac and the day she rejoiced, saying, "God has brought me laughter" (Genesis 21:6). Her laughter had been a long time coming. ... But to be honest, that joyful moment isn't the part of Sarah's life that touches me most. While there are rich lessons to be gathered from God's ability to create life in a dead womb, the long, drawn-out silent stretch that took up most of her life is the part of her story that both fascinates and disturbs me. ... There's wisdom to be gained in freezing Sarah's story right in the middle, before the part about Hagar and the astonishing words she heard the Lord speak through the tent door.
>
> What are we to make of this? How are we to go on when some major piece of our lives is missing or broken? Are we to put our lives on hold and wait for him finally to come through for us? There's no escaping the fact that while nothing is too hard for the Lord, he's not afraid to keep me waiting. Is that how we're supposed to live? How much of our lives do we let slip away while we drum our fingers restlessly waiting to graduate, get married, have a baby, buy a house, or get that big break at work? What do we do in those long stretches when life comes to a standstill because of God's silence, when day after day you're looking at the same problems, the same unchanged heart, the same unhealed body? ...
>
> The problem I wrestle with most is how to live in the silence. Sarah's eighty-nine years is an awfully long time to wait before discovering God's purpose for your life. Caught in God's silence, "We cannot see the end from the middle and must walk by faith, not by sight." It's the hardest thing we ever do. I think there's more to learn from Sarah's failures than from her eleventh-hour triumph.[19]

Sarah's long silence reminds me of Job. For years he beseeched God to speak to him, to let him know he was not forgotten. Mocked by all, even his friends, he steadfastly maintained his faith in his God. He never veered from his testimony. "Though he slay me, yet will I trust in him" (Job 13:15). Sarah did likewise.

Throughout all the years that her passionate hope for a child was not realized, she kept working beside her husband. Forgetting her own agony, she worked as a team with her husband, committed to the one true God and spreading the good news of his reality. Rabbi Adin Steinsaltz puts it this way: "When the turning point came, a new relationship was formed between them. They underwent a name change, becoming Abraham and Sarah, as an indication of rebirth. Abraham was circumcised; Sarah entered the female cycle once again. This transformation provides the symbolic meaning of the story of the patriarchs." He notes that in earlier generations, if spiritual influence was passed down from one person to another, it was passed from teacher to pupil. In this instance, "the spiritual tie" received was reinforced by a "biological tie," by the "birth of the child who would transmit the model throughout the generations of his descendants." Consequently, Abraham and Sarah were not only the "spiritual forbears of the Jewish people," but also the biological ancestors. "The meaning of the name 'Children of Israel' could be made tangible only when the relationship between them underwent another level of change and became a blood tie, a biological link. It thus became the relationship that bore Isaac, in order that he, and only he, could continue the line arising from the union of Abraham and Sarah to form the nation of Israel."[20]

Abraham and Sarah *were* a team. Together they were the founders of a new covenant. God did not make his covenant with Abraham alone. Rabbi Joseph Soloveitchik notes

> Not only did man and woman achieve human dignity together at creation, both in God's image, but they also attained together, and only together, covenantal sanctity, being elected by God to be the founders of a new faith. Their covenantal interdependence is further indicated by the fact that the Torah does not dwell on Abraham's life after Sarah's death. Though he survived her by many years, he knew that his mission as the father of the covenantal community was concluded, and that from that point, all he had to

do was to act out the last part of the drama and walk off the covenantal stage and make room for someone else to succeed him. Only two items remained for him to complete: to purchase ... a burial place for Sarah and to arrange for the marriage of his son Isaac. The latter story is told not to portray the story of Abraham, but to acquaint us with the second mother of the covenantal community, Rebecca, who succeeded Sarah. The concluding verse of this episode clearly informs us that the vacancy was filled. "And Isaac brought [Rebecca] into his mother Sarah's tent and he married her. She became his wife and he loved her. Isaac was then consoled for the loss of his mother" (Genesis 24:67). Now the covenant could be resumed, because there was a mother, not only a father, in the covenantal leadership.[21]

As Bakan accurately points out, "Not all the offspring of Abraham are Israelites: the Israelites stem only from Sarah. Sarah is more definitely the ancestor of the Israelites than Abraham."[22]

The House of Israel is only part of Sarah's legacy. Her life itself articulates a myriad of lessons worthy of emulation.

---

[1] Tammi Schneider, *Sarah: Mother of Nations*, (New York: Continuum, 2004), 99.

[2] Anne Roiphe, *Water from the Well: Sarah, Rebekah, Rachel, and Leah*, (New York: William Morrow, 2006), 90.

[3] Shera Aranoff Tuchman and Sandra E. Rapoport, *The Passions of the Matriarchs*, (Berrien Springs, MI: KTAV Publishing House, Inc., 2004), 67.

[4] Tuchman and Rapoport (2004), 68.

[5] Tuchman and Rapoport (2004), 68–69.

[6] Roiphe (2006), 92.

[7] Tuchman and Rapoport (2004), 93–94.

[8] Tuchman and Rapoport (2004), 94.

[9] Louis Ginzberg, *The Legends of the Jews, Volume 1*, (Baltimore: The Johns Hopkins University Press, 1937), 286–287.

[10] Ginzberg (1937), 287–288.

[11] Tuchman and Rapoport (2004), 78.

[12] Midrash Tanchuma (Chaye Sarah, note 3) quoted in Tuchman and Rapoport (2004), 79.

[13] Victor H. Matthews, *Manners and Customs in the Bible*, (Peabody, Massachusetts: Hendrickson Publishers, 1988), 11.

[14] Thomas Cahill, *The Gifts of the Jews: How a Tribe of Desert Nomads Changed the Way Everyone Thinks and Feels*, (New York: Nan A. Talese/Doubleday, 1998), 88.

[15] Savina J. Teubal, *Sarah the Priestess: The First Matriarch of Genesis*, (Athens, Ohio: Swallow Press, 1984xd), 94.

[16] Matthews (1988), 12–13.

[17] Matthews (1988), 28.

[18] Tuchman and Rapoport (2004), 81.

[19] Carolyn Custis James, *Lost Women of the Bible*, (Grand Rapids, Michigan: Zondervan, 2005), 77–78.

[20] Adin Steinsaltz, *Biblical Images: Men and Women of the Book*, (New York: Basic Books, 1984), 28.

[21] Joseph B. Soloveitchik, *Man of Faith in the Modern World: Reflections of the Rav, Volume Two*, (Hoboken, New Jersey: KTAV Publishing House, 1989), 86-87.

[22] Teubal (1984), 95.

Chapter 7
Seeking Rebekah

As I listened to Sister Julie Beck's talk at the BYU Women's Conference in April 2010, her words hit me with all the force of a two-by-four. She said

> I spent quite a few months this last winter studying about Rebekah from the Old Testament. I have been taken by her mission and what she had to do. I love Rebekah and have learned so much from her. I feel that she is one of the women at the head of the house of Israel, and as my father spoke about the house of Israel, her life and mission was on my mind. I have loved studying her characteristics, her circumstances, her blessings, her journeys, her family, her experiences, and her challenges. She had a very full mortal experience. It had its highs and its lows. I have learned that she was one of the most pivotal and important people in the history of mankind, certainly in the house of Israel. Without a Rebekah, the house of Israel would not have been brought forth. Without a Rebekah who knew who she was, the house of Israel would not have been brought forth. Without a Rebekah who knew her responsibilities in the house of Israel, that house would not have come to pass. Without a Rebekah who knew how to receive revelation, the house of Israel would not have been brought forth. Without a Rebekah who understood the blessings of the priesthood, the house of Israel would not have been brought forth.[1]

Sister Beck went on to say that "each of us in our day is as important to our generation and our time as Rebekah was in her time. ... The success of the house of Israel is now dependent on millions of Rebekahs who understand what their place and mission is on the earth."[2] What gave Rebekah the insight and drive to play such a critical role in the development of the house of Israel? What was she made of?

Before we ever meet Rebekah, (whose name in Hebrew is Rivkah), we hear all about her future husband—the golden boy, Isaac. Isaac is the miracle child, born to a ninety-year old mother who was long past the age of childbearing. Isaac is the chosen recipient of the covenant of Abraham, the heir of promise. He is not chosen by any mortal; his destiny is *divinely* decreed. However, the weight of this destiny does not exclude him from the nightmare of all nightmares: being offered up as a human sacrifice to God. Just ask his father Abraham, who went through the experience himself, yet lived to tell about it. Isaac survives and proves his willingness to submit to God's word.

Abraham has lost his beloved wife Sarah. He has buried her, and has complied with the most grueling commandment he has ever received from the one true God. And because Isaac still lives, Abraham must find the perfect wife for his son. With so much riding on Isaac, the girl has to be incredibly special. Abraham's advanced age precludes his seeking a bride for his son himself, so he enlists his faithful servant, presumably Eliezer, to search for this exceptional creature. This man knows his master's world intimately, and he realizes the great importance of his task. He is trusted implicitly. His is indeed a sacred mission.

Abraham takes this trusted servant aside and makes him swear an oath that he will not choose a bride from among the Canaanites—the uncovenanted inhabitants among whom he now dwells—but rather find a bride from Abraham's own blood and lineage.

> And Abraham said unto his eldest servant of his house, that ruled over all that he had, Put, I pray thee, thy hand under my thigh: And I will make thee swear by the LORD, the God of heaven, and the God of the earth, that thou shalt not take a wife unto my son of the daughters of the Canaanites, among whom I dwell: But thou shalt go unto my country, and to my kindred, and take a wife unto my son Isaac. (Genesis 24:2–4)

Putting the hand under the thigh was an action that accompanied the most solemn kinds of oaths in the ancient world. There is much speculation among biblical scholars as to exactly what gesture is being referred to here. Some commentators consider the expression a euphemism for cupping the genitals.[3] The Interpreter's Bible notes that this is "a reference to an oath by the genital organs, emblems of the life-giving power of deity."[4] Undoubtedly, it was also a reference to the token of the covenant that God had made with Abraham, the most solemn of all covenants. Abraham's seed and the seed of his future posterity must pass *through* the token of this covenant.[5] Perhaps it was also like having Eliezer swear by the emblem of his own future descendants that he would perform this most sacred task.

After the oath is given, the servant mentions a concern with his mission. "Peradventure the woman will not be willing to follow me unto this land: must I needs bring thy son again unto the land from whence thou camest?" (Genesis 24:5). Realizing the covenant nature of the land upon which he now dwells, Abraham rejects this possibility, remembering the promise God has given him that "unto thy seed will I give this land" (Genesis 12:7). He says that under no circumstances will Isaac go to live in another land. The servant has already sworn an oath to find a bride for Isaac, but now Abraham requires him to swear another that he will not take Isaac back to Abraham's homeland, even at the cost of failing to retrieve the sought-after bride.[6] "And if the woman will not be willing to follow thee, then thou shalt be clear from this my oath: only bring not my son thither again" (Genesis 24:8).

Both Abraham and his servant have ultimate faith that God will provide a way that a suitable bride might be found for the heir of the covenant. The lack of detail provided by his master motivates the servant to inquire further of Abraham's God and plead for divine guidance. He sets off with his entourage of ten camels and travels to the land of Aram-naharaim (Hebrew for "Aram of the Two Rivers"), to the city of Nahor—an expedition of 850 miles. With his retinue of men, supplies, and gifts, the journey of this caravan likely took him a month to complete.

When they arrive, the servant causes the camels to kneel down beside the well outside the city at evening time, the time when women come to draw water. He prays in a very unusual way, setting up a series of conditions—a test which the desired young woman must pass to signal to the servant that he had indeed pinpointed the correct girl for Isaac. He has received imprecise instructions for a precise errand, and he *needs* divine assistance in order to accomplish it. He uses a Hebrew phrase which means literally, "make it happen before me now."[7] This lets us in on the state of his mind—he is totally counting on and in fact *expecting* divine help on his errand. He knows he cannot be successful on his own, and he is desperate for assistance from Abraham's God.

I like how the Interpreter's Bible describes the situation:

> So Eliezer prayed. That was his first way of seeking guidance. He had an errand on which he could invoke God's blessing, and he trusted that a wisdom higher than his own would light his way. But he did not assume that this guidance would be arbitrary. It would enlist his wisdom and his consecrated common sense. Presently the girls of the countryside would be coming to draw water from the well where he had halted with his camels. If there should be one among them whom God intended as the bride of Isaac, how should

he, Eliezer, know her? By something that she wore? By some particular feature of her looks? No. There was a more important criterion than that—the criterion of her spirit. The girl who should be the quickest in discernment, the kindest, the swiftest to help— that was the girl he would be seeking.[8]

He is asking God to bring fulfillment to the promise he has made to his master time and again. He is setting the parameters, and he is asking that God comply with them. Then, and only then, will he know he has found the right young woman. He prays,

> O LORD God of my master Abraham, I pray thee, send me good speed this day, and shew kindness unto my master Abraham. Behold, I stand here by the well of water; and the daughters of the men of the city come out to draw water: And let it come to pass, that the damsel to whom I shall say, Let down thy pitcher, I pray thee, that I may drink; and she shall say, Drink, and I will give thy camels drink also: let the same be she that thou hast appointed for thy servant Isaac; and thereby shall I know that thou hast shewed kindness unto my master. (Genesis 24:12–14)

These are amazing stipulations. The number of camels may seem random, but it makes the task that the servant is requesting daunting, at best. One camel can drink twenty-five to thirty gallons in a single session, which would require Rebekah to fill her five-gallon pitcher half a dozen times. Multiply this by ten, and the young woman would have had to make over *fifty* trips to the well.[9] Abraham did not specify that the desired bride be in prime physical condition, but she would have had to have been or she could not have performed the tasks specified by the servant. Perhaps unwittingly, he is setting the bar exceptionally high. Abraham is going to get even more than he asked for.

Such tests as those designed by Eliezer are strict, both in formulation and in result, and presuppose that there is divine control in the events manifest. The conditions are set. When he asks, "Please, lower your jar that I may drink," the maiden will respond, "Drink, and I will also water your camels." Once those events occur in sequence, Eliezer will have received his sign and will *know* that she is the one decreed for Isaac.

Right on cue, Rebekah arrives at the well. The question is asked and answered.

> And it came to pass, before he had done speaking, that, behold, Rebekah came out, who was born to Bethuel, son of Milcah, the wife of Nahor, Abraham's brother, with her pitcher upon her shoulder. And the damsel was very fair to look upon, a virgin, neither had any man known her: and she went down to the well, and filled her pitcher, and came up. And the servant ran to meet her, and said, Let me, I pray thee, drink a little water of thy pitcher. And she said, Drink, my lord: and she hasted, and let down her pitcher upon her hand, and gave him drink. And when she had done giving him drink, she said, I will draw water for thy camels also, until they have done drinking. And she hasted, and emptied her pitcher into the trough, and ran again unto the well to draw water, and drew for all his camels. (Genesis 24:15–29)

It seems that God is one step ahead of Eliezer, for as soon as he has finished shaping his conditions into pleas of petition, God has directed Rebekah's entrance on the set. Mere coincidence? Such stuff is the provender of romance novels. Of course it was no accident; it was orchestrated from on high. The narrator elaborates on the word *virgin*, stating that "neither had any man known her," so that there can be no question as to her purity. Joseph Smith adds in his translation, "And the damsel being a virgin, being very fair to look at, such as the servant of Abraham had not seen, neither had any man known the like unto her" (Gen. 16:24 JST). It is surprising that the narrator eliminates the sense of suspense that *might* be building by his disclosure of Rebekah's heritage, because he has been doing such a great job up until this point.

Rebekah's response is even more than Eliezer had hoped for. She is willing not only to water the camels, but also to stick around until they have finished drinking, in case they want seconds. Eliezer must have been thunderstruck. Not only is this girl stunningly beautiful, but she *runs* to take care of the camels.

I can identify with Eliezer to some degree. When I was in the third grade, I felt a measure of the desperation he felt that day at the well. In the spring of the year, our grade school held "Field Day" right before summer vacation. This was a special occasion because the girls got to wear pants to school. Every other day of the year, we had to wear dresses. I remember my mother taking me to Grand Central and buying me a new "Field Day" outfit. It had turquoise-blue shorts and a sleeveless, blue plaid top with silver threads woven into the plaid. It was the coolest!

I was a tall, skinny kid with little to no athletic ability. When we would choose sides in class before PE, I would inevitably be picked last. In my new blue outfit, I readied myself for the ordeal of choosing sides for the kick soccer team.[10] As I had anticipated, I was again chosen last. It was humiliating, but alas, I was used to it. I was assigned to left field—the safest place for one so unqualified—and the game began. As I sat in left field, I thought about how cool it would be if I got lucky, caught a fly ball, made the winning out, and was a hero for once in my life. In Sunday School, we had been learning about prayer, and that if you prayed and had enough faith, God would give you the answer to your prayer. Right at that moment, I was so sick of the mortification that accompanied every elementary school team activity that I could have screamed. I drew an "X" on the ground with my sneaker and silently prayed: "If I stand on this 'X' with my arms out, will you please let me catch a fly ball?" It was the bottom of the ninth inning with two outs. Our team was one run ahead, and the other team was up, with the bases loaded. Their best kicker was up. I stood on the "X" and closed my eyes, dutifully holding out my arms. Well, you can probably guess the end of the story. (I wouldn't be telling it if it didn't happen just as I had prayed.) The kick was high to left field, and I caught it! I was so excited. Everyone was in shock. That day I learned that my Heavenly Father really cared about me: a gangly, skinny girl with braids. He remembers "every creature of his creating" (Mosiah 27:30).

After having this experience as a young girl, I was deeply moved when I read the story of Rebekah fulfilling Eliezer's very specific prayer. God is indeed involved in the lives of his children.

I have often wondered why Eliezer designed the "camel test." Why was it so important to him that the young woman go out of her way to such a degree? I read an article online called "Rebecca and the Camel Test" that provided me with interesting insights.

> There was an essential characteristic that Eliezer was looking for in a potential wife, something ingrained—part and parcel—in the family of Abraham: boundless lovingkindness (*hesed*). What made Abraham's *hesed* unique was not that he welcomed and catered to his guests in the most generous and impeccable manner, but rather that he actively searched for the opportunity to do such deeds. He wasn't happy to merely serve those who came to him; he would go

out to the crossroads, anxious to be of service. Abraham was an initiator, treasuring the chance to help another. This was the quality he looked for in the future wife of Isaac.[11]

Think about it. When Eliezer and all his able-bodied men parked their camels by the well, they were by no means helpless. Eliezer was not a feeble man begging for a drink. Rebekah was of noble birth, the daughter of Bethuel of Aram-naharaim, not a servant girl used to hauling water from wells to slake camels' thirst. But she radiated her *hesed* when she immediately gave Eliezer drink and offered to haul water for the camels. She saw the opportunity to do something kind. She didn't stop and judge whether Eliezer's retinue of servants should have been drawing their own water, and she didn't question whether she was really needed. She simply "hasted" to perform the work unassisted while the men sat by and watched in wonder. She had one motivation, to show *hesed* to another human being. She jumped at the chance to do service, just as Abraham would have. Here, Rebekah teaches all of us to challenge ourselves to be initiators in giving service, to look for situations where we can be of service, proactively, without judging whether there are others around who could—or *should*—be doing it.[12]

Eliezer must have thought, "Is this girl too good to be true?"

---

[1] Julie Beck, "Choose Ye This Day," BYU Women's Conference, p. 2.

[2] Ibid.

[3] Jack M. Sasson, "The Servant's Tale: How Rebekah Found a Spouse," *Journal of Near Eastern Studies*. (Chicago: University of Chicago Press, 2006.) 65.4, p. 249.

[4] _____, *The Interpreter's Bible*. (Abingdon Press: New York, 1952), p. 652.

[5] Today we speak of children born to parents sealed in the new and everlasting covenant of marriage as being "born *in* the covenant," but anciently, the idea was that one was "born *through* the covenant."

[6] *The Interpreter's Bible* (1952), 653.

[7] See Sasson, 251.

8 *The Interpreter's Bible*, 654.

9 See Camille Fronk, *Women of the Old Testament*, (Deseret Book: Salt Lake City, 2009) 51 and Sasson, 251.

10 For those of you who do not know what this game is, I will try to describe it. The rules are similar to baseball, but instead of a bat and a pitched baseball, the "pitcher" would roll a soccer ball on the ground to the player who was up at "bat," and he or she would kick it and round the bases.

11 Ester Vilenkin, "Rebecca and the Camel Test: A Lesson in Giving," *The Jewish Woman*, http://wwwchabad.org/theJewishWoman/article_cdo/aid/763991/jewish/Rebeca-and-the-Camel-Test.htm, March 22, 2011.

12 Ibid.

Chapter 8
Wooing Rebekah

It has been a good day. Eliezer's prayer has been heard and answered. Now he just has to convince Rebekah to leave her home and accompany a complete stranger to the land of the Canaanites. No big deal, right? Does he dare ask for the dew on the ground instead of on the fleece?[1] A little confirmation never hurt anybody.

While Rebekah is drawing the water for the camels, Eliezer has a lot of time to consider his situation. It must have taken her hours, after all. Eliezer decides to give God another chance to clarify his will. Jack Sasson of Vanderbilt University has noted, "In the ancient Near East, it was the practice in matters of discovering the will of the gods to seek affirmation, even when an answer was straightforward. ... In Israel ... the *urim* and *thummin* were recast even when the initial answer was clear as a bell."[2] This is not so much a new test but merely a confirmation of the previous trial.

> And the man wondering at her held his peace, to wit whether the Lord had made his journey prosperous or not. And it came to pass, as the camels had done drinking, that the man took a golden earring of half a shekel weight, and two bracelets for her hands of ten shekels weight of gold; And said, Whose daughter art thou? tell me, I pray thee: is there room in thy father's house for us to lodge in? And she said unto him, I am the daughter of Bethuel the son of Milcah, which she bare unto Nahor. She said moreover unto him, We have both straw and provender enough, and room to lodge in. And the man bowed down his head, and worshipped the Lord. And he said, Blessed be the Lord God of my master Abraham, who hath not left destitute my master of his mercy and his truth: I being in the way, the Lord led me to the house of my master's brethren. (Genesis 24:21–27)

A word about the gifts that Eliezer bestows upon Rebekah. "Why only one earring?" I always wondered. After I learned a bit of Hebrew I looked it up. The Hebrew word is *nezem* and means "nose-ring."[3] No wonder the King James translators changed it to *earring*. Nose rings weren't in fashion in seventeenth-century England, but they were during Rebekah's era. Nose rings were usually one to two inches in diameter and were pinched on the right nostril. (No piercing needed.)

The two bracelets given to her were symbolic of a man and woman being bound in marriage, a "pair" of bracelets. The weight of the two pieces of gold jewelry could have purchased five slaves. These lavish gifts assured Rebekah's family that she would be well provided for in her marriage to Isaac.[4]

The two questions that Eliezer asks Rebekah are designed to discern two vital bits of information: what her pedigree is and whether she is married. ("Is there room in your *father's* house for us to spend the night?") Had she been married, she would have offered the hospitality of her husband. She gives the appropriate replies, and Eliezer can relax for the moment. She is of the right lineage, and she is unmarried. But Abraham had specified one final stipulation—that the young woman be willing to freely leave her homeland and accompany Eliezer back to Canaan. *This* is the challenge that now possesses his mind.

> And the damsel ran, and told them of her mother's house these things. And Rebekah had a brother, and his name was Laban: and Laban ran out unto the man, unto the well. And it came to pass, when he saw the earring and bracelets upon his sister's hands, and when he heard the words of Rebekah his sister, saying, Thus spake the man unto me; that he came unto the man; and, behold, he stood by the camels at the well. And he said, Come in, thou blessed of the Lord; wherefore standest thou without? for I have prepared the house, and room for the camels. And the man came into the house: and he ungirded his camels, and gave straw and provender for the camels, and water to wash his feet, and the men's feet that were with him. And there was set meat before him to eat: but he said, I will not eat, until I have told mine errand. And he said, Speak on. (Genesis 24:28–33)

Laban, Rebekah's brother, addresses Eliezer as "blessed of the Lord." This response must have been a further confirmation to Eliezer's heart and mind that this household revered his master's God. We see traditional acts of hospitality present: the offering of food, the feeding of animals, and the washing of feet[5] for Eliezer and all his men, who have finally become visible here. Abraham's servant is eager to tell his story, however, and refuses the meal until he has been heard.

> And he said, I am Abraham's servant. And the Lord hath blessed my master greatly; and he is become great: and he hath given him flocks, and herds, and silver, and gold, and menservants, and

maidservants, and camels, and asses. And Sarah my master's wife bare a son to my master when she was old: and unto him hath he given all that he hath. (Genesis 24:34–36)

Eliezer introduces himself to the family and proceeds to sing his master's praises. He emphasizes the vastness of his master's wealth and power, reassuring the family that their daughter will be provided for in royal fashion if she agrees to marry Isaac. Eliezer points out how Abraham's God has led him to Rebekah, and reinforces just how precious Isaac is to his parents. He is a miracle child, conceived in his mother's old age. Continuing, he repeats the stipulation Abraham placed on him when he set out on his quest.

> And my master made me swear, saying, Thou shalt not take a wife to my son of the daughters of the Canaanites, in whose land I dwell: But thou shalt go unto my father's house, and to my kindred, and take a wife unto my son. And I said unto my master, Peradventure the woman will not follow me. And he said unto me, The Lord, before whom I walk, will send his angel with thee, and prosper thy way; and thou shalt take a wife for my son of my kindred, and of my father's house: Then shalt thou be clear from this my oath, when thou comest to my kindred; and if they give not thee one, thou shalt be clear from my oath. (Genesis 24:37–41)

The future bride must come willingly. Eliezer is worried that he cannot keep his oath if the young woman will not come with him, but Abraham provided an "escape clause" in this solemn oath: "And if the woman will not be willing to follow thee, then thou shalt be clear from this my oath: only bring not my son thither again" (Genesis 24:8). The servant was under oath until Rebekah agreed to go with him; he would be freed from the oath only if she did *not* consent to go with him. This was a second test in the divine selection process. Eliezer needs to know what the family thinks before he proceeds. He issues them a polite ultimatum: "And now if ye will deal kindly and truly with my master, tell me: and if not, tell me; that I may turn to the right hand, or to the left" (Genesis 24:49). In other words, "Let me know if this is working for you, otherwise I'm out of here." The narrative continues

> Then Laban and Bethuel answered and said, The thing proceedeth from the Lord: we cannot speak unto thee bad or good. Behold, Rebekah is before thee, take her, and go, and let her be thy master's son's wife, as the LORD hath spoken. And it came to pass,

> that, when Abraham's servant heard their words, he worshipped the Lord, bowing himself to the earth. And the servant brought forth jewels of silver, and jewels of gold, and raiment, and gave them to Rebekah: he gave also to her brother and to her mother precious things. And they did eat and drink, he and the men that were with him, and tarried all night. (Genesis 24:50–54a)

The lavish gifts that Eliezer gives to the bride's family reflect the marriage customs of the time. Abraham would have been expected to pay a "bride price" to compensate parents for the loss of their daughter and to indicate his ability to provide for his family. The earring and bracelets already given to Rebekah at the well also constitute part of this bride price.

In this verse we are suddenly confronted with the presence of Rebekah's father, referred to by one biblical commentator as the "peek-a-boo Bethuel,"[6] whose presence is limited to this one verse. In his record, Josephus quotes Rebekah as saying, "My father was Bethuel, but he is dead,"[7] and Rebekah's mother plays a major role. Bethuel may very well have been deceased, as borne out in the text. Rebekah takes Eliezer to "her mother's house," not her father's house (Genesis 24:28); Rebekah's brother, Laban, transacts the betrothal arrangements rather than Bethuel; Eliezer gives gifts to Rebekah's "brother and to her mother" without mentioning her father; and when good-byes are said, only her brother and mother are mentioned (Genesis 24:55–60). The lone reference to Bethuel is questionable and was perhaps added at a later time.

As he relates the tale of his mission to his master's homeland, Eliezer wisely divides his objective into two steps. First, he will get the family to agree to the betrothal, and then he will secure the bride's consent. He has done his job well, emphasizing his master's wealth and virtues and accentuating God's role in selecting Rebekah. He now gives the family the right to decide the matter. When the family says, "We cannot speak unto thee bad or good," they are using a Hebrew idiom that means "anything at all." They believe that the whole encounter with Rebekah has been God's doing and agree to have Rebekah become the wife of his master's son. Eliezer is overcome with gratitude that his first purpose has been accomplished. With the agreement of the family and the distribution of the gifts complete, Eliezer must now comply with Abraham's added stipulation to his charge—the young woman herself must be ready to leave her home. The narrative continues:

> And they rose up in the morning, and he said, Send me away unto my master. And her brother and her mother said, Let the damsel abide with us a few days, at the least ten; after that she shall go. And he said unto them, Hinder me not, seeing the Lord hath prospered my way; send me away that I may go to my master. And they said, We will call the damsel, and enquire at her mouth. And they called Rebekah, and said unto her, Wilt thou go with this man? And she said, I will go. (Genesis 24:54b–58)

The servant is explicit in his desire to get on the road. He has not come on such a long journey just to chitchat, after all. This, however, is a big deal. The new bride has to be prepared for a wedding, both physically and emotionally. She must prepare herself mentally to leave her girlhood home and set up housekeeping in a distant land. At this point, Eliezer plays his trump card: This whole mission is the will of divinity, and the test was designed not just to pinpoint the proper bride, but also to *deliver* her to her husband. They do not ask Rebekah, "Are you ready to go with this man now?" but instead ask her if she is willing to go with him *at all*. Everything depends on her answer. Eliezer does not falter, but once again leaves the matter in God's hands. This is the last and most crucial test. With three short words, "I will go"—actually only one word in Hebrew—Rebekah passes it. The matter is settled. Like her future father-in-law, Abraham, she leaves her homeland and family because of a divine injunction.[8] This is only the first of many parallels between Rebekah and Abraham that we will see in ancient literature.

> And they sent away Rebekah their sister, and her nurse, and Abraham's servant, and his men. And they blessed Rebekah, and said unto her, Thou art our sister, be thou the mother of thousands of millions, and let thy seed possess the gate of those which hate them. And Rebekah arose, and her damsels, and they rode upon the camels, and followed the man: and the servant took Rebekah, and went his way. (Genesis 24:59–61)

In all probability, Laban does not know he is echoing the Lord's promise to Abraham when he blesses Rebekah to be "the mother of thousands of millions." Years before Abraham ever had children, God promised him that his seed would be as numerous as the stars in the heavens or the sands of the seashore (See Genesis 15:5; 22:17) This is the extraordinary covenant God made with the man who would establish his people on the earth. Somehow, Rebekah knows of her destiny within this covenant, and she is willing to get started immediately. This is indeed "a match made in heaven."

> And Isaac came from the way of the well Lahai-roi; for he dwelt in the south country. And Isaac went out to meditate in the field at the eventide: and he lifted up his eyes, and saw, and, behold, the camels were coming. And Rebekah lifted up her eyes, and when she saw Isaac, she lighted off the camel. For she had said unto the servant, What man is this that walketh in the field to meet us? And the servant had said, It is my master: therefore she took a vail, and covered herself. And the servant told Isaac all things that he had done. And Isaac brought her into his mother Sarah's tent, and took Rebekah, and she became his wife; and he loved her: and Isaac was comforted after his mother's death. (Genesis 24:62–76)

This is a love story. The narrator wants to make sure that we notice that there were sparks flying from the moment Isaac laid eyes on Rebekah. The English text says that Rebekah "lighted off her camel," but the Hebrew text says that she "fell" off her camel. One does not just "alight" from a six-foot camel, at least not until it is made to kneel. Maybe she was so excited to see her intended groom that she wasn't properly balanced and fell. What an entrance that would have been! A true *I Love Lucy* moment.

Isaac takes Rebekah as his wife and he *loves* her. I have to explain how amazing the use of the word *love* is in this verse. It is virtually *never* used in the Old Testament. When a man takes a wife, he takes her, and that's that. The narrator never uses the *ahav* word—"love." But here he does. Isaac loves Rebekah when he first sees her, and he apparently loves no one but her all his life. This example of monogamy is highly unusual in a society where polygamy was common.

Shera Tuchman and Sandra Rapoport cite several rabbinic commentators who underscore this immediate connection between Isaac and Rebekah. "Z'ror Hamor states unequivocally that when Isaac and Rebekah's eyes met across the field, they knew that each was the other's intended mate. *Mishna d'Rabi Eliezer*, a commentary on *Midrash Rabbah*, characterizes Isaac as extraordinarily handsome. The commentator uses the Hebrew phrase *yefeh to'ar*, an expression used very sparingly in the Bible and only to describe the physical beauty of heroes and heroines like Joseph, Rachel, and Esther."[9] Rashi quotes, "She saw him majestic, and she was dumbfounded in his presence."[10]

According to Netziv, just as God "directed Eliezer to encounter Rebekah at the well, so too is God orchestrating the apparent chance meeting between Isaac and Rebekah in this open field. The commentator is certain that it is God's design that Rebekah's initial encounter with Isaac set the tone for their future relationship."[11] According to this commentator, God wants their relationship to be magical—full of romantic fantasy. Theirs would not be a marriage with daily bickering and verbal sparring. From her first glance at Isaac, Rebekah is enamored with her husband. She views him as almost divine.

This initial meeting will set the pattern for how Rebekah views Isaac. She will not have the heart to challenge him, even when "the truth is on her side." She will be obligated to "find other methods to achieve her objectives." Just why this commentator chooses to portray Rebekah as being "driven to furtive methods to achieve her righteous ends" is a mystery. Certainly the matriarch Sarah had been forthright in confronting Abraham "in order to achieve her righteous ends." We are told by this commentator that Rebekah, the second matriarch, "will achieve her goals be *avoiding* confrontation with Isaac." We know that this cannot be because Rebekah is timid. She has demonstrated that she is definitely *not* timid, as she defies her family's wishes for her to remain longer at home before departing with Eliezer to meet her future husband. Netziv intimates that God wishes Isaac to be cushioned by his wife and shielded from any contention. He hints that Rebekah's mission is to comfort her husband's spirit as she transmits the sacred covenant and God's promises to the next generation. Perhaps Isaac's trauma and triumph at his own near sacrifice was "wrenching enough for one lifetime."[12]

One rabbinic commentator, Rashbam, amplifies Eliezer's report to Isaac, noting that "Eliezer enumerated the miracles which pervaded his visit in Aram-Naharayim in order to make it absolutely clear to Isaac that God's presence at every step of his quest is the evidence that it was *God* who chose this girl Rebekah to fulfill Isaac's destiny."[13]

There is an interesting legend surrounding the story of Isaac taking Rebekah into his mother's tent, signaling that she is the new matriarch. In *The Book of Legends* the story reads:

> Isaac brought her into the tent [and behold, she was like] his mother Sarah. As long as Sarah lived, a cloud [of glory] hovered over the entrance to her tent. After she died, the cloud disappeared. But when Rebekah came, the cloud returned. As long as Sarah lived, her doors were wide open to wayfarers; at her death, such openness ceased. But when Rebekah came, openness returned. As long as Sarah lived, blessing was dispatched into the dough she baked; at her death, such blessing ceased. But when Rebekah came, the blessing returned.[14]

Abraham recognized the crucial role that Isaac's future wife would play in passing on the covenant that God had bestowed on him and Sarah. Therefore, he was willing to expend vast resources in his quest for the perfect bride for his miracle son. The covenant must be safeguarded at whatever price was required. Just receiving it was not enough. Passing the covenant on was key.

---

[1] See Judges 6:37–40.

[2] Jack M. Sasson, "The Servant's Tale: How Rebekah Found a Spouse," *Journal of Near Eastern Studies*. Chicago: University of Chicago Press. 65.4 (2006), 255.

[3] Francis Brown, *The Brown-Driver-Briggs Hebrew and English Lexicon*, (Peabody, Massachusetts: Hendrickson Publishers, 1979), 633 entry 5141.

[4] Camille Fronk Olson, *Women of the Old Testament*, (Salt Lake City: Deseret Book, 2009), 54.

[5] Providing water to wash the feet of a guest in the ancient Near East was a gesture inviting the guest to relax. Sasson (2006), 257 fn. 54.

[6] Sasson (2006), 261.

[7] Flavius Josephus, *Antiquities of the Jews* in "The Complete Works of Josephus," (Grand Rapids, Michigan: Kregel Publications, 1981), 33.

[8] See Sasson (2006), 262–263.

[9] Shera Aranoff Tuchman and Sandra E. Rapoport, *The Passions of the Matriarchs*, (Jersey City, New Jersey: KTAV Publishing House, Inc, 2004), 116.

[10] Avivah Gottlieb Zornberg, *Genesis: The Beginning of Desire*, (Philadelphia: The Jewish Publication Society, 1995), 142.

[11] Tuchman and Rapoport (2004), 116.

[12] Tuchman and Rapoport (2004), 116–117.

[13] Tuchman and Rapoport (2004), 119.

[14] Hayim Nahman Bialik and Yehoshua Hana Ravnitzky, *The Book of Legends* (New York: Schocken Books, 1992), 42–43.

Chapter 9
The Revelation

Isaac and Rebekah. It seems like a match made in heaven. The miracle son finally gets the perfect girl: worthy, beautiful, eager to serve, and strong, both physically and emotionally. The precious covenant will be passed forward. Except for one *small* detail. After twenty years of marriage, Isaac and Rebekah are still childless. I can imagine Rebekah's monthly disappointment at finding that she is not with child. And then, to add insult to injury, she has to watch her father-in-law, decades past his one hundredth year, and his new wife bring forth not just one son but *six*. She must have been in agony, the very definition of one's heartstrings being wrenched. It would have been hard to watch a sister give birth when you yourself are childless, but your centenarian *father-in-law*? She undoubtedly felt like a failure, especially by the standards of the ancient world.

Why does God allow Rebekah to go through such excruciating disappointment? Why does she—and indeed, all the matriarchs—have to endure the stigma of infertility? What is the purpose of this mortification? I like the answer provided by Anne Roiphe in *Water from the Well*. She writes that conception is a common event, not viewed by mankind as miraculous. "Only by withholding pregnancy from the most central women in this story could it be made clear that God alone is the instrument of human survival, the grantor of our deepest wishes, the source of life itself." The long period of childlessness that afflicted Sarah and Rebekah, and then Rachel should not be viewed as a test of their patience and virtue, or as a literary device to create suspense in the plot of the story. It is "proof that God is ever the giver of life and man is ever the supplicant, and that the nation of people that God had selected to fulfill his plans would disappear in an instant were it not for the divine affection that has surrounded them throughout their days."[1]

Pirkei d'Rabbi Eliezer relates how a disheartened Isaac is inspired to bring his beloved wife Rebekah to Mount Moriah, the place where God had saved his life. At the top of the mountain, Isaac prays that the God who once delivered him from death would now empower his wife to bear his covenant child.[2] Isaac's prayer is answered and his beloved Rebekah conceives.

However, the pregnancy is fraught with difficulties.

> And the children struggled together within her; and she said, If it be so, why am I thus? (Genesis 25:22a)

The commentaries are full of explanations for Rebekah's anguish. Ibn Ezra suggests that Rebekah asks her neighbors who had given birth if the violent movements she feels within her are normal. They tell her that it is not so.[3] *Midrash Rabbah* adds that Rebekah goes from tent to tent seeking confirmation that her distress is normal, but receives no answer that satisfies her. Rashi comments that Rebekah's pregnancy is filled with so many complications that she wonders why she had ever desired to bear a child in the first place. She questions, "I never expected this pregnancy to be easy, but these pains are so unbearable that I must question my overwhelming desire to bear a child."[4] Ramban claims that Rebekah's suffering is so excruciating and impossible to bear that she cries, "Would that I did not exist—that I should die now! Or even that I should have never been born!"[5] Maharal, responding to Ramban, interprets Rebekah's cry differently. She says only three words in Hebrew: *why*, *this*, and *I (am)*. He suggests a softened translated of *anoki*, or *I am*. "'Why then am I sitting passively, why do I not investigate? It is my task to seek out explanations.' ... 'And she went to seek God.'"[6]

Rebekah must have been aware of the dangers of childbirth. She has undoubtedly witnessed or been aware of the death of a mother during childbirth. Perhaps she is not just fearful for her own life, but for the life within her. She is carrying Isaac's son, the heir to the precious covenant bestowed by God upon Abraham and his descendants. After twenty years of infertility, the fear of a miscarriage must have plagued her. At this point, she realizes that her anguish is beyond the range of normalcy and that both her life and the life of her child are at risk.[7]

Rebekah decides that she must discover for herself the reason she is in such great distress. With none of her neighbors knowing what is going on and her life hanging in the balance, she decides to go to the one person who will surely have the answer. She will go to God directly.

Pirkei d'Rabbi Eliezer states that Rebekah revives sufficiently from her great turmoil and announces to her retinue that she will travel to

Mount Moriah alone to seek God's guidance. She had gone to this holy place nine months before with her husband to pray for a child. God had twice answered Isaac in his desperation, and now Rebekah is counting on the Lord to reveal to her the true cause of her anguish.[8]

> And she went to enquire of the Lord. And the Lord said unto her, Two nations are in thy womb, and two manner of people shall be separated from thy bowels; and the one people shall be stronger than the other people; and the elder shall serve the younger. (Genesis 25:22b–23)

After quoting these verses, Elder Bruce R. McConkie paraphrases the words of the Lord: "That is to say, 'To you, Rebekah, I reveal the destiny of nations that are to be born that are yet in your womb.'"[9] Rebekah's pointed question to her God is the first by a woman recorded in the Hebrew Bible.[10] Rebekah asks, and the Lord answers her. He does not use an intermediary. He answers Rebekah directly. He reveals to her the reason she is experiencing such overwhelming pain: She is carrying twins who are struggling within her.[11] To her alone is the destiny of her children revealed—the elder of her sons is destined to serve the younger. As far as we know from scripture, Isaac never knows about this prophecy. Without the aid of an ultrasound or an obstetrician, Rebekah now knows she will deliver healthy twin boys, and she knows which one will be Isaac's successor.

Why does the Lord disclose this crucial information to Rebekah and not Isaac? Perhaps he trusts her, as a loving mother, to keep both of her rival sons alive. Perhaps he knows that she possesses the strength to make sure that the seed of the Jewish nation will continue uncorrupted by idol worship and that her posterity will remain a God-fearing people. God entrusts the task of ensuring the proper succession of the covenant to Rebekah. She needed to hear God's voice more than anyone in the world.[12] Elder Bruce R. McConkie affirms, "Rebekah is one of the greatest patterns in all the revelations of what a woman can do to influence a family in righteousness."[13]

> And when her days to be delivered were fulfilled, behold, there were twins in her womb. And the first came out red, all over like an hairy garment; and they called his name Esau. And after that came his brother out, and his hand took hold on Esau's heel; and his name was called Jacob: and Isaac was threescore years old when she bare them. And the boys grew: and Esau was a cunning hunter, a man of

the field; and Jacob was a plain man, dwelling in tents. And Isaac loved Esau, because he did eat of his venison: but Rebekah loved Jacob. (Genesis 25:24–28)

Netziv discloses that Isaac loves Esau because he catered to Isaac's love of venison. Rebekah's preference for Jacob is based on his character, not upon anything he could give her.[14] Knowing that God foretold his destiny before his birth undoubtedly influences her special love of Jacob. In him, she sees the manifestation of God's word, his devotion to the one true God, and the future of an upright people who will keep God's covenant.

And Jacob sod pottage: and Esau came from the field, and he was faint: And Esau said to Jacob, Feed me, I pray thee, with that same red pottage; for I am faint: therefore was his name called Edom. And Jacob said, Sell me this day thy birthright. And Esau said, Behold, I am at the point to die: and what profit shall this birthright do to me? And Jacob said, Swear to me this day; and he sware unto him: and he sold his birthright unto Jacob. Then Jacob gave Esau bread and pottage of lentils; and he did eat and drink, and rose up, and went his way: thus Esau despised his birthright. (Genesis 25:29–34)

After being out hunting all day, Esau is famished. In Hebrew, Esau says, "Let me gulp down some of this red stuff." The word *gulp* comes from the root *laat*, which means "to swallow greedily."[15] A sage indicates that this word for gulping in Hebrew is the word used for feeding animals, and he concludes that Esau is uncouth and ill-bred like an animal.[16] (Esau is also known as Edom partly because of this incident, *edom* being the Hebrew word for "red.") Knowing Esau's lifestyle and the lack of value he put on his birthright, Jacob offers him some of the lentil soup if he will sell him his birthright. Esau callously replies, "I am about to die! What good will the birthright do me then?" Jacob is persistent in asking him to swear an oath that he will sell him the birthright.

We next see a series of verbs denoting Esau's actions: he *swears*, he *sells* the birthright for the pottage, he *eats* (gulps), he *drinks*, he *gets up*, and *leaves*, thus disparaging his birthright but satisfying his physical needs. Ohel Yaakov points out that this series of verbs shows that Esau scorned his birthright. There is no hint in the text that Esau showed regret—or any emotion at all—during this hurried meal and immediate withdrawal. The commentator notes that "Esau went on his merry way, sated, happy, and carefree. This is not the portrait of a man who regretted his hasty decision."[17]

Some time after the birthright incident, there is famine in the land. As Isaac and Rebekah and their twins journey to Egypt to find food, they stop at Gerar. There, God appears to Isaac and tells him not to continue on to Egypt, but to stay in the land of Canaan, where he promises to bless him. God reaffirms his covenant with Isaac, saying:

> [U]nto thee, and unto thy seed, I will give all these countries, and I will perform the oath which I sware unto Abraham thy father; And I will make thy seed to multiply as the stars of heaven, and will give unto thy seed all these countries; and in thy seed shall all the nations of the earth be blessed; Because that Abraham obeyed my voice, and kept my charge, my commandments, my statutes, and my laws. (Genesis 26:3–5)

Isaac is greatly blessed by God while he dwells in Gerar. The Philistines envy him because of his prosperity. Abimelech, the king, asks him to leave the city, and he obeys. In the valley of Gerar, Isaac's men dig another well to find water, and he contends with Abimelech's shepherds over water rights. Isaac has re-excavated two of Abraham's wells, but the local shepherds have claimed the water for themselves. Isaac decides that life is too short to fight over wells, so he decides to concede the wells, and move on. He settles in Be'er Sheva where he digs another well and builds another altar to God. God again appears to Isaac, promising him protection. Although Isaac has acquiesced to all the demands of his shepherds, Abimelech follows him to Be'er Sheva with the captain of his army and a "friend," and desires to contract a covenant of peace with him. He sees that Isaac is a man of great power. He realizes that the Lord has blessed him greatly, for Isaac has multitudes of servants and herds and flocks. Perhaps Abimelech reasons that if the Lord is supporting a man so lavishly, it would not be wise to be on his bad side. So now, after abandoning three wells just to avoid contention, Isaac makes a feast for everyone who has made his life miserable. He has certainly taken the high road. This is the Isaac that Rebekah adores.

---

[1] Anne Roiphe, *Water from the Well: Sarah, Rebekah, Rachel, and Leah*, (New York: William Morrow, 2006), 130.

2 Shera Aranoff Tuchman and Sandra E. Rapoport, *The Passions of the Matriarchs*, (Jersey City, New Jersey: KTAV Publishing House, Inc., 2004), 132.

3 Tuchman and Rapoport (2004), 138.

4 *Midrash Rabbah* 63:6 quoted in Tuchman and Rapoport (2004), 138.

5 Tuchman and Rapoport (2004), 139.

6 Avivah Gottlieb Zornberg, *Genesis: The Beginning of Desire* (Philadelphia: The Jewish Publication Society, 1995), 159.

7 Ibid.

8 Tuchman and Rapoport (2004), 139-140.

9 Bruce R. McConkie, "Our Sisters from the Beginning," *Ensign*, January 1979, 40.

10 Tammi J. Schneider, *Mothers of Promise: Women in the Book of Genesis*, (Grand Rapids, Michigan: Baker Academic, 1987), 50.

11 One sage said that every time Rebekah passed a place of worship, Jacob would struggle in the womb and try to come out, and that every time she would pass a shrine to an idol, Esau would push himself forward and try to emerge. See Roiphe (2006), 132.

12 See Roiphe (2006), 132–133 and Tuchman and Rapoport (2004), 142.

13 McConkie, "Our Sisters from the Beginning," *Ensign*, January 1979, 40.

14 Tuchman and Rapoport (2004), 143.

15 Francis Brown, *The New Brown-Driver-Briggs-Genesius Hebrew and English Lexicon*, (Peabody, Massachusetts: Hendrickson Publishers, 1979), 542 entry 3938.

16 Roiphe (2006), 141.

17 Tuchman and Rapoport (2004), 146.

Chapter 10
The Blessing

Many years pass. When Esau turns forty, he marries two Hittite women, Yehudit and Basmet. His father does not arrange these marriages. Esau does it on his own. He does not even ask permission from his parents. The text (Genesis 26:34) simply states that he did it. When Isaac was the same age, Abraham had made elaborate preparations so that his son would marry within the covenant, but it was not so with Esau's generation. And Isaac pays the price for his lack of foresight. Genesis 26:35 states that these wives "were a grief of mind unto Isaac and to Rebekah." These young women had been raised to worship alien gods—the goddess of fertility, the god of crops, the god of war. They were accustomed to their ways. It must have been especially hard for Isaac who had been *visited* by the one true God on two occasions.

By this time, Isaac is feeling his age. He is blind and feeble and does not know how much longer he will live. (He will actually live another thirty years, but on this day, he does not feel like it.) He says to his oldest son, Esau:

> **Behold now, I am old, I know not the day of my death: Now therefore take, I pray thee, thy weapons, thy quiver and thy bow, and go out to the field, and take me some venison; And make me savoury meat, such as I love, and bring it to me, that I may eat; that my soul may bless thee before I die. (Genesis 27:2–4)**

Isaac wants to make sure that the covenant will be passed on to his heir before he dies. Besides his enormous wealth, he will be passing on the covenantal blessing he inherited from Abraham. Isaac obviously knows nothing about Esau selling the birthright to Jacob for a mess of pottage, and Esau is not about to volunteer this information. The birthright son is entitled to a double portion of the inheritance—which would mean, in Esau's case, that he would get two-thirds of his father's wealth. He has much at stake here. It is not surprising that he is not forthright about selling his birthright to his younger brother.

Did Jacob tell his mother about the sale? We are not specifically told so in the text, but Rebekah has her own inside information. This moment is filled with drama, because *we* know that *Rebekah* knows that

Esau—although he is the elder son—is not the one chosen to receive the blessings of the covenant. Isaac, unknowingly, is about to bestow the blessing on the wrong son.

Biblical scholars throughout the ages have tried to explain away Rebekah's subsequent actions. At the same time, they struggle to maintain the righteousness of the patriarch Isaac and his ignorance of God's will. They often question why Rebekah does not trust in her husband to do the right thing, and give the covenant blessing to the son that was meant to have it.

Modern commentator Yehuda Nachshoni points out that Rebekah possesses two key pieces of information that Isaac lacks. The first thing Isaac does not know is that he is about to become the victim of a ruse. The blessing he is about to give to Jacob is only the natural consequence of the chain of events put into play when Esau despised his birthright and sold it to Jacob in Genesis 25:24. As the possessor of the birthright, Jacob is entitled to all the rights and privileges of the firstborn son. And second, Isaac does not recognize the corrupt character of his eldest son, and that he is not worthy to receive the blessings of the covenant.[1] Rebekah discerns all of this and is faced with the dilemma of what action to take. Ramban suggests that Rebekah has prudently concealed the prophecy in her heart for forty years, expecting at all times that her husband's own prophetic ability would give him the insight into which of his sons should receive the covenantal blessing.[2]

> And Rebekah heard when Isaac spake to Esau his son. And Esau went to the field to hunt for venison, and to bring it. (Genesis 27:5)

Imagine Rebekah watching Isaac grow old. She sees him grow blind and become feeble. She sees his innocent love of Esau, and his love of the game his son brings him. She idolizes this man. She knows that the Lord has appeared unto him twice. She knows he is the possessor of the precious covenant given to Abraham. And yet, she dares not let him out of her sight. She dares not get out of earshot for fear that her beloved Isaac might spontaneously decide to bestow his covenantal blessing on Esau while *Jacob* is the one worthy to receive it. She is in quite a predicament.

The commentators discuss how it is that Rebekah overhears Isaac's conversation with Esau. Netziv says that Rebekah listened carefully whenever Isaac spoke with Esau in private because she was so concerned for Jacob. Ohr Hachayim believes that Rebekah possesses prophetic ability and is not just an expert eavesdropper. This prophetic ability enables her to be constantly aware of Isaac's words, even when he is not in her presence. Perush Yonatan concurs with Ohr Hachayim, but adds that only by a divine *command* to have Jacob designated as the heir would such a noble woman as Rebekah have orchestrated the events that follow.[3]

Rebekah knew which son God wanted for his story, and which one was unworthy to be a part of the covenant. It was her destiny to provide a means for Jacob to receive the blessing that granted the inheritance of the covenant. She had to be decisive. So much was riding on her action. What if she did not act? Would God have to pick another group to be his chosen people? Was there even another group available? God gave Rebekah the intelligence to figure a way out of this impossible predicament. He gave her the spiritual insight that convinced her she had to act to save the covenant, and the conviction to do what was right. He knew he could count on her to pass on the covenant.[4]

> And Rebekah spake unto Jacob her son, saying, Behold, I heard thy father speak unto Esau thy brother, saying, Bring me venison, and make me savoury meat, that I may eat, and bless thee before the Lord before my death. Now therefore, my son, obey my voice according to that which I command thee. Go now to the flock, and fetch me from thence two good kids of the goats; and I will make them savoury meat for thy father, such as he loveth: And thou shalt bring it to thy father, that he may eat, and that he may bless thee before his death. (Genesis 27:6–10)

Rebekah is about to engineer a scenario that will have profound ramifications throughout the generations. Rebecca directs Jacob to "Hearken to my voice," which is *bekoli* (*in my voice*) in Hebrew. Netziv notes that whenever this phrase is used in the Bible, it is imperative for the listener to follow the speaker's directions to the letter. By her word choice, Rebekah indicates to her son that the tactics she is about to employ are motivated by divine direction.[5]

Ohr Hachayim also vindicates Rebekah's plan in his commentary. He concludes that her plan to substitute her son Jacob for Esau and thus ensure that he will receive the patriarchal blessing is the only option open to her. The commentator pictures Rebekah at the moment of exigency. The blessing is about to be given, and she is forced into acting decisively. She is aware that she is about to mislead her husband, and on top of that, to influence her son to be a participating accessory. She knows that it is crucial that she prevent Isaac's blessing from being given to the wrong son. The commentator amplifies Rebekah's instructions to her son after she tells him to hearken to her voice. "Now heed my words, Jacob my son. While my advice might appear to be deceitful, and may not seem right to you, I am asking you to trust me and comply with the Bible's positive command to honor your mother. For I am in receipt of God's prophecy in this matter." Ohr Hachayim reminds his audience of the Bible's teaching to obey the instructions of a prophet in such a temporary crisis situation as Jacob is facing, even if, on the surface, it seems to go against established law.[6]

In this manner, the commentaries make great effort to stress that Rebekah's actions are appropriate because she has received God's revelation on the matter. She takes those actions because Isaac's are in direct conflict with the words that God has communicated to her about the destinies of her two sons before they were born. Sarah felt compelled to cast out Hagar and Ishmael in order to assure that Isaac would receive the promise given by God to Abraham. Likewise, Rebekah's actions are driven by a desire to see that the son identified by God before birth receive the promised blessing.

> And Jacob said to Rebekah his mother, Behold, Esau my brother is a hairy man, and I am a smooth man: My father peradventure will feel me, and I shall seem to him as a deceiver; and I shall bring a curse upon me, and not a blessing. And his mother said unto him, Upon me be thy curse, my son: only obey my voice, and go fetch me them. (Genesis 27:11–13)

Jacob has reservations that he can convince his father that he is Esau, because of their physical dissimilarities. He does not want the blessing to backfire and result in a lifelong curse. To me, his feelings are very understandable. In fact, I am surprised Rebekah is able to talk him into going along with her plans. She must indeed have been certain she was acting according to divine will, and being so empowered, was very convincing. She assures her son that he has nothing to worry about.

After all, she has inside information. She knows how the story will end, even though it seems rather uncertain at that moment. God has assured her that Jacob was to prevail. Her confidence inspires Jacob to action, and he is off to go and do.

> And he went, and fetched, and brought them to his mother: and his mother made savoury meat, such as his father loved. And Rebekah took goodly raiment of her eldest son Esau, which were with her in the house, and put them upon Jacob her younger son: And she put the skins of the kids of the goats upon his hands, and upon the smooth of his neck: And she gave the savoury meat and the bread, which she had prepared, into the hand of her son Jacob. (Genesis 27:14–17)

The word translated as "goodly" describing Esau's raiment is from the Hebrew word *kamodah*, which connotes something "costly" or "precious."[7] Some sages say that the garments in which Rebekah clothed Jacob were those made by God for Adam and Eve, and now that Esau has sold his birthright to Jacob, these precious garments rightfully belong to him.[8] Louis Ginzberg describes these garments as being the high-priestly raiment in which God had clothed Adam. Adam passed these garments on to Noah, who gave them to Shem, who bequeathed them to Abraham. Abraham passed them on to his son, Isaac, who then passed them on to Esau, the older of his two sons. Rebekah thought that since Jacob had bought the birthright from his brother, he had thereby come into possession of the garments as well. "There was no need for her to go and fetch them from the house of Esau. He [Esau] knew his wives far too well to entrust so precious a treasure to them; they were in the safe-keeping of his mother."[9]

Another midrash goes even further with this idea. The rabbis ask the question, "Esau had several wives, so why did he keep this clothing with his mother?" They answer, "Esau knew his wives' doings [i.e., their idolatrous actions] and therefore preferred to have his mother keep his garments. After Jacob had received the blessings from his father, he said: 'It is not proper for the wicked Esau to wear this tunic.' What did he do? He dug and buried it in the ground."[10]

Rebekah, knowing that this covenantal blessing will be "before the Lord" (see Genesis 27:7), is aware of the formality of the occasion.[11] For this reason, she carefully clothes him in the sacred vestments of the birthright son. Since Rebekah alerts us to the ritual nature of this blessing, we can widen our view of the seemingly simple dialogue between Isaac and Jacob.

Rebekah prepares the savory delicacies in the special manner she knows Isaac loves. She drapes the skins of the two kid-goats across Jacob's hands and neck. Isaac will not be able to "see" his son Esau, but Jacob will "feel" like Esau. Her beloved husband's eyes have become dim, but Rebekah will help him to "see" clearly in bestowing the blessing upon the proper son. She will be his *eyes*. She is acting as guardian of the covenant, and is in control of the destiny of the house of Israel. Without her, the nation would not have been born. Elder Bruce R. McConkie has said of her, "Women are appointed, Rebekah-like, to be guides and lights in righteousness in the family unit, and to engineer and arrange so that things are done in the way that will result in the salvation of more of our Father's children."[12]

Genesis Rabbah describes Rebekah as accompanying her son Jacob as far as Isaac's tent flap. There, she says to him, "Till now I was obligated to you [out of my love for you, and I did what I could to help you]. From now on your Creator will help you."[13]

> And he came unto his father, and said, My father: and he said, Here am I; who art thou, my son? And Jacob said unto his father, I am Esau thy firstborn; I have done according as thou badest me: arise, I pray thee, sit and eat of my venison, that thy soul may bless me. (Genesis 27:18–19)

Isaac asks his son who he is. Here, Jacob gives the name of his firstborn brother to his patriarch father, in order to legitimize the blessing. That name is a key word that he knows his father will be listening for. In all probability, this was one of the instructions from Rebekah when she twice enjoined Jacob to "obey my voice." He undoubtedly feels that he is entitled to bear the name of the firstborn, since Esau had forfeited it willingly in the lentil episode. Jacob could identify himself as the firstborn by virtue of this trade of birthright for food. He then answers that he has been faithful in doing what his father has commanded him, and now desires a further blessing.

> And Isaac said unto his son, How is it that thou hast found it so quickly, my son? And he said, Because the Lord thy God brought it to me. And Isaac said unto Jacob, Come near, I pray thee, that I may

> feel thee, my son, whether thou be my very son Esau or not. And Jacob went near unto Isaac his father; and he felt him, and said, The voice is Jacob's voice, but the hands are the hands of Esau. And he discerned him not, because his hands were hairy, as his brother Esau's hands: so he blessed him. And he said, Art thou my very son Esau? And he said, I am. And he said, Bring it near to me, and I will eat of my son's venison, that my soul may bless thee. And he brought it near to him, and he did eat: and he brought him wine, and he drank. (Genesis 27:20–25)

Rebekah has anticipated the signs of recognition that Isaac would be looking for in her son. Isaac must test the birthright son to make sure he is not there unworthily. Rebekah has prepared Jacob's hands so that he will pass the test of recognition put forth by Isaac.

> And his father Isaac said unto him, Come near now, and kiss me, my son. And he came near, and kissed him: and he smelled the smell of his raiment, and blessed him, and said, See, the smell of my son is as the smell of a field which the Lord hath blessed: Therefore God give thee of the dew of heaven, and the fatness of the earth, and plenty of corn and wine: Let people serve thee, and nations bow down to thee: be lord over thy brethren, and let thy mother's sons bow down to thee: cursed be every one that curseth thee, and blessed be he that blesseth thee. (Genesis 27:26)

Following the ritual meal, Isaac entreats his son to come close and kiss him. While in this mutual embrace, he is satisfied that the tokens of recognition have been met. All his doubts seem to disperse, and Isaac blesses Jacob with the coveted patriarchal blessing. Remarkably, the central message of Isaac's blessing echoes the revelation given to Rebekah during her troubled pregnancy, that her elder son would serve the younger. Isaac blesses Jacob to be lord over his brother and prophesies that his mother's sons would bow down to him.

Just after Jacob leaves his father's tent after receiving the blessing, Esau returns. It could not have been better scripted in a Hollywood blockbuster. It reminds me of the moment the prophet Samuel appears just as Saul has finished making the offerings before battle, a thing he was not authorized to do. Perhaps if he had waited a few moments for Samuel, he would not have lost his kingdom.[14]

> And it came to pass, *as soon as* Isaac had made an end of blessing Jacob, and Jacob was yet scarce gone out from the presence of Isaac his father, that Esau his brother came in from his hunting. And he also had made savoury meat, and brought it unto his father, and said unto his father, Let my father arise, and eat of his son's venison, that thy soul may bless me. And Isaac his father said unto him, Who art thou? And he said, I am thy son, thy firstborn Esau. And Isaac trembled very exceedingly, and said, Who? where is he that hath taken venison, and brought it me, and I have eaten of all before thou camest, and have blessed him? yea, and he shall be blessed. (Genesis 27:30–33, emphasis added)

Esau confronts Isaac. Isaac begins to tremble. A close reading of the text indicates that he must have been more than suspicious with so many things about the blessing that didn't seem quite right, like Jacob's voice and the goat skins impersonating hairy hands. Isaac questions Jacob and doubts his identity as Esau. Ramban states that Isaac trembles because he realizes that his favorite son has forfeited his blessing forever. Isaac realizes that once the blessing has been bestowed—even unknowingly—it cannot be reversed. Rashi agrees with Ramban and adds that even when Isaac realizes that he has blessed the wrong son, the blessing should remain with Jacob, saying "and he shall be blessed." By saying this, Isaac has confirmed the blessing upon Jacob. Rashbam explains that in a stroke of comprehension, Isaac realizes that his cherished Rebekah has ascertained what he did not: that *Jacob*, not Esau, was the one worthy to receive the covenantal blessing. He verbally authenticates Jacob's blessing and ceases to tremble.[15]

Esau is devastated when he learns that Jacob has received the blessing. Why the change of heart now, I wonder? Not that long ago, he "despised his birthright." Perhaps he now wants the blessing for himself just because someone else has it. He cries out bitterly and asks his father for a blessing. Isaac confers one upon him, albeit a lesser one. Esau is filled with a desire for revenge, and he vows to bide his time until Isaac dies. When that happens, he vows, "then will I slay my brother Jacob" (Genesis 27:41).

> And these words of Esau her elder son were told to Rebekah: and she sent and called Jacob her younger son, and said unto him, Behold, thy brother Esau, as touching thee, doth comfort himself, purposing to kill thee. (Genesis 27:42)

Ramban comments that Rebekah discovers Esau's secret plan for revenge when he boasts to his friends that he intends to take revenge on Jacob, and she is told of his brazen threats. Rashi, along with other sages, ascribes a different meaning to the words "these words of Esau were told to Rebekah." He attributes Rebekah's prophetic gifts with enabling her to detect the hatred lodged in Esau's soul. He states that the vengeful feelings in Esau's heart were revealed to her by divine inspiration. Radak concurs with Rashi and actually calls Rebekah a prophetess.[16]

Rebekah acts on this knowledge and calls Jacob to her. Using the same phrase she had used earlier in telling him to seek the blessing—"hearken to my voice"—she urges him to escape to her brother in Haran. Jacob listens. But Rebekah has more work yet to do. She is a wise woman. She has followed Abraham's servant to the land of promise. She has provided heirs for Isaac. She now needs to ensure that the son who has rightly received the covenantal blessings will survive. She does not want her entire life to have been for nothing.

Even if Jacob is not killed, Rebekah realizes that the blessing Isaac has just given him will have been in vain if he marries a wife who is not supportive of the sacred covenant. If Jacob takes a wife "from the daughters of Heth" as Esau did, he will not be able to pass on the patriarchal priesthood to his posterity. He would thus lose the birthright and the patriarchal authority that is so precious to her. As matriarch, Rebekah needs to ensure that the blessings and ordinances of the covenant are given to her posterity.

At my house, if *I* have an idea, it might or might not prove to be a good one. However, if the idea originates with *my husband*, it is *always* a good idea. And my house might not be the only house in which that is true. The next verses in the text seem like they are a *non sequitur* in the rest of the story. Perhaps Rebekah's house is a bit like mine. It might be a good idea to get Jacob out of town to protect his life, but if Isaac is the one to think of the idea, it will no doubt be a stupendous idea. Rebekah cries out to Isaac:

> I am weary of my life because of the daughters of Heth: if Jacob take a wife of the daughters of Heth, such as these which are of the daughters of the land, what good shall my life do me? (Genesis 27:46)

We might have expected Rebekah to dash into Isaac's tent and say, as suggested by Tuchman and Rapoport, "Husband! Esau is planning to kill his brother Jacob! You must aid me in separating our warring sons. You must prevail upon Esau to leave Jacob be, and send Jacob away, out of Esau's reach."[17] Instead she complains to Isaac about Esau's pagan wives. Why does she do this? Up to now, she has acted with decisiveness and insight. What is she up to?

Netziv indicates that Rebekah is doing what she has always done—protecting Isaac from any uncomfortable situations. She brings up the subject of her irritating daughters-in-law rather than the murder plot to shield Isaac from Esau's true aim. One midrash relates that to persuade Isaac, Rebekah blows her nose and casts [the mucus] away [to say that they were as disgusting to her as the mucus that comes from one's nose]. She says, "The Hittite women squabble with one another."[18] Alshich suggests that besides wanting to protect Isaac and keep her two sons from killing each other, she also seeks to acquire a full-fledged legitimate blessing for Jacob before he flees to Haran.[19]

The three words Rebekah utters to Isaac are, literally, *lama li chaim*: "what - to me - life". This is her final speech in the Bible. She used these words forty years before when she prayed for God to explain the torment within her womb, afraid she would miscarry after twenty childless years of marriage. Here, this same fear resurfaces. She worries that if both her sons marry unworthy wives—as Esau has already done—then the irreplaceable legacy given to Abraham will remain incomplete through Isaac's posterity. In her revelation from God, she learned that her younger son would rule over the elder. Her ardent desire is that Jacob inherit the blessings of the precious covenant. If this were not to be so, then her whole life would be rendered meaningless.

Julie Beck makes this comment:

> We learn from Rebekah that she was weary of her life because of the daughters of Heth. Those were the women who were not in the covenant. ... Now, Rebekah gave up everything—she left her family and her homeland to go form an eternal family because she

wanted these blessings. And of her two sons, she had one left; and of the daughters of the land, there was not one who could form an eternal marriage with her son. She needed to see that her righteous son got the blessings. Rebekah used her influence to see that the priesthood blessings and keys passed to the righteous son. It's a perfect example of a man who has the keys and the woman who has the influence working together to ensure their blessing.[20]

Isaac calls Jacob to him and blesses him, and charges him to follow his words.

> Thou shalt not take a wife of the daughters of Canaan. Arise, go to Padan-aram, to the house of Bethuel thy mother's father; and take thee a wife from thence of the daughters of Laban thy mother's brother. And God Almighty bless thee, and make thee fruitful, and multiply thee, that thou mayest be a multitude of people; And give thee the blessing of Abraham, to thee, and to thy seed with thee; that thou mayest inherit the land wherein thou art a stranger, which God gave unto Abraham. (Genesis 28:1–7)

We can only imagine the joy that fills Rebekah's heart as she watches Isaac *voluntarily* and *deliberately* blessing their son Jacob. The mission of her lifetime—passing the covenant to a worthy son—is at last accomplished! Her joy, however, is mixed with sorrow because she knows that the only way to keep Jacob safe is to have him leave her. He must journey to Padan-aram and make his way to her brother's family. I wonder if she knows that she will never see him again.[21]

---

[1] Shera Aranoff Tuchman and Sandra E. Rapoport, *The Passions of the Matriarchs*, (Jersey City, New Jersey: KTAV Publishing House, Inc., 2004), 156.

[2] Ibid.

[3] Tuchman and Rapoport (2004), 157.

[4] See Anne Roiphe, *Water from the Well: Sarah, Rebekah, Rachel, and Leah*, (New York: William Morrow, 2006), 154.

[5] Tuchman and Rapoport (2004), 158–159.

[6] Tuchman and Rapoport (2004), 159.

[7] Francis Brown, *The Brown-Driver-Briggs Hebrew and English Lexicon*, (Peabody, Massachusetts: Hendrickson Publishers, 1979), 326 entry 2530.

[8] Roiphe (2006), 156.

[9] Louis Ginzberg, *Legends of the Jews, Volume One*, (Baltimore: The Johns Hopkins University Press, 1937), 332.

[10] *Genesis Rabbah* 65:16; *Pirkei de-Rabbi Eliezer*, ed. Higger, chap. 24 as quoted "Rebekah:Midrash and Haggadah," accessed March 8, 2014 at http://jwa.org/encyclopedia/article/rebekah-midrash-and-aggadah.

[11] Many times in the Old Testament, "before the Lord" refers to a male Israelite appearing at the temple for certain holy day celebrations.

[12] Bruce R. McConkie, "Our Sisters from the Beginning," *Ensign,* January 1979, 40.

[13] *Genesis Rabbah* 65:17 as quoted in *Pirkei de-Rabbi Eliezer*, ed. Higger, chap. 24 "Rebekah:Midrash and Haggadah," accessed March 8, 2014 at http://jwa.org/encyclopedia/article/rebekah-midrash-and-aggadah and Tuchman and Rapoport (2004), 161.

[14] See 1 Samuel 13:8–14.

[15] Tuchman and Rapoport (2004), 163.

[16] Tuchman and Rapoport (2004), 165–166.

[17] Tuchman and Rapoport (2004), 166–167.

[18] *Genesis Rabbah* 67:11 as quoted in *Pirkei de-Rabbi Eliezer*, ed. Higger, chap. 24 "Rebekah:Midrash and Haggadah," accessed March 8, 2014 at http://jwa.org/encyclopedia/article/rebekah-midrash-and-aggadah.

[19] Tuchman and Rapoport (2004), 167.

[20] Julie Beck, "Teaching the Doctrine of the Family," *Seminaries and Institutes of Religion Satellite Broadcast*, August 4, 2009.

[21] See Tuchman and Rapoport (2004), 168–169.

Chapter 11
Jacob's Quest

Rebekah has received the wish of her heart. She has witnessed the passing of the precious covenantal blessing to her beloved son Jacob. Her joy should be full. And yet, she has moved her husband to direct Jacob to seek a wife who is a part of God's covenant people. Does Rebekah urge Jacob to run to Padan-aram to avoid Esau's wrath, or does she urge him to flee to her father's house in order to engage a bride from among her own family? The sages credit her with doing both. Rashbam says that she knew Isaac could not survive the knowledge that Esau has vowed to slay Jacob. Chizkuni notes that, while Rebekah seeks to find a worthy spouse for Jacob, she also desires to separate her feuding sons.[1] In her last spoken words found in Genesis, she both protects her husband *and* directs Jacob's future.[2]

Rebekah knows that Jacob's safety depends on his departure to a distant land. His brother Esau is enraged and thirsty for revenge because of the blessing incident. She is willing to let Jacob go, even though it is the hardest thing she has ever done. It is difficult to part from the son who has become so close to her, but the journey will be dangerous for Jacob. He does not dare remain at home a moment longer. He must flee now—alone.

Jacob has received a charge from his father: "Thou shalt not take a wife of the daughters of Canaan. Arise, go to Padan-aram, to the house of Bethuel thy mother's father; and take thee a wife from thence of the daughters of Laban thy mother's brother" (Genesis 28:1). Isaac continues by bestowing the covenantal blessings of Abraham upon Jacob, moments before he flees to Padan-aram. Nehama Leibowitz points out that earlier, when Isaac thought he was blessing Esau, he blessed him with "[a]bundance, fatness, power, and dominion—all material blessings. But the Abrahamic mission, the blessings of seed and the promise of the land, were not bequeathed to Esau, since such a spiritual blessing cannot be conferred by succession but only granted to the one who is deserving of it."[3] Isaac *knowingly* bestows the blessings of the covenant upon Jacob because Esau had violated his parents' trust by marrying Hittite wives who bring grief into Isaac's and Rebekah's lives. Such behavior rendered him unworthy of the covenantal blessing. Leibowitz argues that the scriptural record itself proves that although Isaac sought to bless his firstborn son Esau first, he reserved the *covenantal* blessings for his younger son. She believes that Rebekah's "switch" did not alter Isaac's intention.[4]

Traveling solo in the wilderness is not a good idea. Such a perilous journey was usually undertaken under the protection of a caravan. Such a decision did not require much rational deliberation. Who in his right mind would attempt to cross the desert—where there would be robbers, predators, and not much water—by himself? And besides that, Jacob does not *know* the people he is seeking. He has nothing. Nothing, that is, but the incredible promise he has just received from his grandfather Abraham through the hands of his father Isaac. The one true God had chosen Abraham and his descendants to bless all the families of the earth (see Genesis 12:3). Jacob must absolutely believe in the promises of that covenant in order to to undergo the dangers of such a journey. But again, these are incredible promises. The blessings of the promised land are conditional upon his marriage within the covenant and his return to the land of his birth. Even if he can find such a wife and return home safely, there is still Esau to consider. Would he ever lose his desire for revenge? Would he stalk Jacob for the rest of his life? Jacob has much to consider. He decides to sleep on it. And then something amazing happens.[5]

> And Jacob went out from Beer-sheba, and went toward Haran. And he lighted upon a certain place, and tarried there all night, … and he took of the stones of that place, and put them for his pillows, and lay down in that place to sleep. And he dreamed, and behold a ladder set up on the earth, and the top of it reached to heaven: and behold the angels of God ascending and descending on it. And, behold, the Lord stood above it, and said, I am the Lord God of Abraham thy father, and the God of Isaac: the land whereon thou liest, to thee will I give it, and to thy seed; … and in thee and in thy seed shall all the families of the earth be blessed. And, behold, I am with thee, and will keep thee in all places whither thou goest, and will bring thee again into this land; for I will not leave thee. … And Jacob awaked out of his sleep, and he said, Surely the Lord is in this place; … How [full of awe] is this place! This is none other but the house of God, and this is the gate of heaven. And Jacob vowed a vow. (Genesis 28:10–17, 20)

Jacob dreams a dream, and what an awesome dream it is. He sees the God of Abraham and Isaac. God reaffirms the promises of the covenant that he made to his grandfather Abraham and to his father Isaac and extends them to Jacob and to all his descendants. He is full of wonder.

Jacob ponders on the vision of the ladder.[6] The rungs of a ladder allow those who use it to travel from the earth, upon which its base rests, to the point where the ladder reaches. This ladder seems to connect heaven to earth, because *angels* are using it. What could it mean? Could it suggest that the things of the earth and the things of heaven are *connected*? Samuel Dressner proposes the idea that the presence of angels climbing up and descending the ladder suggests that the ladder can be ascended—God's world is perhaps not as distant from man's world as he might believe. God has created a "staircase of the spirit" that humans can learn to ascend. The ladder is an avenue for communication between man and God. "It is the promise of the covenant."[7]

In this remarkable dream, God assures Jacob that he need not fear the harrowing journey through the desert, for God will be with him. God will bring Jacob back, the promised land will be his, and his descendants will bless all the families of the earth. The passage between heaven and earth is intimately connected with the journey to Haran to seek a wife who can be a partner in a life lived in God's covenant.[8]

Like his father and grandfather before him, Jacob is ready to accept the responsibilities of the covenant. He vows to continue in the covenant. He realizes that his life is more than just the life of one man. His life is intertwined with the purposes of heaven. In order to honor heaven's claim on his life, he must find a wife who will accept the covenant and help him pass it on to his descendants. This directive and the "charge of succession" will guide Jacob's life. Dressner admonishes, "The children of Israel were not to marry frivolously; personal feelings must give way to destiny." When future generations read about the monumental efforts expended by the patriarchs and matriarchs in order to preserve the covenant, they will gain strength to find worthy spouses so that the covenant can be maintained.[9]

Jacob takes the stone that he has used as a pillow[10] and erects a monument to his vow.[11] He calls the place Beth-el—meaning

"House of God" in Hebrew—because God has indeed been here. Robert Alter notes that "stones are Jacob's personal *motif*: from the stone at his head, to the stone marker, then the stone upon the well that he will roll away, and the pile of stones he will set up to mark his treaty with Laban."[12]

After this phenomenal experience at Beth-el, Genesis 29:1 records that "Jacob lifted up his feet" and continued on his journey. Although eyes are often lifted up, here feet are being lifted up. Rashbam suggests that Jacob's jubilation after his vision at Bethel gives a lightness to Jacob's step as he travels on his long eastward quest. Buoyed by God's promises, Jacob proceeds on his journey to find a bride with a light heart.[13]

> And he looked, and behold a well in the field, and, lo, there were three flocks of sheep lying by it; for out of that well they watered the flocks: and a great stone was upon the well's mouth. And thither were all the flocks gathered: and they rolled the stone from the well's mouth, and watered the sheep, and put the stone again upon the well's mouth in his place. (Genesis 29:2–3)

Road-weary from his long travels, Jacob sees first the well, and then the flocks. He notes the great size of the stone on the well's mouth, and the narrator explains that each shepherd of the area must wait until all the flocks and shepherds are present in order to have the manpower necessary to lift the huge stone off the mouth of the well. Radak points out that the massive size and weight of the stone was historically necessary to the sustaining of a desert society, ensuring that no single outlander could approach their well and empty their precious water supply. The size of the stone and its girth made it infeasible for a single individual to grip and remove it from its place. It necessitated the communal effort of all the united shepherds to remove the stone from the mouth of the well and water the flocks.[14] Netziv notes that the stone was not massive in size, as much as it was wide, thin, and heavy, like a giant stone wheel, challenging any one person's capability to dislodge it from its place on top of the well.[15]

> And Jacob said unto them [the shepherds], My brethren, whence be ye? And they said, Of Haran are we. And he said unto them, Know ye Laban the son of Nahor? And they said, We know him. And he said unto them, Is he well? And they said, He is well. (Genesis 29:4–6a)

Jacob addresses the shepherds at rest beside the well. He carefully seeks to ascertain his location by asking where they are from. Finding that he has arrived at his destination, he asks if they know Laban, son of Nahor. Those familiar with biblical genealogy know well that Nahor is not Laban's father, but rather his grandfather. So why does Jacob use this name to discover if it is the home of Laban, his mother's brother? Kli Yakar states that Jacob does this in order to reveal Laban's character in a shrewd manner. By specifically relating Laban to Abraham's honorable brother, Nahor, rather than to the unsavory Bethuel, Jacob was allowing the shepherds to tell him what he needs to know in a veiled fashion. Are the daughters of Laban fit candidates to be brides for the grandson of Abraham? According to Netziv, when Jacob asks whether all is well with Laban, he wants more than a surface answer. He wants to know details about the character of Laban and his household. Unknowingly, these shepherds inform Jacob that his uncle Laban is a close spiritual kin to Nahor and that Laban's daughters might indeed be worthy prospects as future wives for Abraham's descendants. Also, according to Alshich, when Jacob asks if Laban is "at peace" (*shalom*) and the shepherds answer using the same word, *shalom*, Jacob has learned two pieces of information. First of all, a man who is "at peace" with his pagan neighbors who practice idolatry is one to be viewed with caution. In addition, Laban's daughters are pure and undefiled. Because Laban is so much "at peace" with his neighbors, his daughter feels secure appearing at the public well alone, knowing that she will not be accosted by hostile men.[16]

> [The shepherds said], behold, Rachel [Laban's] daughter cometh with the sheep. And [Jacob] said, Lo, it is yet high day, neither is it time that the cattle [sheep] should be gathered together: water ye the sheep, and go and feed them. And they said, We cannot, until all the flocks be gathered together, and till they roll the stone from the well's mouth; then we water the sheep (Genesis 29:6b–8).

Here we see the beginning of a *big* change in Jacob. The text is scant in describing the drama of his first meeting with and Rachel, but the sages fill in the blanks left by the scriptural text. Chizkuni asserts that Jacob is instantly attracted to Rachel and is eager to speak with her face-to-face. When he sees her driving the flocks of her father, he fears that the shepherds are only waiting for her arrival so they can take their sheep out to graze together. Chizkuni interprets Jacob's near-order to them to leave as a maneuver enabling him to have time alone with Rachel. Netziv adds that Jacob is enchanted by Rachel from the moment he sees her. He dismisses the shepherds so that he can have time alone with her.[17]

Jacob must have recalled the family stories about Abraham's servant meeting his mother Rebekah at the well. Love stories in the Bible often begin with encounters at wells. This was apparently the standard operating procedure for meeting women in the ancient world. A pretty good idea, actually, since water was scarce and needed to be drawn from the well every day. One did not observe many men fetching water either, that was certain.

> And while [Jacob] yet spake with them [the shepherds], Rachel came with her father's sheep: for she kept them (Genesis 29:9).

Rachel's role as a shepherdess suggests several things about her character. Shepherds must guide and care for their flocks, succoring and nurturing their charges. Dressner notes that when Moses, the shepherd at Midian, chased a lost sheep to a dangerous cliff and returned it to the flock, heaven marked him as now being worthy to guide the flocks of Israel. The Lord himself is referred to as a shepherd in Psalm 23. In time, Rachel will become the "legendary shepherdess and mother of all Israel," as her suffering people receive comfort as they pass her tomb while they travel to exile.[18]

While most other women in the ancient Near East spend their time within the walls of their homes or tents tending to domestic duties, Rachel is comfortable outdoors, roaming free in the hills with the sheep. In the fields, Rachel develops the quality of self-reliance, even "audacity." These qualities continue to grow throughout her life, and even become legends which follow her after her death. She has the backbone to defy her father by leaving him and confiscating his idols. She alone among the barren matriarchs complains to her husband that he has not given her children.[19] Acknowledging Rachel's distinctive independence, her behavior on meeting Jacob is not unexpected.

Rachel arrives at the well to fulfill her assignment to tend her father's sheep. The Zohar asks, "What was special about Rachel that she was summoned to this crucial meeting?" The commentary responds that "Rachel's beauty was so exquisite that she served God's purpose by riveting Jacob's eyes and heart so completely, that it acted as a magnetic force, causing Jacob to cease his wandering, stake his claim and set down roots in Haran in order to possess her."[20]

Alter's translation of Genesis 29:10 reads: "And it happened when Jacob saw Rachel daughter of Laban his mother's brother and the sheep of Laban his mother's brother that he stepped forward and rolled the stone from the mouth of the well and watered the sheep of Laban his mother's brother."[21] Knowing that Rachel is his uncle's daughter—and confident that she is his ordained mate—Jacob displays astonishing strength, rolling back the huge stone "as easily as a cork is drawn from a bottle," as one sage describes it.[22] Alter comments on this action: "The 'Homeric' feat of strength in rolling away the huge stone single-handed is the counterpart of his mother's feat of carrying up water for ten thirsty camels. Though Jacob is not a man of the open field, like Esau, we now see that he is formidably powerful—and so Rebekah was not unrealistic in fearing the twins would kill each other should they come to blows."[23]

When water is drawn after meeting a young lady at a well in a foreign land, it is a cue to the audience that a betrothal scene is about to commence. But this vignette is the polar opposite of Isaac's chosen bride appearing at the well. Instead of the usual go-between, the prospective groom *himself* appears at the well, and it is *he*—not the maiden—who draws the water. To do so, he must deal with the mammoth stone, stones being Jacob's signature motif in Genesis.[24]

"And Jacob kissed Rachel, and lifted up his voice, and wept" (Genesis 29:11). What a wealth of meaning is compressed into these seven words. Samuel Dressner states, "A minimum of words, a maximum of meaning."[25] There is a Hebrew pun between "he watered" *(vayasq)* and "he kissed" *(vayishaq)*.[26] Alshich comments that Jacob's cry was instinctual, an expression of his ecstasy and relief, because Rachel was so very beautiful. Rabbi Abraham, son of Ramban, adds that Jacob's cry is a prayer of thanksgiving to God for guiding him to the perfect woman.[27]

The Bible does not contain a love story more splendid than the love story between Rachel and Jacob. In fact, few such love stories equal it in tenderness and poignancy in the three thousand years of literature which follow. Jacob is on his own. He does not have the luxury of an arbitrator or lavish gifts. All he has to offer is himself. Jacob and Rachel's passion is spontaneous and irrepressible. Jacob knows at first glance that this girl was the one his mother had envisioned for him. However impetuous, this love is certain, and it grows into an ever-deepening union, able to outlast much anguish.

---

[1] Shera Aranoff Tuchman and Sandra E. Rapoport, *The Passions of the Matriarchs*, (Jersey City, New Jersey, KTAV Publishing House, Inc., 2004), 181–182.

[2] Genesis 27:46: "And Rebekah said to Isaac, I am weary of my life because of the daughters of Heth: if Jacob take a wife of the daughters of Heth, such as these which are of the daughters of the land, what good shall my life do me?"

[3] Nehama Leibowitz, *Studies in Beresheit*, (1973), 277–278.

[4] Tuchman and Rapoport (2004), 182, 183.

[5] See Samuel H. Dressner, *Rachel*, (Minneapolis: Fortress Press, 1994), 21–22.

[6] Robert Alter, *Genesis: Translation and Commentary*, (New York: W. W. Norton and Company, 1996), 149 fn 12.

"*[A] ramp*. Although its etymology is doubtful, the traditional rendering of 'ladder' is unlikely. As has often been observed, the references to both 'its top reaching the heavens' and 'the gate of heaven' use phrases associated with the Mesopotamian ziggurat, and so the structure envisioned is probably a vast ramp with terraced landings."

[7] See Dressner (1994), 23.

[8] See Dressner (1994), 24.

[9] Dressner (1994), 25.

10 Alter (1996), 148, fn 11. "There is scant evidence elsewhere of a general (and uncomfortable) ancient Near Eastern practice of using stones as pillows. Rashi, followed by some modern scholars, proposes that the stone is not placed under Jacob's head but alongside it, as a kind of protective barrier. The stone by which Jacob's head rests as he dreams his vision will become the pillar, the commemorative or cultic marker (*matsevah*) at the end of the story."

11 Alter (1996), 150 footnote 18. "Cultic pillars—Jacob ritually dedicates this one by pouring oil over its top—were generally several feet high. If that is the case here, as such it would have required … Herculean strength to lift the stone. We are then prepared for Jacob's feat with a massive weight of stone in the next episode."

12 Alter (1996), 148 fn 11.

13 Alter (1996), 151, fn 2 and Tuchman and Rapoport (2004), 184.

14 Tuchman and Rapoport (2004), 184–185.

15 Tuchman and Rapoport (2004), 184.

16 Tuchman and Rapoport (2004), 186–187.

17 Tuchman and Rapoport (2004), 188–189.

18 See Dressner (1996), 34.

19 See Dressner (1996), 35–36.

20 Zohar, 153b, quoted in Tuchman and Rapoport (2004), 191.

21 Alter (1994), 152.

22 Pirkey de Rabbi Eleazar (Warsaw, 1852) 36 in Dressner (1996), 31.

23 Alter (1994), 152.

24 Alter (1994), 148, footnote 11. Again, Alter reminds us that there are many stones that mark Jacob's life—this stone that he removes from the mouth of the well, the stone that was his pillow at Bethuel, the stone monument he erects after his dream, and the stones he erects as a marker to commemorate his peace with Laban as they leave each other for the last time.

[25] Dressner (1996), 30.

[26] Alter (1994), 152, fn 11. Also, Tuchman and Rapoport (2004), 194. These two words, although identical in Hebrew, arise from two different root words, *shakoh*, meaning "to give to drink," and *nashok*, meaning "to kiss."

[27] See Tuchman and Rapoport (2004), 195.

Chapter 12
Rachel and Leah: The Agony and the Ecstasy

There is an old adage that says, "The course of true love never did run smooth." Actually, it was Shakespeare.[1] This is an understatement as far as Jacob is concerned. He was lucky in finding the love of his life as soon as he gets into town, but, alas, things soon change.

The Genesis text reports little conversation between Jacob and Rachel at the well after "the kiss." We are left wondering, "What does Rachel do when Jacob kisses her? Does she kiss back?" The Talmud fills in the voids in the Genesis text. It informs us that when Jacob sees Rachel and kisses her, he immediately asks for her hand in marriage, and she consents. At that time, she has feelings of foreboding because she knows her father well. She tells Jacob that her father is a cunning man, and she fears that Jacob will encounter problems in the marriage negotiations for her hand. Jacob replies, "I am your father's brother," seeking to console Rachel with the knowledge that he, Jacob, was equal to her father in "maneuvering ability" to her father. "How will he try to trick me?" asks Jacob. Rachel tells him, "I have a maiden sister who is older than I, and my father will not betroth me before her. He will surely try to give her to you in marriage in my stead." In order to prevent this from happening, Jacob gives Rachel secret signs that only the two of them would know, so that only Rachel would be able to reveal them to him at the time of their marriage. In this way, Jacob can be sure that Laban's deceit would be beaten.[2]

Being thus reassured, Rachel runs to her father's house to tell him that his nephew has arrived, has moved the great stone on the well's mouth single-handedly, and has watered his flocks. Alter notes that hurrying home to tell the news of a guest's arrival—usually with the verb *ruts*, meaning "to run," as it is here—is another conventional requirement of a betrothal type-scene.[3]

When Laban, Rachel's father, hears from his daughter that his sister's son Jacob has arrived, he *runs* to the well to receive him, *hugs* him, *kisses* him, and *brings* him back to his house. Rashi elaborates on all the action verbs that describe Laban's behavior toward Jacob. Laban remembers that the last visitor from the land of Canaan brought along with him ten camels carrying rich gifts for his sister Rebekah's bride price. Rashi notes that although Laban runs to the well, he sees no caravan. Laban then *embraces* Jacob in order to detect any hidden bags of gold on his person. Next, he even *kisses* Jacob to see if he has secreted valuable jewels in his mouth.[4]

Jacob is not ignorant of these maneuvers by his cunning uncle. He describes in detail all the events of the last few weeks of his journey. According to Sforno, Jacob tells Laban that he is not penniless, but rather is escaping the fury of his twin brother. His mother has advised him to seek temporary sanctuary with her brother. Ohr Hachayim attributes Jacob with the ability to immediately perceive the cunning nature of Laban's character. While Jacob appears to be telling Laban about his weeks on the run, he is actually communicating to his uncle that he can fend for himself, even in dangerous territory, and that he does not intend to freeload off of Laban's hospitality. By informing Laban that he obtained the birthright that should have belonged to Esau and by relating that he obtained the coveted Abrahamic blessing from his father, Jacob is letting Laban know that he has finally met his match in matters of shrewdness.[5]

We learn that Jacob has been staying with Laban for a month, tending his flocks, when his uncle calls his "bone and flesh" into him and asks, "Because you are my kin, should you serve me for nothing? Tell me what your wages should be?" (Genesis 29:15). This is apparently more than a friendly chat. It is a facade for the negotiation of a betrothal agreement for Rachel. As justification for this idea, notice how the text reads in Genesis. At this point, before Jacob can answer, the two daughters of Laban are introduced.

> And Laban had two daughters: the name of the elder was Leah, and the name of the younger was Rachel. Leah was tender eyed; but Rachel was beautiful and well favoured. (Genesis 29:16–17)

According to Rashbam, Genesis presents Leah and Rachel at this point in the narrative because Rachel will be the price point of the negotiation. Jacob intends to ask for her hand in marriage as his salary.[6] Much tradition surrounds the relationships between these two sisters. According to one midrash, Leah and Rachel are twin sisters who are fourteen years old when Jacob comes to their father's house, and they are consequently twenty-one years old at the time of their marriage to Jacob.[7]

Both girls are described as beautiful. Rachel is exquisite in both form and feature, while Leah's eyes are singled out as her best feature. The Hebrew adjective used to describe Leah's eyes is *rakhot,* which can be interpreted as "soft, tender, delicate, or gentle."[8] If used in a negative connotation, however, the word can also be construed as "weak." Hardly a nice way to introduce a beautiful girl.

Shera Tuchman and Sandra Rapoport point out that the Talmud does not point out Leah's weak eyes in order to highlight something negative about her character. Quite the opposite, in fact. The Talmud teaches us of Leah's righteous and sensitive qualities from the use of the word *rakhot.* Leah has overheard two townspeople speculating about possible matches. The townspeople have matched up her aunt Rebekah's two sons with her father's two daughters, saying, "The older daughter, Leah, is a match for the older son, Esau. And the younger daughter, Rachel, is a match for the younger son, Jacob." Leah becomes horrified at the prospect of marrying Esau, a well-known outlaw. As a result, she cries so fiercely that her lovely eyes become weakened. Even so, this unhappy consequence is a result of her moral integrity in refusing to marry a man with a deplorable reputation. Ohel Yaakov elaborates on the Talmudic reference, adding that Leah's effusive tears are shed as she prays that God stay the decree that she must marry Esau. Radak states unequivocally that both sisters were equally lovely, although Leah's eyes are dimmed by her tears.[9]

Another version on this midrash is found in "The Book of Legends," Sefer Ha-Aggadah. Rav states that the fact that Leah had weak eyes is no disgrace to her but a cause for praise. "So she sat the crossroads asking all passersby, 'The older one—what kind of a person is he?' and was told 'A cunning hunter [Genesis 25:27], a wicked man, given to robbing people.' 'And the younger—what kind of a person is he?' 'A quiet man, dwelling in tents.' At this Leah wept so much that her eyelids seemed to disappear."[10] Talk about crying your eyes out ...

Meanwhile, back at the negotiating table, Laban awaits an answer to his question about what Jacob's wages will be. Genesis reads: "And Jacob loved Rachel; and said, I will serve thee seven years for Rachel thy younger daughter" (Genesis 29:18). What is the nature of Jacob's love for Rachel? She is heartbreakingly beautiful, it is true, but we tend to view Jacob's initial infatuation with Rachel as something otherworldly. Rachel is precisely the girl his parents have hand-picked for him to marry. Be that as it may, many arranged brides are not received in quite the way Jacob receives Rachel. She may have looked great at the well after Jacob's long, hot journey, but he has been here for a month now. He has most likely seen her at her daily tasks, helping with household chores, to say nothing of the conversations they would have had as they tended Laban's sheep. And yet the luster does not seem to have rubbed off of Rachel. The magic is still there.

Ohr Hachayim explains that Rachel's beauty ignites a "chemical reaction" within Jacob. This reaction is the palpable essence of a lasting relationship. Without it, a man may be tempted to look at another woman. The Bible's focus on Rachel's exquisite beauty and its magnetic hold on Jacob gives us a glimpse into the power of Jacob's obsession with her. The commentator of *Midrash Rabbah* augments the simple words of his speech, in light of Jacob's knowledge of the duplicitous nature of Laban's character. In reality, Jacob is saying, "I will work for seven years, but *only* for Rachel (not for Leah), your younger daughter (in case you were thinking of substituting some impostor from the marketplace with the same name, or even your older daughter, by pretending that her name is Leah."[11]

> And Jacob served seven years for Rachel; and they seemed unto him but a few days, for the love he had to her. (Genesis 29:20)

While Rachel was beautiful and desirable and on a pedestal, how could seven years of hard labor seem but a few days? Love, with all its pains and ecstasies, is in the eye of the beholder. In Victor Frankl's book, *Man's Search for Meaning*, the thing that enabled some inmates at the camp to survive while others perished was their obsession with an idea or a person who gave meaning to the terrible days. The ardor of Jacob's seven years of labor could be vaporized by the image of his Rachel before him.[12] How much more romantic can you get?

Marriage contracts in Old Testament times were generally negotiated by the bride's father interacting with the groom or the groom's agent. Agreements included the amount of a bride's dowry, money that would be returned to the woman in the event of a divorce, the responsibility of support, and other clauses relating to the groom's fidelity.[13] Generally, the bride's father included the bride price in the woman's dowry. Not so with Laban. He negotiated a bride price that included seven years of labor as a shepherd from Jacob. The bride price appears to have originated anciently as compensation for a daughter's lost services in her father's household. It also gave the prospective bridegroom a chance to show off his ability to provide support for his new family.

Laban does not seem to have provided a dowry for his daughters, other than the gift of Zilpah and Bilhah. This failure to provide for his daughters engenders deep-seated resentment in Rachel and Leah against their father, one of the only things they can agree upon. When Jacob counsels with them about returning to the land of Canaan, they express their hostility toward their father, saying, "Are we not counted of him strangers? For he hath sold us, and has quite devoured our money" (Genesis 31:15). Perhaps the sisters had computed the bride price—which would have been at least seventy shekels—and felt that they had been cheated out of the expected marital security fund.[14]

A bride price did not necessarily have to be paid in a lump sum. Rachel was undoubtedly pleased by the price she fetched, since it was huge by contemporary standards. She must have felt like a "ten-cow wife." The minimum annual wage for an assistant shepherd was about ten shekels of silver. In addition, as master shepherd, Jacob would have qualified to receive a fifteen to twenty percent increase in the flock as wages, besides living expenses. Even though the chief shepherd had to absorb the losses from death, theft, and disease, his potential for remuneration was much higher than ten shekels per year.[15]

The dowry was the most important material consideration in a marriage contract. It usually far exceeded the bride price and was a wife's opportunity to inherit from her father. Tradition dictated that the dowry be worth about a tenth of the father's estate. The dowry gave stability to the new marriage, and was a strong financial deterrent to divorce, since the dowry had to be returned in the event the marriage was dissolved. During the marriage, such property could be sold only with the wife's approval.[16]

For seven years, Rachel and Jacob made preparations for their marriage. When the seven years were over, Jacob came to Laban to demand his bride. Alter translates this as, "Give me my wife, for my time is done, and let me come to bed with her" (Genesis 29:21).[17] Jacob is quite explicit here with his anxiousness to at last possess his precious Rachel. Laban calls his fellow shepherds together and prepares a feast for the wedding. According to *Midrash Rabbah*, Laban colludes with his companions to keep Jacob around another seven years. He tells them about his plan to substitute Leah for Rachel in the marriage tent. He assures them that the lovesick Jacob will stay around another seven years for Rachel, and they can continue to enjoy the extra water and prosperity his presence has provided. The shepherds are conscience-stricken about their part in the plot, and while the wedding guests are singing praises to Jacob, the men chant "Hee leah, hee leah," which means "She is Leah" in Hebrew. This phrase also has a double meaning; it is a wedding song refrain, and perhaps a subtle attempt to warn Jacob that Laban was switching the sisters.[18]

Rachel and Leah must have been close, even if they were not twins. When Rachel learns of her father's plot to substitute Leah in the bridal chamber, she must make a decision. She is torn by her love of Jacob and empathy for her sister's situation. According to one midrash, Rachel chooses not to put her sister to shame. She does not want Leah to be given to the dishonorable Esau, over which possible betrothal she has wept so many bitter tears. She could not bear the thought that Leah would be utterly humiliated when Jacob discovered that their father had played such a devious trick on him. According to one source, Rachel taught her sister the secret signals that she and Jacob had agreed upon to identify each other in case Laban attempted a deception. She suggests that Leah use the private signs—touching Jacob's right toe, thumb, and earlobe—to mislead her inebriated bridegroom in the darkness of the bridal tent.[19] Support for these assertions is purportedly derived from the Old Testament text itself: "In the morning, behold, it was Leah" (Genesis 29:25). Since the veiled bride knew the signs, Jacob believed her to be Rachel. One commentary adds the detail that the two sisters' voices were so similar that Jacob could be fooled in the dark.[20]

Another midrash gives a slightly different version of events. It concurs with the argument that Laban would not have succeeded in deceiving Jacob without Rachel's involvement. Rachel has to choose between her love for Jacob and her compassion for her sister, and she decides in favor of the latter. In one of the most extreme descriptions of Rachel's act of self-sacrifice, Rachel secrets herself under Jacob and

Leah's bed on their wedding night. "When Jacob spoke with Leah, Rachel would answer him, so that he would not identify Leah's voice."[21]

One commentary recounts the conversation that took place on the morning after. After a night of Jacob calling, "Rachel," and Leah responding, Jacob says, "'How could you have deceived me, you daughter of a deceiver?' She said to him, 'And is there a book without faithful readers? [I know your story, so I followed your example.] Did not your father call you 'Esau' and you answered him accordingly? So you called me by a name other than my own and I answered accordingly.'"[22] Is she suggesting that turnabout is fair play?

Jacob immediately confronts Laban saying, "What is this thou hast done unto me? Did not I serve with thee for Rachel? Why did you deceive me?" (Genesis 29:25). One commentator, Ohr Hachayim, states that Jacob is not just angry at the substitution of Leah for Rachel—who was specifically named in the marriage contract—but at the underhanded way that Laban went about the whole matter. He says that if Laban had just explained the local custom to him and told him he could not marry Rachel without first marrying Leah, he would have complied. This would have spared Leah the humiliation of spending her wedding night trying to impersonate her younger sister and the mortification of knowing that her husband would have never married her unless it were under a guise. Jacob might have been disinclined to marry Leah, but he would have done so if that was the only way he could marry his beloved Rachel.[23] It was the ultimate "bait and switch."

Laban's response to Jacob's query was, "It must not be so done in our country, to give the younger before the firstborn," and then offered him Rachel for an additional seven years labor—without the waiting period this time. Hearing this, Jacob is even more furious because the assertion that the elder must be married before the younger was false. If there were such a custom, Rachel and he would have known about it. Jacob could have had the marriage annulled, but his options were limited. There were no legal courts to which he could appeal, and he could not return home for fear of Esau. James Baker states, "A patriarchal potentate had created a case-specific law. Jacob could have Rachel along with Leah or not at all."[24] He agreed to Laban's conditions, and at the end of the week set aside for the observance of Leah's marriage, he wed Rachel. (It was the custom at that time to celebrate a seven-day marriage feast so that nomadic family and friends could gather and reacquaint themselves before departing for remote lands.[25])

Why did Laban promise his younger daughter in the first place, we might ask? Dressner feels that it was a way to get seven years of free labor from Jacob. He also believes that Laban's public response to Jacob revealed an additional message meant for Jacob's ears alone. The assertion of the older child's rights over the younger child's was designed to push an emotional button in Jacob. Laban knew he was especially vulnerable on that subject. Had not Jacob, the younger brother, taken the birthright from Esau? Laban mocks Jacob and his heritage, insinuating that "Maybe in *your* country, proper conduct might not always be observed, but in *our* country, we respect the traditions of the fathers." Dressner puts it this way: "For what was most precious to Isaac—the birthright—Jacob beguiled Esau; for what was most precious to Jacob—Rachel—is he beguiled."[26] After this, what could Jacob say?

Alter notes that Jacob's "guilty consciousness" is augmented by Laban's referring to Leah as the firstborn (*bekhirah*). He observes that throughout history, the story of the switched brides is a meting out of poetic justice to Jacob—the deceiver deceived, deprived by darkness of the sense of sight as his father was by blindness, relying like his father on the misleading sense of touch."[27]

The story continues with Rachael and Leah as Jacob's two wives, sisters vying for the attention of their husband. While the Chinese character for "chaos" is *not* made up of two "woman" characters under one "roof" character, I thought it might have been quite apropos.

---

[1] William Shakespeare, *A Midsummer Night's Dream*, Act 1, scene 1, line 134.

[2] Shera Aranoff Tuchman and Sandra E. Rapoport, *The Passions of the Matriarchs*, (Jersey City, New Jersey, KTAV Publishing House, Inc., 2004), 198.

[3] Robert Alter, *Genesis: Translation and Commentary*, (New York: W. W. Norton and Company, 1996), 153 fn 12.

[4] Tuchman and Rapoport (2004), 199 and Alter (1996), 153, fn 13.

⁵ Tuchman and Rapoport (2004), 199.

⁶ Tuchman and Rapoport (2004), 201.

⁷ *Seder 'Olam Rabbah ii* as quoted in Emil G. Hirsch and M. Seligsohn, "Rachel," Jewish Encyclopedia.com accessed June 3, 2011 at http://www.jewishencyclopedia.com/view_friendle.jsp?artid=57&letter=

⁸ Tuchman and Rapoport (2004), 201–202.

⁹ Bava Batra 123a in the Talmud, quoted in Tuchman and Rapoport (2004), 202.

¹⁰ Hayim Naham Bialik and Yehoshua Hana Ravnitzky, editors, *The Book of Legends: Sefer Ha-Aggadah*, (New York: Schocken Books, 1992), 47.

¹¹ Tuchman and Rapoport (2004), 205–206; see also Samuel Dressner, "Rachel," (Minneapolis: Fortress Press, 1994), 44.

¹² Dressner (1994), 40 and Viktor E. Frankl, *Man's Search for Meaning: An Introduction to Logotherapy*, (New York: Washington Square Press, 1963), 121.

"Nietzsche's words, 'He who has a *why* to live for can bear with almost any *how*,' could be the guiding motto for all psychotherapeutic and psychohygienic efforts regarding prisoners. Whenever there was an opportunity for it, one had to give them a *why*—an aim—for their lives, in order to strengthen them to bear the terrible *how* of their existence."

¹³ James Baker, *Women's Rights in Old Testament Times*, (Salt Lake City: Signature Books, 1992), 39.

¹⁴ Baker (1992), 41.

¹⁵ Baker (1992), 59 fn11.

¹⁶ Baker (1992), 43.

¹⁷ Alter (1996), 154.

¹⁸ Jacob Neusner, *Genesis Rabbah: The Judaic Commentary to the Book of Genesis, A New American Translation, Volume III*, (Atlanta, Georgia: Scholars Press, 1985), 41 and *Midrash Rabbah* (70.19) quoted in Tuchner and Rapoport (2004), 211–212.

[19] Babylonian Talmud, Megillah 13b in Dressner (1994), 46. See also Naomi Mara Hyman, "*Biblical Women in the Midrash: A Sourcebook*, (Northvale, New Jersey: Jason Aronson, Inc., (1997) 59–60.

[20] Commentary on Torah Temima in Tuchman and Rapoport (2004), 216.

[21] *Lam. Rabbah* [ed. Vilna] petihtah 24, as quoted in "Rachel: Midrash and Haggadah," accessed March 8, 2014 at http://jwa.org/encyclopedia/article/rache-midrash-and-aggadah. Also Neusner (2004), 41–42.

[22] Neusner (2004), 41. *Genesis Rabbah* 70.19.

[23] Tuchman and Rapoport (2004), 217–218.

[24] Baker (1992), 42.

[25] Baker (1992), 60 fn 12.

[26] Dressner (1994), 45.

[27] Alter (1996), 155, fn 26.

Chapter 13
The Baby Derby[1]

After the week of feasting in celebration of Leah's wedding, Laban gives Rachel to Jacob as a wife. "Laban gave Rachel *to him* to be a wife *to him* (Genesis 29:28; my translation, emphasis added). The Hebrew text in Genesis repeats the words *to him* twice, emphasizing that Rachel was his true mate. Ohr Hachayim writes that "Jacob perceives that Rachel—not Leah—will be the mainstay of his home."[2] James Baker notes, "in a polygamous marriage, more than one woman might be *a* chief wife, but only one woman, the first chronological wife, would be *the* chief wife. Both Rachel and Leah were chief wives."[3] Something tells me that this could prove problematic.

Laban has transacted a contract for Leah and Rachel, has paid a dowry for each (in the gifts of Zilpah and Bilhah), and received a bride price for each (seven years of labor). Although Leah is the first wife chronologically, Jacob's intent was that Rachel be the first (and only) wife. Jacob marries Leah only through her father's deception. He does not technically confirm his marriage to Leah until his marriage contract with Rachel is reaffirmed. So Rachel's contract remains the first contract, and Leah's the second. Thus Rachel is *the* chief wife, and Leah is *a* chief wife.[4] Only a lawyer would be able to make sense of this complicated language. No wonder that the relationships in the family are tangled.

Genesis next tells us that Jacob "loved" Rachel, and that Leah was "despised." Of course the term "despised" has emotional intimations, but Robert Alter points out that the word is also a technical, *legal* term for the unfavored co-wife.[5] Leah reinforces the emotional interpretation of this word as she names her sons. She constantly seeks her husband's love, which she thinks will be won for her by bearing sons to him. Fertility seemingly gives her no satisfaction, as her heart is set on winning Jacob's love. In the same light, Rachel gets no satisfaction from her husband's love. She only wants a son.

Samuel Dressner says it this way, "The Rachel-Leah conflict centers upon the contest between *love* and *motherhood*."[6] Rachel is loved but barren. The Lord has opened Leah's womb, but with the birth of each child, she expresses her unrequited love for Jacob in the name she gives her son. She names her first son "Reuben" and says, "because

God saw my suffering, and now my husband will love me" (Genesis 29:32). Reuben is thus interpreted as *reu'ben*, "see, a son," but Leah immediately converts the verb to apply to God. She says, "Because God saw how I was suffering"—without Jacob's love—"perhaps now"—with the birth of the son I have given him—"my husband will love me." Radak adds to this, "as much as he loves my sister." For Leah, no matter how much she loves her child, he is not her paramount objective. Her longing is fastened upon her husband.[7]

Not long after this birth, "Leah again becomes pregnant, and gives birth to a son, and she says, 'because God heard that I am hated, he also gave me this one.' And she named him Simeon'" (Genesis 29:33). The Hebrew word *shama*—which means "to hear" or "to listen and understand"—is the source of the name Leah chooses for her son. With the birth of each son, she articulates her unrequited love for Jacob. With her third son, Levi—which means "to accompany" or "to stay with"—she says, "Now will my husband be joined to me" (Genesis 29:34). His name can also be a play on the word *lev*, meaning "heart." By the time she bears her fourth son, Judah, she uses the naming process to express her gratitude to God for giving her four sons. *Hodah* means "to give thanks" or "to glorify." This verb is used frequently in psalms of thanksgiving. Leah no longer verbalizes the hope of winning her husband's affection, but simply praises God for granting her sons.[8] She then takes a break from childbearing. We are not told why this is so. Is it a natural occurrence, or has Jacob stopped visiting Leah's tent?

Try to imagine yourself in Rachel's shoes during this period of time, watching as her sister easily conceives and bears four sons in quick succession. What must have been going through her mind and heart? Torat Hachida examines the complexity of her emotions. He reminds us that, while Rachel might have fallen in love with Jacob at first sight, she had also had a close relationship with Leah all her life. That close attachment to her sister impelled her to disclose the secret signs she had formulated with Jacob so that Leah would not be humiliated publicly at her wedding festivities. Rachel might also have feared that her father would decide not to allow her to marry Jacob as an additional wife, making him lost to her forever. In addition, perhaps she feared Jacob would change his mind and decide not to marry her, also. This commentator points out that even with these divergent, competing allegiances—to her promised bridegroom, to her older sister, to her father, and even to her own happiness—Rachel acts as a hero and reveals the passwords to her sister. The commentator says, "She walked through the minefield of emotions and found the clear and righteous path. This act of Rachel's was a great and meritorious act."[9]

At this point in the Genesis text, we glimpse the only recorded conversation between Rachel and Jacob. In utter frustration at not being able to bear children, she says to Jacob, "Give me sons, for if you don't, I'm a dead woman" (Genesis 30:1, Alter's translation).[10] Rashi describes how Rachel begs Jacob to pray for her to be able to conceive a child. She firmly believes that if she does not conceive, she would be as if she were dead. The Talmud states that one who is childless equates herself with one who is dead. The super-commentary on Torah Temima explains the source of Rachel's agony through the use of metaphor. She believes that one's children are the "thread that connects one generation to another." Consequently, for a woman who is barren, this life-line has been suddenly severed, and it is as if she is dead. Netziv agrees, highlighting Rachel's belief in this life perspective. It is not surprising that with this viewpoint, even with Jacob's "passionate devotion" to her, Rachel continues to be dissatisfied. Without children to follow after her, the love between her and Jacob seems empty and meaningless. She is passionate about passing on the Abrahamic covenant and its promises to the generations that follow. She wants to be "remembered long after she is gone."[11]

Jacob reacts to Rachel's emotional pleading by becoming angry: "And Jacob was incensed with Rachel, and he said, 'Am I instead of God, who has denied you the fruit of the womb?'" (Genesis 30:2, Alter's translation).[12] Author Avivah Gornberg sheds further light on this conversation. He argues that this dialogue, the only one recorded between Jacob and Rachel, can perhaps be best understood in light of "the dynamics of desire and frustration." These commentators do not view Rachel as "having a female tantrum" or "threatening her husband with dire consequences if he does not 'give' her children." Instead, Rachel is merely describing "a dull meaninglessness, a loss of sap in her life." As we comprehend this, we begin to see Jacob's anger in a new light. "It is painful for him to hear his wife—whom he loves for herself, not as a means of procreation—declare so plainly that her primary passion is not for him."[13]

Alter observes that the author of Genesis makes an artful deviation from the standard annunciation scene here. According to the convention of such a story, the childless wife will visit an oracle or be visited by an angel or a messenger from God to tell her that she will give birth to a male child. Instead, Rachel entreats her husband, who appropriately answers that he cannot play God's role in the annunciation narrative. Rachel then resorts to the alternative of bearing a child through her servant, just as Sarah did with Hagar. Rachel's demand is for "sons," not just *a* son. Some might interpret this as Rachel inadvertently prophesying her own death, trying to give birth to an additional son.[14]

Rachel presents Jacob with her own solution to her childlessness, offering her maid Bilhah to him as a surrogate wife. The Hebrew text of Genesis reads, "that she may bear a child upon my knees, and I will also be *built up* through her" (Genesis 30:3–4). To place a newborn on someone's knees was a sign of adoption. She uses the word *ibaneh* from the word *banah* (*to build*) which plays on the word *ben*, meaning "son."[15] These are the same words Sarah used when she offered her maid Hagar to Abraham. Rachel names the first son of this union Dan, which means "he judged" in Hebrew, because "God has judged me, and he has also heard my voice, and has given me a son" (Genesis 30:6). She apparently interpreted this as, "God has judged my desire for a son to be worthy, and granted me my desire." Bilhah conceives again and bears a second son whom Rachel names Naphtali. The origin of this name could come from two sources: *ptil*, meaning "connecting cord" or "thread," (twisted); or *naphtulay*, meaning "struggles," or "wrestlings."[16] This undoubtedly refers to Rachel's complicated relationship with her sister, with all its twists and turns—once intimate, but now tainted with envy for Leah's many sons.

Not to be outdone in the baby derby, Leah offers her handmaid Zilpah to Jacob as a wife. She has not borne any children for some time, and any children born to Zilpah will be imputed to Leah. She will name them and raise them, and such actions have the potential for further securing Jacob's love for her. Netziv presents a more magnanimous view of Leah, attributing her motivation for giving Zilpah to Jacob as a sign of her compassion for Zilpah's unmarried state. Leah also attempts to allay Zilpah's envy of Bilhah, whom Rachel had elevated from handmaid to legal wife. She believes she could do as much for Zilpah. Her sons will have the same status and property rights as Jacob's other sons. Da'at Zekeinim prompts us to remember that Zilpah and Bilhah are also Laban's daughters, but they are called "handmaids" because they were born to his concubine.[17] The situation has become *extremely* complicated. Through Zilpah, Gad ("good fortune has come,") and Asher ("fortunate" or "praiseworthy") are born. Rachel is still the only wife that is an *akarah*—a barren woman. She is *hungry* for a child.

The Genesis text tells us that during the wheat harvest, Leah's young son Reuben finds mandrakes in the field and brings them to his mother. We are privy to the one and only conversation between the two sisters found in Genesis. Their words reveal what is most important to each. "Then Rachel said to Leah, Give me, I pray thee, of thy son's mandrakes. And she said unto her, Is it a small matter that thou hast taken my husband? and wouldest thou take away my son's mandrakes also? And Rachel said, Therefore he shall lie with thee tonight for thy son's mandrakes" (Genesis 30:14–15). Leah aches for her husband's love, while Rachel longs for a child. They negotiate an exchange—a portion of the mandrakes for one night with Jacob in Leah's tent.

As in other cultures, mandrakes (*dudaim*), were believed to possess aphrodisiac qualities and to promote fertility. The aphrodisiac function is augmented by the similarity of sounds to *dodim*, which in Hebrew means "lovemaking."[18] Rachel is desperate to get her hands on what she identifies as a fertility-inducing plant. This episode with the mandrakes illustrates that although Leah has conjugal rights that cannot be denied, it is Rachel who directs Jacob's nighttime arrangements. After all, she is *the* chief wife. We might wonder why Leah castigates Rachel for "taking away [her] husband," when Leah knows that Jacob never intended to marry her in the first place, Rachel being the object of his desire. Radak attempts to explain this by saying that Leah is expressing her feelings of rejection by Jacob. Because he spends more nights with Rachel, trying to help her conceive, Leah holds her sister responsible for Jacob abandoning her.[19] Normally, connubial rights would be shared equally, but Rachel easily gets the lion's share of Jacob's nights.

Alter says it this way: "In his transactions with these two imperious, embittered women, Jacob seems chiefly acquiescent, perhaps resigned. When Rachel instructs him to consort with her slavegirl, he immediately complies, as he does when Leah tells him it is she who is to share his bed this night. In neither instance is there any report of response on his part in dialogue." Leah uses a particular idiom for sexual intercourse (literally "to me you will come"). This term is ordinarily reserved "for intercourse with a woman the man has not previously enjoyed." This might be an indication that "Jacob has been sexually boycotting Leah," and could easily explain just what Leah is referring to when she says to Rachel, "You have taken my husband."[20]

After a night with Jacob, the mandrake-less Leah becomes pregnant with yet another son, whom she names Issachar. This name is a double pun on the word *sakhar*—which means "wages" or "reward", signifying a fee paid for hiring something. Thus, the name *Issachar* arises from the conditions of his conception, bartering the mandrakes for a night with Jacob and also the sense of reward Leah feels when she bears another son.[21] When her sixth son is born, Leah's constant craving for Jacob's love is again revealed. She calls him Zebulun. Rashi postulates that the name is derived from the Hebrew word *zebul*, which means "dwell with" or "to honor."[22] Alter argues that phonetic connections in the naming process can be rather loose, citing that the Hebrew word meaning "gift," *zebed*, shares only two consonants with Zebulun, and the meaning for *zabal*, "to exalt," is nothing more than an educated guess.[23] Leah then gives birth to a daughter, Dinah, and rests securely in her position as a matriarch in the house of Israel.

At this point in the Genesis narrative, it seems all hope is lost for Rachel. But then we read

> And God remembered Rachel, and God hearkened to her, and opened her womb. And she conceived, and bare a son; and said, God hath taken away my reproach: And she called his name Joseph; and said, The Lord shall add to me another son. (Genesis 30:22–24)

Motherhood has been Rachel's obsession during her entire married life, and the reproach of her infertility has been removed in one fell swoop with the birth of this son. Yet the name she chooses for her son does not contain a reference to Jacob, as his other sons' names do. The fact that "God remembered" Rachel, and "God listened" to her reflect the certainty that Rachel, after first entreating her husband to pray for a child for her, took it upon herself to offer her *own* prayers to God. She was confident that someday he would hear and answer her prayers for a child. When Jacob balked, she took the initiative and approached God herself. And "God listened."

Some sages have taught that it was not just Rachel who prayed for this child. They propose that the opening of Rachel's womb was a result of the combined prayers of Jacob *and* Leah *and* Bilhah *and* Zilpah, in addition to Rachel herself. "The sages were imagining a friendship among the women, a loyalty that surpassed rivalry, as they spoke to God in one voice for the sake of Rachel. Rabbi Hanina said that all the women of the camp prayed that Rachel would have a son saying, 'We have sufficient.'"[24]

Rachel's long-awaited pregnancy erases the long years of barrenness and humiliation. Rachel names her son Joseph, which comes from the word *yasaph,* meaning "to increase". By beginning Joseph's name with the Hebrew letter *yod*—which signals the future tense—Rachel is supplicating God to add yet another son. "The Lord will add another son to me." Most new mothers are so overwhelmed at the birth of their first child—the hard labor, the utter fatigue, the new levels of pain—that the thought of having another child is far from their minds. And yet here Rachel is already entreating God for another son. She has used another form of this same Hebrew word: *asaph*, which means "to add," or "to gather." God has "gathered" away her shame. In this manner, Joseph's name reflects Rachel's gratitude that she no longer has to bear the shame of being a barren woman, but also includes an entreaty for the future. Her reproach as a barren woman is gone, but her role as a mother is just beginning. The determination of this righteous woman to be part of handing down the covenant of Abraham is heroic. This resolve is the primary function of the patriarchs and matriarchs.

So, how will this change the dynamics of Jacob's family? Legally, the firstborn son enjoyed both the rights of the inheritance of property and the patriarchal blessing, which bestowed on the recipient the leadership of the family. The birthright son enjoyed a double portion of his father's inheritance. If a father had five sons, he would divide his estate into six portions, the firstborn son receiving two shares, or one-third of the shares, while the other sons each received one-sixth. With this extra revenue, the birthright son was expected to support the women of the family: the son's mother, the childless wives of the family, his unmarried sisters, and any other women returning to the home because of divorce or widowhood. This son was also obligated to find husbands for his sisters and provide them with a dowry.[25]

In Jacob's family, just who *was* the birthright son? Chronologically, the birthright son is Reuben, Leah's oldest son. But Joseph is the firstborn son of *the* chief wife. This question is of critical importance to a mother like Leah, whose social standing and economic well-being would be affected. By the time Joseph is seventeen, Jacob has made his choice clear by giving Joseph a special coat denoting family leadership. Not an enviable place to be in if you have ten big brothers. Hugh Nibley teaches that this coat was the garment the Lord gave Adam in the garden of Eden, which was passed through Seth to Shem, then to Isaac and finally to Jacob.[26]

---

[1] I must give credit for this chapter title to Michael Wilcox, who used this phrase in one of his Old Testament classes. I loved it and thought it perfectly described the goings-on of the first years of Jacob's marriage.

[2] Shera Aranoff Tuchman and Sandra E. Rapoport, *The Passions of the Matriarchs*, (Jersey City, New Jersey, KTAV Publishing House, Inc., 2004), 219.

[3] James Baker, *Women's Rights in Old Testament Times*, (Salt Lake City: Signature Books, 1992), 44.

[4] Baker (1992), 45.

[5] Robert Alter, *Genesis: Translation and Commentary*, (New York: W. W. Norton and Company, 1996), 155 fn 31.

[6] Samuel Dressner, *Rachel*, (Minneapolis: Fortress Press, 1994), 53.

[7] Tuchman and Rapoport (2004), 228–229.

[8] Alter (1996), 157, fn 35.

[9] Tuchman and Rapoport (2004), 235.

[10] Alter (1996), 158.

[11] Talmud (Nedarim 64b) quoted in Tuchman and Rapoport (2004), 237–238.

[12] Alter (1996), 158.

[13] Avivah Gottlieb Zornberg, *Genesis: The Beginning of Desire*, (Philadelphia: The Jewish Publication Society, 1995), 210.

[14] Alter (1996), 158, fn 2.

[15] Alter (1996), 159, fn 3.

[16] Tuchman and Rapoport (2004), 248 and Francis Brown, *The New Brown-Driver-Briggs-Genesius Hebrew and English Lexicon*, (Peabody, Massachusetts: Hendrickson Publishers, 1979), 836. Entries 6616, 6617, 5319.

[17] Tuchman and Rapoport (2004), 251.

[18] Alter (1996), 160 fn 14.

[19] Tuchman and Rapoport (2004), 257.

[20] Alter (1996), 160, fn 16.

[21] Alter (1996), 161, fn. 18.

[22] Tuchman and Rapoport (2004), 264.

[23] Alter (1996), 161, fn 20.

[24] Anne Roiphe, *Water From the Well: Sarah, Rebekah, Rachel, and Leah*, (New York: William Morrow, 2006), 228.

[25] Baker (1992), 50–51.

[26] Hugh Nibley, *Ancient Documents and the Pearl of Great Price*, transcript of videorecorded class, 2.

Chapter 14
Rachel's Legacy

Soon after Joseph's birth, Jacob asks Laban for permission to return to his own land. We might ask, "Why does Jacob wait until this precise moment to beg leave of his father-in-law?" Commentators have proposed various theories. Perhaps only now the fourteen years of Jacob's contracted labor have been completed. Perhaps now that Rachel has borne a son, Jacob does not fear that Laban will marry her off to someone else. Perhaps now Jacob feels that he could return to his father with his chosen wife. If Jacob returned with a beautiful but barren Rachel, his father might wonder if he had selected a beautiful wife only for the pleasure she would give him. Now that she has given birth to Joseph, Jacob feels free to return home at last. Abrabanel explains that Jacob is still preoccupied with securing Abraham's covenantal blessing, even after so many years have gone by. Until Rachel gave him a son, he did not feel that he had brought forth the "spiritual heir" worthy to inherit the covenantal blessing. Now that his most favored wife has given birth to his son, he hopes that this son will be worthy to receive this most important blessing.[1]

James Baker brings up the issue of whether or not the marriage between Jacob and Rachel was "metronymic." In this type of marriage, the husband joined his wife's family and the children adopted the name of the mother or her father. Other signs of a metronymic marriage were the absence of a bride price, dowry, or contract and the bride remaining in her father's home. The son-in-law sought his father-in-law's permission when decisions had to be made, and he was subservient to his wife's father in all ways. Jacob's exodus from Padan-aram raises the question, "Did Jacob and Rachel have such a marriage?" Jacob asks Laban for permission to leave his service and for permission to take his wives and children with him. Moreover, he has worked off the bride price demanded by Laban for fourteen years. Why does Jacob feel he needs to ask for what is already his? Baker feels that perhaps Jacob was trying to curry favor with Laban, knowing that he could not leave without permission—if only for practical reasons. Laban later tries to justify his claim that the marriage was metronymic, but Baker feels that both men knew that it was not technically so.[2]

As they talk, Laban acknowledges that he has been blessed by the Lord because of Jacob's service. Laban asks Jacob what would induce him to stay, allowing him to name his price. Jacob says he will continue to shepherd all of Laban's flocks if he can have all the speckled, spotted, or brown sheep. The solid white and black animals will be Laban's. This seems like an unusual request to us as readers. We wonder what Jacob can be thinking. They negotiate another contract, and Jacob stays for six more years.

Apparently, Jacob is attempting some primitive genetic engineering. In order to cause more speckled lambs to be born, he places brown-striped rods in the watering troughs of the sheep, thinking that if they see stripes as they drink, their offspring will be speckled. Amazingly, Laban's solid-color flock produces mottled offspring over time, and Jacob accumulates a vast flock. Although he has employed a superstitious notion in order to accomplish his designs, Jacob later learns that it is the Lord that has blessed him with his wealth. An angel appears to him in a dream and shows him that the flocks being speckled is God's doing, to compensate for all the injustices Laban has inflicted upon Jacob (see Genesis 31:9–12). Jacob notices that Laban's face is not as favorably disposed to him as it once was. He is told in the same dream to return to the land of his father, and that God will be with him.

Jacob sends for Rachel and Leah to come to him in the field where he is tending his sheep. He wants to be far away from the ears of Laban and his sons when he discusses his plans for the future with his wives. He rehearses to them what has happened over the last two decades—how he served their father diligently, only to have his wages changed ten times. Despite Laban's shenanigans, he tells them that God did not allow their father to prevail against him. No matter how Laban altered the terms of their agreement—whether he promised Jacob the speckled animals or the striped ones—God made sure that the results would be to Jacob's advantage. He relates how God sent an angel to him one night in a dream, telling him that God was aware of all the ploys that Laban was attempting in order to outsmart him. As they are about to embark on this treacherous flight from their homeland, Jacob wants to make it explicitly clear to his wives that God has been with him and will continue to be with him. Jacob wants to make sure Rachel and Leah understand that his spectacular prosperity is not the result of his own skill as an animal breeder. It is a compensatory blessing from the Lord. Jacob comprehends that without the active support and cooperation of his wives, he will not be able to follow the divine injunction he has received from the angel.

> And Rachel and Leah answered and said unto him, Is there yet any portion or inheritance for us in our father's house? Are we not counted of him strangers? for he hath sold us, and hath quite devoured also our money. For all the riches which God hath taken from our father, that is ours, and our children's: now then, whatsoever God hath said unto thee, do. (Genesis 31:14–16)

Laban has apparently pocketed all the proceeds of Jacob's fourteen years of labor and has not set aside any for his daughters. Rachel and Leah see themselves as reduced to chattel by their father—not married off, but sold for profit, as though they were not even family. Most commentaries assume it is Rachel who speaks first in this interchange, because her name is listed first. The text of Genesis 31 uses the singular form of the Hebrew verb *vataan*, meaning "to answer," in the phrase translated as "Rachel and Leah answered." If both women had answered, then the text would have used the plural form. According to Sforno, Rachel says, in effect, "Do as God commands, take control of what is yours and go! You have no need to seek my father's permission."[3]

Athalaya Brenner makes an interesting observation about this "family council." Only when the family is threatened from the outside do the sisters finally cooperate with each other. After Jacob points out to them that their father had completely devoured the bride price he exacted from him, the only emotion recorded in the scriptures for the sisters is fury against their father who has robbed his own daughters. When Rachel and Leah feel that the continuity of the covenant family line is jeopardized, they unite. We will see them do this again when the family is about to encounter Esau.[4] Tammi Schneider feels that the sisters' relationship with each other has healed at this point. They would rather be with each other than with their father.[5]

Rachel's place as the mother of Jacob's son is now firmly established, and she is more than willing to flee from her father's house. She is also determined that nothing happen to her young son or her husband. Laban has made a practice of grazing his flocks at a distance of three days journey from Jacob's herds. The time approaches when Laban must shear his sheep. Sheep-shearing in the Bible is a very elaborate practice involving feasting and large numbers of men, which would provide a marvelous cover for Jacob's escape. Rachel knows her father well. She recognizes that his anger would indeed be great when he returned from the shearing and found his family gone. She desires to maximize the time and distance between her father and the escaping family. She acts with courage and decisiveness and, unbeknownst to her husband, enters her father's tent and steals his teraphim, or household gods.

For centuries, commentators have puzzled over Rachel's theft of her father's teraphim. As a firm believer in the God of Abraham, why would she steal Laban's idols? Here is a sampling of their various opinions.

Netziv postulates that Rachel took the idols because they were her father's means of divination, and she feared that, returning and finding his daughters and grandchildren gone, Laban would consult them to determine their whereabouts. Rashi states that Rachel took the gods in order to remove her father from their idolatrous influence, in an attempt to uproot idolatry from her father's house.[6] Another author postulates that the motive for Rachel's theft might have been an attempt to preserve her inheritance. C. H. Gordon writes, "The [household] gods apparently constituted the title to the chief inheritance portion and leadership of the family."[7] Rachel's desire to possess the household gods could therefore be interpreted as an attempt to have Jacob recognized as the leader of the family after Laban's death.

However, could Rachel have really thought that possession of these gods could hold sway or legal validity regarding her father's estate when her father was still living? If Rachel was so interested in Jacob's position as leader of the family, was this the best way to do it? What was she thinking? William Whitson offers yet another explanation. Over a thousand years after Rachel's time, Near Eastern women were still in the habit of taking their household gods along when going into a foreign land. Rachel was leaving for a distant land and had no thought of returning. Perhaps she wanted to take a treasured family heirloom with her.[8] Rachel's true reason for taking the teraphim remains a mystery for now.

On the third day after Jacob's flight, Laban is informed of his escape. He gathers men and pursues Jacob for seven days, until he finally catches up to Jacob's group at the Mountain of Gilead. Although it would have taken Jacob much longer to travel with his flocks and family, a pursuit party traveling quickly might feasibly cover the distance in a week. The text refers to this speed of travel as *dalaq*—the Hebrew word which also means "to burn" and seems to derive its meaning from the rapid movement of fire—instead of using the usual verb for "pursue."9 Laban pitches his tent, and that night he has a dream in which God says to him, "Watch yourself, lest you speak to Jacob either good or evil" (Genesis 31:24). Another translation reads, "Do not attempt to manipulate Jacob with your words by offering him incentives, or by threatening him."10 Laban asks Jacob:

> What hast thou done, that thou hast stolen away unawares to me, and carried away my daughters, as captives taken with the sword? Wherefore didst thou flee away secretly, and steal away from me; and didst not tell me, that I might have sent thee away with mirth, and with songs, with tabret, and with harp? And hast not suffered me to kiss my sons and my daughters? ... And now, though thou wouldest needs be gone, because thou sore longedst after thy father's house, yet wherefore hast thou stolen my gods? (Genesis 31:26–28, 30)

Laban's words are indeed ironic, for it is Rachel who has taken the teraphim, but only the reader knows this. Laban will be hard pressed to replace Jacob and will sorely miss the remarkable prosperity that accompanied his service in Laban's fields. He knows why Jacob has fled secretly—he would not have been allowed to leave openly.

Jacob separates Laban's accusations into two components, the first being, "Why did you depart secretly?" To this, he answers that he was afraid that Laban would take his wives—Laban's daughters—away from him by force. To the second question, "Why did you steal my gods?" he invites Laban to search the entire caravan. Jacob knows that *he* has not taken them, and since he has taught his entire household to believe in the one true God, he is sure that Laban will not be able to find his teraphim anywhere in the caravan. In fact, he underscores this statement by pronouncing the death penalty on the person in whose possession Laban finds the idols, death being the penalty for idolatry.

> Now Rachel had taken the images, and put them in the camel's furniture, and sat upon them. And Laban searched all the tent, but found them not. And she said to her father, Let it not displease my lord that I cannot rise up before thee; for the custom of women is upon me. And he searched, but found not the images. (Genesis 31:34–35)

Rachel seems as cool as a cucumber during the search. She knows that the camel saddle upon which she sits will not be searched. Anne Roiphe explains why. A woman during her menstrual period was not to be touched by a man, and her sitting down in his presence while bleeding was permissible. Rachel's sitting down on the camel saddle effectively contaminated the area, preventing a search. It was said at that time that a man who passed between two menstruating women could fall dead.[11] The whole scenario is a stroke of genius on Rachel's part. The episode becomes even more impressive when the fact of her pregnancy is revealed. She is anything *but* menstruating.

Jacob—who for years has suppressed his resentment against his father-in-law—takes the failure of Laban's search for his teraphim as an opportunity to vent his frustration. He describes, in detail, his scrupulous honesty during his twenty years in Laban's employ, despite Laban's continuous altering of his wages. Jacob contends that if God had not warned Laban in a dream not to harm Jacob, Laban would even now rob him of all that was his.

Laban responds by refusing to concede the point that the entire caravan belongs to Jacob. He adheres to his belief that Jacob's wives are, first and foremost, *his own* daughters, the sons they bore to Jacob *his own* sons, and the flocks that Jacob shepherded under his contract with Laban remain *Laban's*. Finally, after seeing that his daughters and grandchildren are attached to Jacob, he relents and invites Jacob to make a pact. Perhaps he fears to use the forces he has brought with him because of the divine warning he received. Alter comments on what happens next.

> Invited to make a pact, Jacob immediately resorts to the language of stones, as after the Bethel epiphany and in his first encounter with Rachel at the well. Thus, in sequence, the stones are associated with religious experience, and now politics. Here, there is a doubling in the use of stones: a large stone as a commemorative

pillar (and border marker) and a pile of smaller stones as a commemorative mound.[12]

The two men then make a pact never to harm each other. The treaty-vow is confirmed by a sacred meal. (The term *zevah*[13] refers to both a ceremonial meal and a sacrifice.) They offer a sacrifice and partake of a shared meal symbolic of their covenant. Laban and Jacob part on good terms, and Laban returns with his entourage to his home in Padan-aram, a great ending to a potentially explosive situation.

After Laban leaves, Jacob turns his attention to his journey homeward and his meeting with his estranged brother, Esau. He sends messengers promising gifts and livestock, all offerings of peace. Jacob gets word that Esau has received his message, and is now approaching with four hundred men. Jacob has no idea what Esau's reaction to him will be after these twenty years. Four hundred men could easily wipe out his entire family and possessions with minimal efforts. Understandably terrified, Jacob divides his family into two camps. He places the handmaids and their children first, Leah and her children next, and Rachel and Joseph in the rear. He must have reasoned that although part of his family might be destroyed by Esau and his men, the ones in the rear might escape harm. He prays earnestly to the God of his fathers to deliver his family from Esau and to fulfill his previous promise of protection.

After seeing his family safely across the river, Jacob encounters an unidentified man. The text is ambiguous as to the nature of the struggle between them, but afterward, Jacob extracts a blessing and is given a new name—Israel. Jacob names the place Peniel which means "the face of God." He says, "I have seen God face to face, and my life is preserved" (Genesis 32:30). While it is still unclear exactly what has happened, Jacob seems sure about the identity of the being with whom he has just spent the night, and he is spiritually bolstered for the dreaded encounter with his brother.

Jacob crosses the river and sees Esau and his four hundred men approaching in the distance. He quickly divides his family into their assigned groups and takes his place at the head of the caravan. Seeing Esau, he bows to the earth seven times as his brother draws near, showing deference and respect. "And Esau ran to meet him, and embraced him, and fell on his neck, and kissed him: and they wept"

(Genesis 33:4). The brothers are reconciled at last. Jacob introduces each member of his family to his brother, saving Rachel and Joseph until last. Jacob entreats Esau to accept gifts in recognition of the reconciliation, which Esau reluctantly accepts, and the brothers part peacefully. Another potential crisis is averted.

As they near his homeland, Jacob and his family journey to Shechem, where Dinah, Jacob's daughter by Leah, is tragically raped, and two of her brothers massacre the entire city in revenge. Jacob next receives word that his mother's nurse, Deborah, has died. Amidst these tragedies, Jacob is buoyed up by the Lord, who repeats the great promises made to him, emphasizing the promises that he will be the father of a great nation and that the land promised to Abraham will be given to him and his posterity. God tells him to go to Beth-el, where this covenant was first given to him, and as was his custom, he erects a stone monument where God spoke to him twenty years earlier.

As they travel onward, still some distance from Ephrath, Rachel begins to feel the pains of labor. Only now do we realize that she is with child, and that her story about "the custom of women" being upon her to justify her inability to rise from the camel saddle before Laban was just that, a story. The labor is hard and long, and the text uses the emphatic Hebrew word *behakshota*. Ibn Ezra extrapolates that her labor was extremely rigorous, so much so that Rachel realizes that this is not merely a difficult childbirth, but that "her very life-blood was flowing from her." Another commentary on Ibn Ezra deduces that she is aware her life—and perhaps that of her child—is hanging by a thread. She realizes she might not be alive to raise her son Joseph, the son she had yearned for all her life.[14] The midwife comforts Rachel with the words, "Fear not, this is also a son" (Genesis 35:17).

Jacob's youngest son is born and Rachel names him with her dying breath—Ben-oni. Rashi translates this as "son of my sorrow," but Jacob called him "Ben-yamin," translated by Ramban as "son of my right hand" or "son of my strength." Since the word *oni*[15] has two interpretations, one being "my sorrow" and the other "my strength," Jacob chose to define his wife's choice of a name in the positive sense, denoting goodness and fortitude, rather than sorrow. Rashbam concentrates his commentary on Jacob's name for his son, "Ben-yamin." He explains that the Hebrew word *yamin* is really intended to be *yamim*, meaning "days." Benjamin, like Joseph, is the son of Jacob's old age, and is doubly precious, especially as Jacob realizes he is not immortal.[16]

Years later in Egypt, the sons of Jacob will tell their unrecognized brother Joseph why they cannot return to their father without Benjamin. Jacob refers to Benjamin as one of the "two sons my wife bore to me" (Genesis 44:27). I wonder how that statement made the other ten brothers feel. How can Jacob say the words "my wife," when he in fact had four? Ramban explains: "When Jacob uses the term 'one wife,' he is referring of course to Rachel, the wife he married *knowingly*. And only two sons were born to this wife, the only wife he also married *willingly*. It is upon Rachel's two sons that Jacob lavished the great love he felt for Rachel, and he showered them with this love as if he had no other sons. The other ten sons, even those born to Leah, were considered, in Jacob's affections, as if they were the sons of concubines."[17]

Jacob makes the decision not to bury Rachel in the cave of Machpelah in Hebron where he will eventually be entombed. Chizkuni presents a practical reason for Jacob's decision to bury her on the roadside. Because Rachel hemorrhaged to death after her most difficult labor and delivery, Jacob fears that transporting her body on the roadway for even a short distance would be inappropriate and unhygienic. The Meshech Chachma bases his commentary on the Talmud, which dictates that the bier of a woman who died in childbirth must never be carried on a roadway; she must be buried immediately "out of a sense of respect for her dignity and sacrifice."[18] So Jacob buries Rachel outside Ephrath, which is near Bethlehem, and sets up a stone pillar on her grave, stones being his trademark. It is said that Rachel was buried alongside the road where, many centuries later, her people would walk on their long journey to exile in Babylon. They believed she would weep for them as they passed by, and would intercede with God in forgiving them and obtaining a promise from God to one day return them to their own land.[19] The site of Rachel's grave was one day destined to fall into the province of the tribe of Benjamin, which also encompassed the very spot where her baby was born.

Another midrash credits Rachel for entreating God to let the children of Israel return from exile. The text states that when Rachel saw the events of the Destruction and the Israelites being sent into exile from their land, she jumped in before God and said: "Master of the Universe! it is known before You that Your servant Jacob's love for me knew no bounds, and he worked for my father for seven years for me." She goes on to recite all the history of Jacob's sacrifices in order to marry her. How, after the seven years were completed and the time came for their marriage, Laban advised Rachel to exchange Leah as the bride. She recounts, "This was exceedingly difficult for me, when I learned of this counsel. I informed Jacob, and I gave him a sign so that he could distinguish between me and my sister, so that my father would not be able to exchange me." She narrates her struggle between her compassion for her sister and her desire for Jacob, deciding, in the end, to save her sister from disgrace, and gave her all the secret signs of recognition she had arranged with Jacob so that he would think that she was Rachel. In addition, she recounts another humiliation, "And this was not all—I went under the bed where he lay with my sister: he would speak with her, and I responded every time, while she remained silent, so that he would not recognize her voice." She pleads with God, saying that she acted kindly with her sister in not allowing her to be shamed. She ends her petition with this question, "What am I, flesh and blood, dust and ashes, that I was not jealous of my rival wife, and that I did not allow her to be shamed and disgraced, but You, merciful living and eternal King, why were You jealous of idolatry that is of no import, and exiled my children who were slain by the sword, and allowed their enemies to do with them as they pleased?" God's mercy was immediately activated and he said, "For your sake, Rachel, I shall return Israel to their place—for there is a reward for your labor [...]. And there is hope for your future—declares the Lord: Your children shall return to their country"[20] According to this source, even after her death, Rachel's heart is drawn out towards her children.

Eighteen years after Rachel's death, Leah passes away, and Jacob buries her in the cave of Machpelah. Shera Tuchman and Sandra Rapoport believe that Leah's burial in the ancestral grave may be very appropriate. "Leah's primary passion ... was, quite simply, Jacob. Her desire for his love informed her entire life. Rachel's primary passion, on the other hand, was her desire for children. She yearned for them above all else, and ultimately gave up her life bearing a son. Their burial places properly reflect their life-passions: Leah is buried beside Jacob for eternity, and Rachel is buried where future generations of Israel will receive her solace."[21]

Perhaps the most stunning resolution to the Rachel-Leah rivalry appears in Hasidic literature. Most scholars translate the Hebrew of Genesis 29:30 as "And [Jacob] loved Rachel more than Leah." Although there are different translations, most interpretations contain the idea that Jacob favored Rachel over Leah. Translators are perplexed over the inclusion of the Hebrew word *gam* (which means "also") that appears after the *he loved*. The Hasidic rabbi Levi Yitzhak renders the verse in this way:

> *He loved Rachel also [i.e. even more] because of Leah.* How does he support this rendition, technically possible but far from obvious? It is clear that while Jacob's purpose in working for Laban was to marry Rachel, Jacob in fact, wed Leah. And it was Rachel [by her silence] who was responsible for this. Now Jacob's love was twofold: he loved her for herself, but he loved her *also*, even more, because she brought him so pious a wife as Leah. This then is what the verse is telling us: *Jacob loved Rachel "also" (gam et Rachel) "because of" Leah (mi-Leah).* Which is to say. It was because Leah became his wife through the efforts of Rachel that Jacob felt an additional measure of love for Rachel over what he felt before. (emphasis in original)[22]

According to Yitzhak's interpretation of this verse, the whole rivalry between the two sisters is turned upside down. There is no conflict between motherhood and love of a spouse, no anguish over the exchange of brides. Samuel Dressner says, "To [Rabbi Yitzhak] the matriarchs are models demonstrating how to overcome family unhappiness through the power of love and the example of piety. Far from Rachel's envying Leah, she was responsible for her marriage; far from Jacob's resenting the deception, he only loved Rachel more. Human kindness and nobility of character conquer society's flaws."[23]

Again, we will have to wait until Rachel writes her memoirs to find out whether Rabbi Yitzhak was correct. Do we prefer the tale of sibling rivalry and struggle, or the one of the test and triumph of Leah's devotion, Rachel's tenderness, and Jacob's love for one wife and honor for the other? However it is interpreted, as Adin Steinsaltz states, "The relationship between Jacob and Rachel became a paradigm of the great, loving historical relationship between God and Israel,"[24] the ultimate love story.

---

[1] Shera Aranoff Tuchman and Sandra E. Rapoport, *The Passions of the Matriarchs*, (Jersey City, New Jersey, KTAV Publishing House, Inc., 2004), 276–277.

[2] James Baker, "Women's Rights in Old Testament Times," (Salt Lake City: Signature Books, 1992), 67–69.

[3] Tuchman and Rapoport (2004), 282–283.

[4] Athalaya Brenner, *The Israelite Woman: Social Role and Literary Type in Biblical Narrative*, (Sheffield, England: JSOT Press, 1985), 94.

[5] Tammi J. Schneider, *Mothers of Promise: Women in the Book of Genesis*, (Grand Rapids. Michigan: Baker Academic, 1987), 71.

[6] Ktziah Spanier, "Rachel's Theft of the Teraphim: Her Struggle for Family Primacy," *Vestus Testamentum*, Vol. 42, Fasc. 3 (July 1992), 405 and Moshe Greenberg, "Another Look at Rachel's Theft of the Teraphim," *Journal of Biblical Literature*, Volume 81, No. 3 (September 1962), 242, fn 16.

[7] Greenberg (1962), 242, fn 16.

[8] Greenberg (1962), 246–247.

[9] Robert Alter, *Genesis: Translation and Commentary*, (New York: W. W. Norton and Company, 1996), 170, fn 23.

[10] Tuchman and Rapoport (2004), 290.

[11] Anne Roiphe, *Water From the Well: Sarah, Rebekah, Rachel, and Leah*, (New York: William Morrow, 2006), 238.

[12] Alter (1996), 174 fn 45.

[13] Francis Brown, *The New Brown-Driver-Briggs-Genesius Hebrew and English Lexicon*, (Peabody, Massachusetts: Hendrickson Publishers, 1979), 257, entry 2077.

[14] Tuchman and Rapoport (2004), 317.

[15] Brown (1979), 20, entries 206 meaning "sorrow" and 202 meaning "vigor or strength."

[16] Tuchman and Rapoport (2004), 320.

[17] Tuchman and Rapoport (2004), 332.

[18] The Talmud (Moed Katan 27b) quoted in Tuchman and Rapoport (2004), 322.

[19] Roiphe (2006), 248.

[20] *Lam. Rabbah* [ed. Vilna] petihtah 24 as quoted in Tamar Kadari, "Rachel: Midrash and Aggadah," accessed March 8, 2014 at http://jwa.org/encyclopedia/article/rachel-midrash-and-aggadah.

[21] Tuchman and Rapoport (2004), 342–343.

[22] Rabbi Levi Yitzhak, *Kedushat Levi*, (Jerusalem, 1958), 53 in Samuel Dressner, *Rachel*, (Minneapolis: Fortress Press, 1994), 72.

[23] Dressner (1994), 72.

[24] Adin Steinsaltz, *Biblical Images: Men and Women of the Book*, (USA: Basic Books, 1984), 52–53.

Chapter 15
In the Beginning

It is impossible to talk about women in the scriptures without talking about Eve. Eve embodies the model for all women because she was *created* by God. He designed her schematics. Every woman can look to Eve when she questions the purpose of her existence. A correct understanding of Eve and the purposes for her creation are absolutely essential to understanding what womanhood is all about. In the book *Lectures on Faith*, the Prophet Joseph Smith states that in order for a person to develop faith in God, he must first gain a correct understanding of both the character and the attributes of Deity.[1] Otherwise, he will not be able to develop true faith in God. Likewise, when a woman has questions about her womanhood and what she is meant to contribute to this life, she must have a correct understanding of woman, as created by God. Why did he do it? What did he intend her to do?

I like the point made by Carolyn Custis James in her book *Lost Women of the Bible*. She argues

> God cast the mold for all women when he created Eve. She embodies the secrets of his original blueprint for us. So we rightly turn to her to understand who we are [as women] and to discover God's purposes for us. We see and evaluate ourselves ... through the definition we draw from her. Which makes Eve both powerful and dangerous. Mistakes with regard to our understanding of her are costly for everyone. Like the missile that launches only the slightest fraction off course, we will miss our ultimate target by light-years if we misinterpret Eve. Conversely, a better understanding of Eve as God created her promises much-needed direction and ensures we have a true target in our sights.[2]

So, if we want to really understand Eve and our legacy as women, we need to begin at the beginning. We must revisit Genesis and examine what God has revealed about Eve and his purposes for her in his heavenly plan. Then, and only then, will we understand what God intended for his daughters during every phase of their lives.

The first information we are given about Eve in Genesis does not mention her by name. It does not even use the word *woman*. We only learn about a being created in the very image of God, only female. Genesis 1:27 reads: "So God created man *in his own image*, in the image of God created he him; *male* and *female* created he them"³ (emphasis added). Clearly, God created man and woman to bear his image. To look like him. To be like him. What an amazing statement, after we have just beheld the creation of a marvelous world, complete with all the amenities. We have been awed by the power and planning and scope of such a project. And the crowning creation is a being who is "in the image" of this all-powerful creator? We cannot comprehend such a thing. And yet it is so.

What does it mean to bear the image of God? In the King James Bible, Psalm 8:4–5, we read: "What is man, that thou art mindful of him? … For thou hast made him a little lower than the angels, and hast crowned him with glory and honor." This English rendition is very different from the literal Hebrew, which reads, "For thou has made him lacking a little from God [*elohim*] (or gods)" (my own translation). What does it mean to be created to lack "a little" from God? The psalmist David interprets the standing God places upon Adam and Eve as one possessing glory and honor, only slightly removed from that of the Creator himself. Adam and Eve are placed in a position to have dominion over God's new creation. As his image bearers, they are to represent God and emulate his ways on the earth. They are to join with him in his labors. He entrusts them with the responsibilities of being his image-bearers. He calls them to be like him. Carolyn Custis James describes this as "the rarest of privileges, the highest of honors, the most daunting challenge imaginable."⁴

In Genesis 1:26, we are made privy to a conversation between the creators of this amazing world. "And God said, Let *us* make man in our image, after our likeness: and let them have dominion over the fish of the sea, and over the fowl of the air, and over the cattle, and over all the earth, and over every creeping thing that creepeth upon the earth" (Genesis 1:26, emphasis added).

Suddenly we have a change in subject. The God we had thought was singular now refers to himself as *us*. Anyone who has studied language knows that nouns and pronouns must agree in both number and gender. And yet we have a singular subject—*God*—with a plural pronoun—*our*. If we examine the original Hebrew word translated "God" in this scripture, we see that it is *elohim*. The "-*im*" ending in Hebrew indicates that the noun is plural, much like "-*s*" in English makes a noun plural.⁵ And not only is this *us* plural, but its images are both male *and* female.

This situation gives rise to the mythology found in the Talmud that man and woman "are essentially parts of a single whole, originally created as one being; but for various reasons—principally the establishment of a different, more complex, and perhaps deeper kind of connection between the two—the whole body is divided. The two half bodies are constantly in search of one another, and find no fulfillment until they are joined."⁶ This is a very romantic notion, although the degree of truth it contains is debatable.

To those with eyes to see, the evidence of the existence of two divine parents is apparent. The apostle Erastus Snow taught, "Deity consists of man and woman. ... How do you know? I only repeat what he says of himself; that he created man in the image of God, male and female created he them. ... There can be no God except he is composed of the man and woman united, and there is not in all the eternities that exist, nor ever will be, a God in any other way."⁷

Genesis 2:7 reads, "And the Lord God formed man (*adam*) of the dust of the ground (*adamah*), and breathed into his nostrils the breath of life; and man became a living soul." The Hebrew word *adam* can be translated as a singular noun ("man"), as a proper name ("Adam"), and as a plural collective noun meaning "mankind" or "humankind." It can also mean "red." These various meanings have spurred many interpretations throughout the centuries. Rabbi Eliezer utilized these meanings in his commentary on the word *adam*. Rabbi Yehuda said that the name *Adam* came from the word *adamah*, or *earth*, from whence he was taken. An English rendition of this Hebrew play on words would be "God formed the human from the dust of the humus⁸." Rabbi Joshua ben Korchah said: "He was called Adam because of his flesh and blood—blood implied by the word red."⁹

> And the Lord God planted a garden eastward in Eden; and there he put the man whom he had formed. And out of the ground made the Lord God to grow every tree that is pleasant to the sight, and good for food; the tree of life also in the midst of the garden, and the tree of knowledge of good and evil. (Genesis 2:8–9)

Thus far there is no mention of Eve.

Next we read, "And the Lord God took the man, and put him into the Garden of Eden to dress it and to keep it" (Genesis 2:15). The Hebrew word translated "dress" is from the Hebrew word *avad*, which means "to serve." When this verb is made into a noun, it means "service" or "worship." The word translated "keep" is from the Hebrew *shamar*, which has the connotation of "to guard" and "to protect," like the keep of a castle where the most precious treasures are safeguarded.

God places Adam in a garden full of trees, all of which have been pronounced "good." He gives him these instructions: "And the Lord God commanded the man, saying, Of every tree of the garden thou mayest freely eat: but of the tree of the knowledge of good and evil, thou shalt not eat of it: for in the day that thou eatest thereof thou shalt surely die" (Genesis 2:16–17). Notice that Eve is not around to receive this commandment. She does not come into existence for another five verses. Next we read

> And out of the ground the Lord God formed every beast of the field, and every fowl of the air; and brought them unto Adam to see what he would call them: and whatsoever Adam called every living creature, that was the name thereof. And Adam gave names to all cattle, and to the fowl of the air, and to every beast of the field; but for Adam there was not found an help meet for him. (Genesis 2:19–20)

Let's see what we have here. Before Eve appears on the scene, the world has been created, Adam has been placed in the Garden of Eden, and he has given names to all the animals, associating with them in what seems to be a real-life wildlife park. He openly communicates with God on a regular basis. What more could he ask for?

J. Reuben Clark puts it this way:

> Adam wandered alone in the glorious Garden in Eden, which he had dressed and adorned—the Garden of Eden with its stately trees, its lovely flowers heavy with sweet odors, its grassy swards, its magnificent vistas with the far reaches of its placid rivers, with its gaily plumed birds, its lordly and graceful beasts, all at peace, for sin was not yet in the world. Through all this magnificence Adam wandered, lonely, unsolaced, uncompanioned, the only being of his kind in the whole world, his life unshared in a solitude of exquisite elegance, and, what was of far greater moment, his mission, as he

knew it to be, impossible of fulfillment, except the Father gave him an helpmeet.[10]

Much like President Clark, John Milton in *Paradise Lost* portrays the loveliness of the Garden of Eden with its many varieties of flora and faunae. However, he conveys to his readers his perception of Adam's loneliness and frustration as he watches the interaction between the animals and yet is unable to communicate with them, try as he might. Adam reaches the conclusion that something is radically wrong. Milton writes:

> They rejoice
> Each with their kind, lion with lioness;
> So fitly them in pairs thou hast combin'd;
> Much less can bird with beast, or fish with fowl
> So well converse, nor with the ox the ape;
> Worse then can man with beast, and least of all.[11]

In other words, Adam is saying, "What's wrong with this picture?" As he proceeds to name the animals, he undoubtedly notices that there are male giraffes as well as female giraffes and that God has pronounced all of these creations as "good." The next thing the Lord says is that something is "*not* good." Up to this point, God has consistently declared everything to be "good," and he needs to remedy the "not good" situation. This is startling news indeed! Something is terribly wrong with the man being alone. So God declares, "It is not good that the man should be alone; I will make him an help meet for him" (Genesis 2:18).

Milton suggests that God has delayed introducing Eve until Adam can fully appreciate her. Seeing Adam's loneliness, God concludes that he is now ready to be introduced to her. Milton describes what Eve will mean to Adam:

> What next I bring shall please thee, be assur'd,
> Thy likeness, thy fit help, thy other self,
> Thy wish exactly to thy heart's desire.[12]

What does "thy fit help" mean? Certainly not that she will be physically fit. It means she would be a perfect match for him—a counterpart, a complement. In fact, she would be his "other self." When Eve appears, Adam is thunderstruck. He has never conceived of such a creature. Milton continues

Under his forming hands a creature grew,
Manlike, but different sex, so lovely fair,
That what seem'd fair in all the world, seem'd now
Mean, or in her summ'd up, in her contain'd,
And in her looks, which from that time infus'd
Sweetness into my heart, unfelt before.[13]

Elder Glen Pace gave a devotional address at BYU entitled "The Divine Nature and Destiny of Women." He discussed man's need for woman philosophically. He said that what Adam felt upon seeing Eve was "much more than that which was generated by Eve's physical appearance. Those feelings flowing into him had as their source her wellspring. His feelings were the direct result of standing in front of one of the daughters of heavenly parents who had a divine nature different from, but complementary to, his own divine nature." He said that "the Father's statement 'It is not good that the man should be alone' had a much more profound meaning than the obvious biological implications. It also went further than providing Adam with 'company.' Adam's ability to obtain the purification necessary to get back into the presence of God was dependent upon his continuous association with Eve."[14]

After quoting D&C 131:1–3, which states that a man cannot obtain the highest degree of the celestial kingdom without entering into the new and everlasting covenant of marriage, he explains why.

> Why can't he obtain it? It's not just because he didn't obey a celestial commandment. It's because he didn't become a celestial being. There is a limit to our spiritual development as long as we are single. There is a spiritual development that can only be obtained when a man and a woman join their incomplete selves into a complete couple. Just as conception requires the physical union of male and female, perfection requires the union of the very souls of male and female.[15]

So what exactly is a "help meet for him?" Nobody uses the word *meet* anymore. Was it supposed to be *helpmate*? O was it *helper*? *Helper* is easier to understand. I had always understood it to mean "an assistant of lesser status." But is this really what God had in mind when he created Eve?

As I studied these words in Hebrew, I discovered that this is not at all the meaning these words are intended to convey. "Help meet for him" in Hebrew is *ezer kenegdo*. When God decided to create another creature so that man would not be alone, he does not merely make a helper for him—he makes an equal partner. David Freedman writes that these words should be translated as "a power equal to man."[16]

In Hebrew, the word *ezer*[17] describes an equal, if not a superior. In the Old Testament, *ezer* is most frequently used to describe how God is an *ezer* to man. It definitely does not have the connotation of a "mere helper" in any of the cases in which it is used. A more accurate translation would be a "power" or "strength." Etymological evidence indicates that *ezer* originally had two roots, one meaning "to rescue" or "to save," and one meaning "to be strong."[18] The verb *azar* means "to succor," "to save from extremity," or "to deliver from death." It refers to the actions of one who gives water to someone dying of thirst, thus saving his life. Samuel Terrien makes the statement, "Far from being a subordinated or menial servant, woman is the savior of man."[19]

Each of these ancient roots began with a different Hebrew guttural sound. Some ancient languages made a distinction between the two roots, while others did not. Hebrew no longer distinguishes between them. About 1500 BC, these two different sounds began to be written with the same sign. Later, the two pronunciations also merged. As a result, when the Bible was written, what had once been two roots of *ezer* had merged into one. With merger of pronunciation and writing came the merger of meanings. Thus, *ezer* could mean both "to be strong" and "to save." In time the root was always interpreted as "to help," which was a mixture of the nuances of both meanings.[20]

The second word which confused me in the Hebrew of Genesis 2:18 was the word *kenegdo,* which traditionally had been translated as "meet for" or "fit for." Because *kenegdo* appears only once in the Bible, scholars had little upon which to base their translations. *Neged* was one of the first words I learned in Hebrew, and I was taught that its meaning was "against." I thought it very strange that God would create a companion for Adam that was "against" him! Later, I learned that the word could also mean "in front of" or "opposite."[21] This still didn't help much. Finally, it was explained to me as being "exactly corresponding to," as when you look at yourself in the mirror. In Mishnaic[22] Hebrew, the root *kened* means "equal." The King James translation of *kenegdo* as "meet for" is based on the seventeenth-century meaning of "meet" as "worthy of," which has long been out of usage. This archaic translation has led to the formation of the word "help-meet" to describe a good wife, although nobody really knew how this was different than "helpmate." Any way you look at it, the meaning intended by the original Hebrew was totally lost. Good wives all want to be "helpmates," but they completely miss the fact that the scripture clearly states that God created woman to be an equal partner to her husband, exactly corresponding to him in every way. There are some obvious differences, but men and women are still considered equal partners in the eyes of God.

The noun *ezer* occurs twenty-one times in the Hebrew Bible. In eight of these instances, the word means "savior." These examples are easy to identify because they are associated with other expressions of deliverance or saving. Elsewhere in the Bible, the root *ezer* means "strength."[23] In 1 Samuel 7:12, Samuel erects a stone to commemorate the "help" God has given them in their victory over the daunting Philistines. In Hebrew, *eben* is "stone" and *ezer* is "help", hence the stone is called Eben-ezer.[24] This is a nice gesture, a sort of ancient plaque to help remember the "help" that God gave you in a battle with your enemies. However, if we look at the story a little closer, we see that it is a little more than ordinary "help" that God has given. I would define "ordinary" help as maybe God strengthening you to be at the top of your game when fighting your enemies. But this is quite a bit more than just bolstering you to fight your best fight. If we back up to verse 10, we find this: "And as Samuel was offering up the burnt offering, the Philistines drew near to battle against Israel: but the Lord thundered with a great thunder on that day upon the Philistines, and discomfited them; and they were smitten before Israel." After dedicating the battle to the Lord, the armies of Israel sat back and watched as the Philistines were given a dose of divine "special effects." During the battle, the Lord demonstrated that he was fighting for Israel as he called the elements into service. The thundering from heaven threw the enemy into confusion, striking a "holy terror" in them. I think I would use the term "rescue" or "deliverance" rather than the anemic "help" translated in 1 Samuel.

Knowing that Adam couldn't fight the battles of earth life alone, God created a companion for him who would fulfill both meanings of *ezer*. Carolyn Custis James advocates that *ezer* is a military word, and the *ezer* is a warrior. Earth is a war zone, and God uses a military word to mobilize Eve into action. She was a woman with a mission. God created her to be man's greatest ally in the battle against the fierce opposition of the enemy of all righteousness. Woman would be a "strength" to man in helping meet all the challenges that earth-life would launch at them—pain, toil, discouragement, rebellion, burnout, and faltering faith. She might even "rescue" him at times with precious insight into the meaning of their trials, or "save" him from discouragement or despair. God created the woman to be an *ezer* to man. To strengthen *and* to save. This is Eve's legacy for all women, not just within the bonds of marriage, but wherever she touches the lives of others in the world at large.[25]

---

[1] See Joseph Smith, *Lectures on Faith*, (American Fork, Utah: Covenant Communications, 2000), 39, 42–49.

[2] Carolyn Custis James, *Lost Women of the Bible*, (Grand Rapids, Michigan: Zondervan, 2005), 29–30.

[3] "The expression 'male and female,' … highlights rather the sexual distinctions within mankind and foreshadows the blessing of fertility to be announced in verse 28."
Gordon J. Wentham, *World Biblical Commentary Volume 1*, (Waco, Texas: Word Books, 1987), 33.

[4] James (2005), 33.

[5] Readers will note that in the *Pearl of Great Price* account of the creation found in the book of Abraham, the subject (God) *is* plural. Abraham 4:1 reads "and they, that is the Gods, organized and formed the heavens and the earth."

[6] Adin Steinsaltz, *Biblical Images: Men and Women of the Book*, (United States of America, Basic Books, 1984), 5.

[7] Brigham Young, *Journal of Discourses*, Volume 19, (London: William Budge, 1898), 269–270.

[8] Notice that the word *humus* refers to "earth," and not to *hummus*, the spread made from chick peas.

[9] Shira Halevi, *The Life Story of Adam and Havah: A New Targum of Genesis 1-26-5:5*, (Northvale, New Jersey: Jason Aronson Inc., 1997), 13.

[10] *J. Reuben Clark: Selected Papers: On Religion, Education, and Youth,* ed. David H. Yarn, Jr. (Provo: Brigham Young University Press, 1984), 59–60.

[11] John Milton, *Paradise Lost* (1667), ed. David Hawkes (New York: Barnes & Noble Classics, 2004), 249; book VIII, lines 392–97.

[12] Milton, *Paradise Lost,* 251; book VIII, lines 449–51.

[13] Milton, *Paradise Lost,* 253; book VIII, lines 470–75.

[14] Glen L. Pace, "The Divine Nature and Destiny of Women," *Brigham Young University 2009–2010 Speeches,* given 9 March 2010.

[15] Ibid.

[16] See R. David Freedman, "Woman, a Power Equal to Man," *Biblical Archaeology Review 09:01 (Jan/Feb 1983).* Herschel Shanks, editor, 56.

[17] Pronounced 'ay-zr'.

[18] See Freedman (1983), 56.

[19] See Samuel Terrien, *Till the Heart Sings: A Biblical Theology of Manhood and Womanhood,* Philadelphia: Fortress Press, 1985) 10.

[20] See Freedman (1983), 58.

[21] Frances Brown, *The New Brown-Driver-Briggs-Genesius Hebrew and English Lexicon* (Peabody, Massachusetts: Hendrickson Publishers, 1979), 617, entry 5048.

[22] The Mishnah is a major work of Rabbinic Judaism, and the first major redaction into written form of Jewish oral traditions, called the Oral Torah. In the study of literature, redaction is a form of editing in which multiple source texts are combined together *(redacted)* and subjected to minor alteration to make them into a single work. Often this is a method of collecting together a series of writings on a similar theme and creating a definitive and coherent work.

[23] See Freedman (1983), 56.

[24] Many readers will be familiar with the beloved hymn "Come, Thou Fount of Every Blessing," which contains the line, "Here I raise my Ebenezer." Few

understand that it refers to this story in 1 Samuel 7:12. (Text by Robert Robinson, lyrics date, 1758; Melody from John Wyeth's "Repository of Sacred Music.")

[25] See James (2005), *Lost Women of the Bible,* 36–37.

Chapter 16
Making Sense of the Rib Story

In order to fully understand the Book of Genesis, a quick history lesson is in order. The original text composed by Moses contained only Hebrew consonants with no vowel letters or vowel "points." These were added by a group of scribes called the Masoretes between 800 and 1000 AD.[1] In addition, there were no spaces between the words, so it was difficult to tell if a letter at the beginning or end of a word really belonged to that word or to its neighbor. Therefore, there is a wide variety of ways a Hebrew text may be interpreted. For example, consider the group of letters "FRSCRNDSVNYRSG." If I give you a hint that this comes from a well-known document in American history, you might have a minute chance of figuring out that this is the first line of the "Gettysburg Address." Otherwise, I think the majority of readers would be totally lost. Right now you might be in awe that any part of the Old Testament was transmitted to us in any recognizable form whatsoever. I am. It also makes me very open to other possible interpretations of biblical passages than the ones we have grown up with.

The account of the creation of woman reads: "And the Lord God caused a deep sleep to fall upon Adam, and he slept: and he took one of his ribs, and closed up the flesh instead thereof; And the rib, which the Lord God had taken from man, made he a woman, and brought her unto the man" (Genesis 2:21–22).

"The rib story" has given rise to many romantic notions about the nature of the relationship between man and woman. One of the most heart-warming is from Matthew Henry, an eighteenth century English theologian. He comments, "The woman was made of a rib out of the side of Adam; not made out of his head to rule over him; nor out of his feet to be trampled upon my him; but out of his side to be equal with him; under his arm to be protected; and near his heart to be beloved."[2] *The Book of Legends* states, "God said: I will not create her from Adam's head, lest she be conceited; nor from the eye, lest she be a coquette, nor from the ear, lest she be an eavesdropper; [nor from the neck, lest she be haughty]; nor from the mouth, lest she be a gossip; nor from the heart, lest she be prone to jealousy; nor from the hand, lest she be light-fingered; nor from the foot, lest she be a gadabout—so He made her from the rib, a part most modest and chaste."³ Not quite so warm and fuzzy, but interesting nonetheless.

For just a moment, let's keep our minds open to some new ideas. Since the biblical record uses the word "rib," let's examine the original Hebrew to see if we can gain any new information. The word used is *tsalot*, which is the plural of *tsela*, a Hebrew word used thirty-two times in the Hebrew Bible. Genesis 2:21–22 is the *only* place where it is translated as "rib," meaning "a bone from the rib cage of a living creature." In all other instances but one, *tsela* refers to the construction of the tabernacle, temple, or ark of the covenant. It refers to "a 'plank,' 'beam,' 'wall,' 'chamber,' or 'side-chamber,' all specifically referring to structural elements of a temple."⁴

Douglas Clark provides some interesting observations. The text reads that from the "rib" he took from Adam, God "made a woman." The word translated as "made" is not the usual *asah* but *banah*, the Hebrew word for *build*. God does this "building" while Adam is asleep. The usual word for *sleep* is not used, but one that can be interpreted as a trance, "an especially deep, wondrous sleep, a divine sleep," hinting at the secrecy of the divine creative process that produced Eve.⁵

Dutch Professor Ed Noort has made the observation that this metaphoric description Eve's creation seems to allude to a child growing in its mother's womb during gestation.

> The way in which the woman is built is not described at all; it is quite likely that the narrator has used the analogy of the growing of a child during pregnancy. In biblical language, a child comes into being in the mystery and darkness of the mother's womb, which parallels the *tardemah* [the "deep sleep"]. There its bones and flesh are made, parallel to *banah* ("built"), and after birth it is welcomed with joy, parallel to the exclamation of Gen 2:23.⁶

Tsela may also reflect a play on words that has been lost in the Hebrew but rediscovered in an ancient Sumerian account of the creation, where the same cuneiform symbol represents both "life" and "rib." Samuel Noah Kramer, the first to decipher cuneiform symbols from Sumeria, points out that the symbol "TI" represents the words for both "life" and "rib." NIN.TI may be read as both "Lady of the Rib" and "Lady of Life."⁷ In the Sumerian version of the creation myth, Enki is cursed by the goddess Ninhursag because he has eaten forbidden plants growing in paradise. Kramer notes the parallel with the biblical paradise narrative, equating Enki's cursing for eating the eight plants with Adam's loss of privilege for eating the fruit of the tree of knowledge of good and evil. As Enki's health begins to fail, the other gods persuade Ninhursag to yield and heal Enki. She creates Nin-ti—the "Lady who Makes Live"—to cure him. Nin-ti then brings Enki back from his near-death condition. David Rohl comments, "When Kramer first translated the ancient text of the Sumerian paradise myth, he immediately saw in this passage an explanation for the biblical story of Adam's rib. The author (or perhaps the later redactor) of Genesis, when he adapted this myth in order to incorporate elements of it into the biblical narrative, was clearly unaware of the fact that the Sumerian tale involved a play on words and so simply translated *ti* as rib. Thus Eve is created from a rib and, because there is no similarity between the Hebrew word for 'rib' (*tsalah*) and 'to make live' (*hayah*) the pun is lost."[8] However, what remains of the hidden meaning is the name Adam gives to his wife in Genesis 3:20—Eve, "the mother of all living." In Hebrew this name is *havah*, derived from the verb *hayah*, which means "to make live."

One Hebrew scholar, Shira Halevi, has reinterpreted the Hebrew text of Genesis 2:21 in different ways. She argues that the writer of the text could have written that God took an *atsmah* (*bone*) from Adam's *tsad* (*side*). There is no need to use "an obscure temple term as an analogy to a man's rib cage."[9] The first interpretation requires no changes in the Masoretic text. The second reading requires revoweling and rearrangement of the consonants, which is perfectly justifiable. She changes the translation from "and he closed up the flesh thereof" to "whom he enclosed in flesh below." Could this refer to the spirit of the pre-mortal Eve being placed in a flesh and blood body? It is not clear, but at any rate, we have an alternative to the rib operation on Adam. In her next reading, she shifts a letter from the beginning of one word to the end of the preceding word. In this way she derives the translation, "and he [Adam] received joyous tidings of marriage."[10]

This translation provides a perfect segue to Adam's recitation in Genesis 2:23–24, "And Adam said, This is now bone of my bones, and flesh of my flesh: she shall be called Woman, because she was taken out of Man. Therefore shall a man leave his father and his mother, and shall cleave unto his wife: and they shall be one flesh." In fact, without this alternate translation, Adam's exclamation makes no sense. Many have argued that "bone of my bones" refers to Eve being made from Adam's rib, but in other verses where this phrase is used, it has nothing to do with creation. Rather, in all seven instances, it refers to the blood ties between uncle and nephew, between brothers, or between relatives in general. Halevi continues, "Following a marriage ceremony, this phrase would declare that the man and the woman were now bound together as though they shared the same parentage. They are now kinfolk in the bloodline sense of the word—lateral relatives of equal standing."[11]

The still-immortal Eve is presented to the still-immortal Adam in the Garden of Eden, a place where Adam and Eve have talked with God. If a place to commune with God is the definition of a temple, then Eden is the consummate type. God himself presents the bride. Jewish tradition corroborates this, affirming that "God [gave] away the bride in the manner of a father."[12] This seems to be the epitome of a temple marriage.

Elder Russell M. Nelson concurs that these verses do indeed refer to the marriage of our first parents. He teaches, "Adam and Eve were joined together in marriage for time and for all eternity by the power of the everlasting priesthood. Eve came as a partner, to build and to organize the bodies of mortal men. She was designed by Deity to cocreate and nurture life, that the great plan of the Father might achieve fruition."[13]

Another point to be made from Genesis 2:23–24 is the change in a man's priorities after marriage. Gordon Wentham notes, "Beforehand, his first obligations are to his parents: afterwards they are to his wife. In modern Western societies where filial duties are often ignored, this may seem a minor point to make, but in traditional societies like Israel where honoring parents is the highest human obligation next to honoring God, this remark about forsaking them is very striking."[14] God is very clear about what *should be* man's first priority.

It is no wonder that only *after* the creation of woman did God say that his work of the sixth day was "very good." The other five days had only been "good." He had corrected the situation that had been pronounced "not good," when Adam was alone in the world. Only now could the whole purpose for creation be realized—the creation of the family.

In her address to seminary and institute teachers, Julie Beck taught

> The Creation of the earth was the creation of an earth where a family could live. It was a creation of a man and a woman who were the two essential halves of a family. It was not about a creation of a man and a woman who happened to have a family. It was intentional all along that Adam and Eve form an eternal family. It was part of the plan that these two be sealed and form an eternal family unit.[15]

After God has united these two in marriage, he blesses them and commands them to "be fruitful, and multiply, and replenish the earth, and subdue it." In other words, he is giving them stewardship for the watch-care of his newly created world, and tells them to "carry on" with the work of creation. He shares his sacred powers of procreation with mere humans. He admonishes them to fill the earth, imparting to them the responsibility of procreation that will assure the continuation of what he has just finished. He says, "Here is the world and all its inhabitants. It is good. In fact it is *very* good. I'm counting on you to keep it going. I entrust this responsibility to you. It's a big one, but I trust you. After all, you had a great teacher."

Adam announces that his new wife shall be called "woman," (*ishah*) because "she was taken out of man." The Hebrew word *adam* is the generic name for "mankind," as opposed to animals, fish, or birds. "Man," in both male and female form, is a species created "in the likeness" of God. Up to this point in scripture, "man," "Adam," and "mankind" are all represented by the Hebrew word *adam*. We are told in Genesis 5:2 that after God created male and female and blessed them, he "called their name Adam." But suddenly we have a change in word usage. Instead of the usual *adam*, the word *ish* is used. This is the first time *ish* has been used in scripture.

So what difference does this make? *Ish* and *adam* both mean "man." Why didn't Adam call his wife the feminine form of *adam*, which would have been *adamah*? (The "h" is the feminine particle, much like "ette" makes Jean into Jeanette.) The reason? *Adamah* means "earth" or "ground." *Adam* shares the same root letters as "earth," "dirt," and "red." Adam is "earthly," being taken from the earth (*adamah*), and associated with the red of blood.[16]

When man and animals are found in parallel phrases in the Bible, *adam* is always used, never *ish*. Mosaic law forbids touching the dead body of an *adam* (*man*), but *ish* is never used in an unclean sense. *Ish* shares consonants with *esh*, which means "fire"—the kind that burns up sacrificial offerings on the altar or that burned the bush on Mount Sinai. The very presence of God was frequently demonstrated by bursts or pillars of fire. *Ish/man* and *esh/fire* are associated with the divine. In the scriptures, the word used for such men as prophets, patriarchs, priests, temple workers or men of wisdom or royalty is always *ish*—never *adam*. Thus, an *ish* is an "elevated man" or a" holy man."[17]

So, Adam, the "Man of Fire," sees his wife in the presence of God. What does he choose to call her? Halevi observes, "If he meant to name her after himself, he would have named her *Adamah*, the feminine counterpart to his own name. Instead, he calls her *Ishah*, the feminine counterpart to *ish*, with all its allusions to holiness and fire."[18]

Halevi points out yet another meaning to the word *ish*, "a meaning never labeled *adam* in scripture—a man who marries a woman. Very often, a woman's *ish* is translated into English as a woman's 'husband.' ... When an *adam* marries an *ishah*, a woman, his status is immediately elevated to that of an *ish*—a man of higher degree. He becomes more like the Diving Being in whose image he was created. Without a woman, a man cannot engage in the most godlike activity available to human beings—making life."[19] Clark further points out that when God "called their name Adam" in Genesis 5:2, "the implication is clear: man was not complete without woman. 'Only through his wife,' wrote Rabbi Samson Raphael Hirsch, 'can man truly become 'man,' for 'only husband and wife together can comprise "Adam." The task is too great for either to perform and must therefore be shared by another.'"[20]

The clear implication of all this was that Adam and Eve were to remain together and to begin God's work of procreation, filling the earth with inhabitants according to God's injunction. Could they do this and remain in the Garden of Eden? We are told in the text, "Therefore shall a man leave his father and his mother, and shall cleave unto his wife: and they shall be one flesh." "Therefore" seems to mean, "In order to accomplish what you have been commanded to do, you have to make a few changes. You need to leave your father and mother."

But whose father and mother? I thought we hadn't had any childbirth yet. We've had man being "formed out of the dust of the earth" and the "build a bone" episode, but nothing about any father and mother. There must be something the Bible has failed to tell us.

Thank heaven for the restoration of ancient texts through modern revelation. Joseph Smith taught that Adam became "of dust a living soul" through being "*born* into the world by water, and blood, and the spirit," and that he must be born the second time by the same three elements.[21] So ends the mystery. Birth is the process of combining the elements of the earth into a living soul. Brigham Young emphasized this point when he said, "When you tell me that Father Adam was made as we make adobes from the earth, you tell me what I deem an idle tale. ... There is no such thing in all the eternities where the Gods dwell."[22] Adam "was made as you and I are made, and no person was ever made upon any other principle."[23] God "created man as we create our children, for there is no other process of creation in heaven, on the earth, in the earth, ... or in all the eternities."[24] The reality of Adam's formation by reproduction may be contained within the text itself, with the word *bara* being translated as "God *formed* man" in Genesis. Botterweck notes in his *Theological Dictionary of the Old Testament* that one of the translations of *bara* in the Septuagint (a Greek translation of the Hebrew Bible) is "to beget," and that the word *bara* may also be related to an Old South Arabic root whose meanings include "to bring forth" and "to give birth to."[25]

Procreation, the one divine power that God saw fit to share with mankind, could not happen in the Garden of Eden. Adam and Eve were not in a state where birth could take place. They were walking and talking with God on a daily basis in their Edenic existence, and yet they were told, "Therefore shall a man leave his father and his mother." How could that situation possibly be improved upon? What could be better than walking and talking with one's divine Father and Mother whenever you wanted? Apparently, something more was at stake. Leaving father and mother was even better than being with God. Many readers of this scripture in Genesis cannot explain it. But, having eyes that see, it is evident that it was Adam and Eve who left their father and mother in order to perform a greater work. They were told to "cleave" to each other and to become "one flesh." According to Strong's Lexicon, cleave means: "abide fast, cleave (fast together), follow close (hard after), be joined (together), keep (fast), overtake, pursue hard, and stick."[26] "One flesh" is the epitome of unity.

[1] Institute for Biblical and Scientific Studies, "Old Testament: Hebrew Text," accessed through http://www.bibleand science.com/bible/sources/hebrew.htm October 11, 2011.

[2] Matthew Henry, *Exposition of the Old and New Testaments (1708–1710)*, accessed through http://en.wikiquote.org/wiki/Matthew_Henry, November 12, 2011.

[3] Hayim Nahman Bialik and Yehoshua Hana Ravnitzky, editors, *The Book of Legends/Sefer Ha-Aggadah: Legends from the Talmud and Midrash*, (New York: Shocken Book, 1994) 19.

[4] Shira Halevi, *The Life Story of Adam and Havah: A New Targum of Genesis1:26-5:5*, (Northvale, New Jersey: Jason Aronson, Inc., 1997), 136.

[5] E. Douglas Clark, *Echoes of Eden: Eternal Lessons from Our First Parents*, (American Fork, Utah: Covenant Communications, 2010), 26.

[6] Ed Noort, "The Creation of Man and Woman in Biblical and Ancient Near Eastern Traditions," in Gerard P. Luttikhuizen, ed. *The Creation of Man and Woman: Interpretations of the Biblical Narratives in Jewish and Christian Traditions*, (Leiden: Brill, 2000), 11.

[7] Rosalyn Lacks, *Women and Judaism: Myth, History, and Struggle*, (Garden City, New York: Doubleday & Company, Inc., 1980), 28. See also Theodor Gaster, *Myth, Legend, and Custom in the Old Testament*, (New York: Harper and Row, 1969), 21.

[8] David M. Rohl, *Legend: The Genesis of Civilisation* [sic.], (London: Century, 1988), 210.

[9] Halevi (1997), 140.

[10] Ibid., 158–159.

[11] Ibid., 163.

[12] Leila Leah Bronner, *From Eve to Esther: Rabbinic Reconstructions of Biblical Women*, (Louisvill, Kentucky: Westminster John Knox Press, 1994), 30.

[13] Russell M. Nelson, "Lessons from Eve," *Ensign*, November 1987, 87.

[14] Gordon J. Wentham, *World Biblical Commentary Volume 1*, (Waco, Texas: Word Books, 1987), 71.

[15] Julie Beck, "Teaching the Doctrine of the Family," *Seminaries and Institutes of Religion Satellite Broadcast*, August 4, 2009.

[16] Biblical scholar Phyllis Trible writes: "Not only does the feminine *adamah* exist in the story prior to the masculine [word] *adam,* but also the latter comes out of the former. From this perspective the "female" both precedes the "male" and provides the material from which he is formed." Phyllis Trible, "Not a Jot, Not a Tittle: Genesis 2–3 After Twenty Years," in *Eve and Adam: Jewish, Christian, an Muslim readings on Genesis and Gender*, Edited by Kristen E. Kvam, Linda S. Schearing and Valarie H. Ziegler, (Bloomington: Indiana University Press, 1999), 440.

[17] See Halevi (1997), 145–147.

[18] Ibid., 148.

[19] Ibid., 149–150.

[20] Clark (2005), 37 quoting Samuel Raphael Hirsch in *T'rumath Tzvi*. Edited by Ephraim Oratz. Translated by Gertrude Hirschler. New York, The Judaica Press, 1986.

[21] See Moses 6:59.

[22] Brigham Young, *Journal of Discourses*, Volume 7, (London: Amasa Lyman, 1860), 285.

[23] Brigham Young, *Journal of Discourses*, Volume 3, Orson Pratt, ed., (London: Orson Pratt, 1856), 319.

[24] Brigham Young, *Journal of Discourses*, Volume 11, (London: B. Young, Jr., 1867), 122.

[25] *Theological Dictionary of the Old Testament, Volume II*, edited by G. Johannes Botterweck and Helmer Ringgren, (Grand Rapids, Michigan: William B. Eerdmans Publishing Company, 1975), 245.

[26] James Strong, *A Concise Dictionary of the Words in the Hebrew Bible* in *The Exhaustive Concordance of the Bible*, (Peabody, Massachusetts: Hendrickson Publishers, 1890), 29 entries 1692, 1693, and 1695.

Chapter 17
The Two Trees

Soon after Adam's creation, he is given stewardship over the Garden of Eden. He has free access to the myriad trees there and may partake of every fruit except one.

> And the Lord God took the man, and put him into the garden of Eden to dress it and to keep it. And the Lord God commanded the man, saying, Of every tree of the garden thou mayest freely eat: But of the tree of the knowledge of good and evil, thou shalt not eat of it: for in the day that thou eatest thereof thou shalt surely die. (Genesis 2:15–17)

And yet, God had commanded Adam to "multiply and replenish the earth" (Genesis 1:28). If the Hebrew text is examined grammatically, it is clear that the commandment not to eat of the fruit is directed to a second-person male: "you, man." From the rest of the chapter, it is evident that Eve does *know* about the commandment. It is undoubtedly relayed to her by Adam, who is only trying to protect her. However, it is obvious from the singular masculine pronouns used in the text that she is not present when the commandment is given. What are the ramifications of this realization? Why does God not wait until *after* Eve is created to give the commandment not to partake of the fruit of the tree?

For millennia, the world has blamed womankind for the consequences resulting from Eve's act in the Garden of Eden. They have assumed that if Eve had not partaken of the fruit, we would all be living in paradise. How wrong they were, on so many counts. As a graduate student at BYU, I took classes from a professor named Valerie M. Hudson who had joined the Church as a young adult. In *The Two Trees*, she relates that she had been taught many misconceptions about Eve from her youth. She grew up in a tradition where "the fact that Eve was created second was taken to mean that she was an appendage to Adam, that she was somehow inferior to Adam, that being derivative of Adam and not derivative of God, that she was two steps away from divinity, not one step as Adam was."[1]

Dr. Hudson suggests that Eve is created second in order to demonstrate Adam's helplessness before the first tree. She asks, "Could it be—two people, two trees—that Eve was foreordained to partake first of the First Tree?" She proposes that partaking of the fruit of the tree of knowledge of good and evil means "to enter into mortality with a mortal body, to enter into full agency, and to have awakened in us the light of Christ." She attributes the purposes of the two trees in the Garden of Eden to the different stewardships of men and women. "It is through women that souls journey to mortality and gain their agency, and in general it is through the nurturing of women ... that the light of Christ is awakened within each soul." Every soul born into mortality comes through a woman. Dr. Hudson goes on: "The fruit of the First Tree symbolizes the gift that women give to every soul that chooses the plan of Christ. It symbolizes the role and power of women in the Great Plan of Happiness. It was not, in this view, right or proper for Adam to partake first from the fruit of the First Tree. It was not his role to give the gift of the fruit of the First Tree to others. It is interesting to think that even Adam, who was created before Eve, entered into full mortality and full agency by accepting the gift of the First Tree from the hand of a woman. In a sense, Adam himself was born of Eve."[2]

While the rest of Christianity bemoans the moment Eve partook of the fruit, Dr. Hudson asks us to consider what we were doing when we, as pre-mortal spirits, watched the goings-on in Eden. She asks, "Are we saying, 'No, no, Mother Eve, don't partake! No, I can't look, don't partake!' Is that what we were doing? What do Latter-day Saints say? 'Mother Eve, please eat the fruit, please, please, please eat the fruit!' And when she did, are we crying and weeping? No, we're shouting and celebrating!" Dr. Hudson explains why she feels it was proper for women to open the door to mortality. She believes that the daughters of God were given at least a glimmer of what would befall them—including rape, forced marriage, sex trafficking, and being treated as chattel throughout much of human history. She feels that "if no *woman* was willing to open the door to mortal life and all that it would mean for women, I don't think it would have been opened, and that would only be just."[3]

Where does this leave Adam and his stewardship? Dr. Hudson asserts that Adam and the sons of Adam are given stewardship over the Second Tree, the Tree of Life. They are to administer all the ordinances and covenants that are necessary for the children of God to return home to their heavenly parents. She states, "Just as the veil into this life is guarded by the women, the daughters of God, so the veil that brings us home, is administered and guarded by the sons of God."

There are also two "hearkenings." "Just as Adam hearkened to Eve in partaking of the fruit of the First Tree, so Eve hearkened to Adam in accepting the fruit of the Second Tree."[4]

While this may seem clear and equitable as we read about these two separate but equal stewardships, in actuality, many of us are far removed from the drama of our births and appreciation for the gift of life we each received upon entering mortality. We are all anxiously engaged in staying on the strait and narrow path that leads to the Second Tree, the Tree of Life or eternal life. We see the sons of God who offer us the fruit of the Second Tree, the ordinances and covenants necessary to enter into God's presence. We see no daughters of God offering us these ordinances. However, we must not forget how we got here. It is important to step back and look again at the *whole* picture that includes both women *and* men. There are two trees and two stewardships. Both are necessary for God's plan to work.

So, how is it that Eve is able to partake of the tree first? We continue with the story in Genesis 3:1 which reads: "Now the serpent was more subtil [cunning][5] than any beast of the field which the Lord God had made. And he said unto the woman, Yea, hath God said, Ye shall not eat of every tree of the garden?" Unfortunately, this translation is ambiguous. Is the serpent saying that God said not to eat from *any* of the trees of the garden? Modern translations render this as "Did God really say, 'You must not eat from any tree in the garden?'"[6] The premise of this question is absolutely false, and Satan's motivation in asking it of Eve is to undermine her assurance that God has her best interests at heart. Eve responds that his assertion is false and that God has allowed them to eat from every tree but one, whose fruit would bring death. "And the woman said unto the serpent, We may eat of the fruit of the trees of the garden: But of the fruit of the tree which is in the midst of the garden, God hath said, Ye shall not eat of it, neither shall ye touch it, lest ye die" (Genesis 3:2–3).

We know from Eve's response to the serpent that she somehow knows about the directive not to eat from the tree of knowledge of good and evil. Adam must have decided to tell her about God's command. In fact, he adds an extra prohibition. He tells her that God commanded them not to even *touch* the fruit. Apparently, he was trying to put a fence around the law, thinking that if she did not touch the tree, she would not eat the fruit. Adam must have assumed that if the fruit would be deadly to him, it would have the same effect upon Eve. It must have seemed logical to him to warn her of its danger. Here, biblical scholar Shira Halevi alleges that Adam made two mistakes. First, he had no business adding to what God had told him, and second, he had no business passing this commandment on to Eve. It wasn't meant for her. She asserts, "It was no sin for her [Eve] to take this fruit for God did not command her not to eat it."[7]

Satan urges Eve to eat of the fruit by telling her that she will not die. Is this a lie? Yes, because she *will* become mortal and die, eventually. But it does not mean that she will die *immediately*, which is perhaps what she anticipated. "And the serpent said unto the woman, Ye shall not surely die: For God doth know that in the day ye eat thereof, then your eyes shall be opened, and ye shall be as gods, knowing good and evil" (KJV Genesis 3:4–5). Robert Alter comments on the grammatical syntax of this verse, saying, "the form of the Hebrew is … infinite absolute, the infinitive followed by the conjugated form of the same verb. … It is the pattern regularly used in the Bible for the issuing of death sentences. 'Doomed to die' is an appropriate equivalent.'"[8]

The *Armenian Apocrypha* adds an interesting element to this verse. Verse 4 reads, "The serpent spoke with Eve: '(That is) not so! God was a man like you. When he ate of the fruit of his tree he became God of all. Because of that God said to you not to eat, lest you become an equal God.'"[9]

The serpent insinuates that God is keeping something good from Eve because he does not want to share his glory as a god. Eve certainly has a lot to think about. She has trusted God implicitly, but this new information causes her to ponder on the tree and its merits. At some point she "saw that the tree was good for food, and that it was pleasant to the eyes, and a tree to be desired to make one wise" (KJV Genesis 3:6). Douglas Clark makes a noteworthy observation about this realization. "That Eve saw that it was good—even *before* she ate the fruit and her eyes were opened!—is a remarkable echo of what God himself had repeatedly done during creation when he surveyed his work and 'saw that it was good.' In Eve's 'seeing,' her godlike capacity was already being manifest."[10]

The serpent has been speaking to Eve, but he uses plural pronouns in addressing her about being "as gods." In an English translation, this is not apparent. He says "*Ye* (plural, man and woman) shall be as gods." I wonder how she thought that would come to pass. Perhaps she pondered the commandment to "multiply and replenish the earth." Clark asks, "Did she remember that the first commandment to multiply and replenish had been given to them both, but the second had come only directly to Adam? … Did she see that these two commandments were related? Did she begin to discern why the great gift of posterity had so far not been realized in the garden? Did she deduce that as long as they remained there, they could never keep the first great commandment?"[11]

Jewish scholar Shira Halevi reports that according to tradition, children were not conceived until after Adam and Eve ate of the tree of knowledge of good and evil, and that the bearing of children was one of the consequences of the Fall.[12] She suggests that this tree could have been called the Tree of Mortality, but that perhaps God wanted to emphasize the type of knowledge gained through mortality. She writes, "Remember, the Garden is also timeless. Without the progression of time, neither death nor birth can occur. Old age and fetal development, as well as the growth and maturity of a baby to adulthood, are all dependent on the forward movement of time—of days and months and years." It could also be argued that opposites did not exist in the garden. "Therefore birth and death, those extreme opposites of mortality, could not exist."[13]

Clark argues that Eve "knew that Adam had been placed in a situation in which he could not, without, Eve's help, achieve his potential, for the command not to eat the fruit had come only to him. It was up to her to take the step that Adam could not take. Only if she ate *first* would he have to eat in order to obey the first great command to multiply. She must eat so her husband could become what he had been created to be, the father of the human race. Eve must eat for his sake and for hers, for the sake of their marriage and mankind."[14]

And so, Eve "took of the fruit thereof, and did eat, and gave also unto her husband [who was] with her; and he did eat" (KJV Genesis 3:6b). We sometimes conveniently forget about Adam's presence during Eve's conversation with the serpent, although the text clearly states that he was "with her." As soon as Eve eats the fruit, she and Adam "were now drastically separated," notes Hugh Nibley, "for they were of different natures."[15] Eve takes action in her role as an *ezer*, a rescuer of the race of mankind. She takes the first step necessary to bring mankind into mortality. Now she needs to bring Adam along with her. Nibley describes how she accomplishes this:

> First she asked Adam if he intended to keep all of God's commandments. Of course he did! *All* of them? Naturally! And what, pray, was the first and foremost of those commandments? Was it not to multiply and replenish the earth, the universal commandment given to all God's creatures? And how could they keep that commandment if they were separated? It had undeniable priority over the commandment not to eat the fruit. So Adam could only admit that she was right and go along ... but it was she who made him see it. This is much more than a smart way of winning her point, however. It is the clear declaration that man and woman were put on the earth to stay together and have a family—that is their first obligation and must supersede everything else.[16]

Halevi offers an alternate translation of Genesis 3:6, derived from changing the vowels placed in the Hebrew text by the Masoretes. Previously, the Hebrew text had no vowels and was open to a variety of interpretations. The text reads

> beneficial to the (*ayin*) eyes
> > to the understanding
> desirable (*lehakasil*) for gaining wisdom
> The same phrases can be voweled differently to produce this translation:
> beneficial for the (*aiyeen*) springs (which is a metaphor for children)
> desirable above (*leshashakol*) grieving childlessness
> This kind of parallel would not be possible with other words for *barren*, because they do not share root letters with *wisdom*. Likewise, there are more common metaphors for children, but *aiyeen*/springs shares root letters with the word for eyes, which in turn means "wisdom."[17]

Halevi also notes that this reading fits the pattern of barrenness among the matriarchs in scripture. If the life stories of Eve and Adam, Sarah and Abraham, Rebecca and Isaac, and Rachel and Jacob are studied, the many common elements become apparent. "The inheritor of the birthright marries a woman of high standing in terms of kinship ties and social status. The couple enjoys comparative[ly] ideal living conditions: wealth, living conditions, and comely bodies. God promises, or in the case of Adam and [Eve], commands numerous posterity. The woman is afflicted with barrenness. In Sarah's case over seventy years, Rebecca suffered seventeen years of long-term infertility, while Rachel endured seven years."

She goes on to point out another element to this pattern, which is important in interpreting Eve's encounter with the serpent. "When it came to bearing and rearing children, the matriarchs took decidedly aggressive roles, while their husbands receded into the background as passive participants." For example, it is Sarah who insists that Abraham take a concubine so that she might be "built up" and obtain children by adoption. Rebekah determines the passage of the birthright through "manipulation, which neither Jacob nor Isaac protested with any strength or will power." Rachel and Leah vie for Jacob's sexual attentions as well as for fertility herbs. Similarly, Eve takes the initiative to "transform covenant promises into reality."[18]

This Jewish scholar might be surprised to learn that she has echoed the message of Relief Society General President Julie Beck. They both characterize these women as lionesses protecting their offspring and the covenant. Halevi notes that just as Adam discovers that paradise without woman was "not good" and lonely, so Eve discovers that paradise without children is incomplete and unfulfilling. Eve's motive is the same as Rachel's. "Give me a child! Give me a child or I shall die!" (Genesis 30:1) "She experiences a natural and universal feminine emotion—the hunger for a child. ... Barrenness conveys only a physical state of infertility. *Shakot*, on the other hand, is a uniquely feminine kind of grief, arising from the anguish of a woman bereaved of her children."[19]

Why did the serpent tempt Eve instead of Adam? Didn't the man have stewardship over all the earth? Halevi again unknowingly concurs with Dr. Hudson when she proposes that it is because Adam does not have the right to make that choice. Adam calls his wife "Eve," which is a derivative of the word for "life." She is the "mother of all living" (Genesis 3:20). She is the one who would bear the pain and most of the responsibility of childrearing. Eve would "bear the most painful and possibly fatal consequences of mortality. ... Adam had neither the right to hold back the means by which [Eve] could conceive life—for such action would be cruel to her natural desires—or to force her to bear children, for such action would unjustly subject her to the physical and emotional pain of bearing and rearing children without her consent." That is the reason why Adam is commanded not to eat the fruit. It is not *his* decision to make. Halevi asserts, "He [God] did not command the woman not to eat the fruit, for it was her right to eat or abstain. Adam remained silent because it was [Eve] who had the most to lose from eating the fruit that would make her mortal."[20]

Adam makes the conscious choice to leave the Garden of Eden in order to remain with Eve and to fulfill the commandment given by their Father to people the newly created earth. He unquestionably knows what he is doing in leaving paradise to come into the less friendly "world." Life outside the Garden of Eden will be fraught with challenges and heartache. His actions foreshadow the Savior's own actions in "leaving his throne to come to rescue mankind."[21]

Gary Anderson writes, "Adam's venturing forth from Eden to earth was typologically suggestive of the incarnation wherein God the Son left Heaven to come to earth to redeem humanity."[22]

No wonder it was likely Adam who, as an angel, came to strengthen the Savior in the Garden of Gethsemane.[23] (See Luke 22:43.) They were both willing to die so that mankind might live.

---

[1] Valerie M. Hudson, transcript of address given at FAIR Conference 2010, accessed at http://www.fairmormon.org/perspectives/fair-conferences/2010-fair-conference/2010-the-two-trees, November 21, 2014.

[2] Ibid.

[3] Ibid.

[4] Ibid.

[5] Robert Alter, *Genesis: Translation and Commentary*, (New York: W. W. Norton & Company, 1996), 11, fn. 1. "The kind of pun in which the ancient Hebrew writers delighted, 'arum, "cunning" plays against 'arumim, "naked" of the previous verse."

[6] *New International Version*, Genesis 3:1.

[7] Shira Halevi, *The Life Story of Adam and Havah: A New Targum of Genesis 1:26-5:5*, (Northvale, New Jersey: Jason Aronson Inc., 1997), 174–175.

[8] Alter (1996), 8 fn. 16–17.

[9] Michael E. Stone, editor and translator, *Armenian Apocrypha Relating to Adam and Eve*, (New York: E. J. Brill, 1996), 25.

An additional reference to man attaining godhood can be found in the Testament of Adam 3:2, in the *Old Testament Pseudepigrapha, Volume 1*, Edited by James H. Charlesworth, (New York: Doubleday, 1983), 994. God speaks to Adam after he partakes of the fruit saying, "Adam, Adam do not fear. You wanted to be a god. I will make you a god, not right now, but after a space of many years."

[10] E. Douglas Clark, *Echoes of Eden: Eternal Lessons From Our First Parents*, (American Fork, Utah: Covenant Communications, Inc., 2010), 53.

[11] Clark (2010), 54.

[12] See 2 Baruch 56:6 in *The Old Testament Pseudepigrapha, Volume 1*, Edited by James H. Charlesworth, (New York: Doubleday, 1983), 641.

[13] Halevi (1997), 180–181.

[14] Clark (2010), 54–55.

[15] Hugh Nibley, *Old Testament and Related Studies*, (Salt Lake City, Utah: Deseret Book Company, 1986). 88.

[16] Nibley (1986), 89.

[17] Halevi (1997), 185–186.

[18] Halevi (1997), 186–188.

[19] Halevi (1997), 189.

[20] Halevi (1997), 190–191.

[21] Clark (2010), 57.

[22] Gary A. Anderson, *The Genesis of Perfection: Adam and Eve in Jewish and Christian Imagination*, (Louisville: Westminster John Knox Press, 2001), 102.

[23] See Bruce R. McConkie, Ensign, April 1985.

"We know that he [Jesus] lay prostrate upon the ground as the pains and agonies of an infinite burden caused him to tremble and would that he might not drink the bitter cup. We know that an angel came from the courts of glory to strengthen him in his ordeal, and we suppose it was mighty Michael, who foremost fell that mortal man might be."

Chapter 18
The Consequences of Mortality

After Adam and Eve partook of the fruit of the tree of knowledge of good and evil,

> the eyes of them both were opened, and they knew that they were naked; and they sewed fig leaves together, and made themselves aprons. And they heard the voice of the Lord God walking in the garden in the cool of the day: and Adam and his wife hid themselves from the presence of the Lord God amongst the trees of the garden. And the Lord God called unto Adam, and said unto him, Where art thou? And he said, I heard thy voice in the garden, and I was afraid, because I was naked; and I hid myself. And he said, Who told thee that thou wast naked? Hast thou eaten of the tree, whereof I commanded thee that thou shouldest not eat? And the man said, The woman whom thou gavest to be with me, she gave me of the tree, and I did eat. And the Lord God said unto the woman, What is this that thou hast done? And the woman said, The serpent beguiled me, and I did eat. (KJV Genesis 3:7–13)

The Hebrew again makes clear with its use of masculine singular pronouns that it was only Adam who received the commandment not to eat of the fruit. This is not apparent in the English translation, because *thee* and *thou* can be interpreted as both singular and plural pronouns. Thankfully, the Hebrew leaves no doubt as to whom God refers.

Why did Eve say she was beguiled or tricked? Jewish scholar Shira Halevi provides enlightenment about this issue. Eve understands that partaking of the fruit will enable her and Adam to reproduce and to gain understanding, and that this is to be desired. However, she does not comprehend how this will come about. "The serpent lied to her when he said, 'You will not certainly die,' for she *would* most certainly die, and she would suffer much on the way to dying." He emphasized the advantages of eating the fruit, but downplayed the unpleasant consequences. Eve's response in Genesis 3:13 suggests another reason for the curse on Satan. The phrase *hi-shee-a-ni*—"he deceived me"—can also be read *hi-see-a-ni*—"he made me feel guilty/responsible."[1]

Reading the Hebrew letter as a *sin* instead of a *shin*—which is entirely allowable—alters the meaning substantially. Now, Satan lays the responsibility for Adam and Eve's childlessness on Eve, "blaming her for their failure to keep the first commandment given to them by the Lord, to multiply themselves and fill the earth with sons and daughters."[2]

Halevi suggests that Adam and Eve have entered a new phase of their existence as their eyes are opened. They have symbolically left their "Garden existence" and have moved forward into a new stage of mortality. "The Garden can symbolize several ideas simultaneously, ... [the] idea of a holy place where humanity lives in the presence of God, or [the] idea of the biological and mental state of childhood."[3]

Our parents have left their childhood behind and are now ready to move forward to fulfill their appointed stewardship. God informs them of the consequences of living in the state of mortality that they have just entered. He first deals with the serpent.

> And the Lord God said unto the serpent, Because thou hast done this, thou art cursed above all cattle, and above every beast of the field; upon thy belly shalt thou go, and dust shalt thou eat all the days of thy life: And I will put enmity between thee and the woman, and between thy seed and her seed; it shall bruise thy head, and thou shalt bruise his heel. Unto the woman he said, I will greatly multiply thy sorrow [*itsabon*] and thy conception; in sorrow thou shalt bring forth children; and thy desire shall be to thy husband, and he shall rule over thee. And unto Adam he said, Because thou hast hearkened unto the voice of thy wife, and hast eaten of the tree, of which I commanded thee, saying, Thou shalt not eat of it: cursed is the ground for thy sake; in sorrow [*itsabon*] shalt thou eat of it all the days of thy life; Thorns also and thistles shall it bring forth to thee; and thou shalt eat the herb of the field; In the sweat of thy face shalt thou eat bread, till thou return unto the ground; for out of it wast thou taken: for dust thou art, and unto dust shalt thou return (KJV Genesis 3:14–19).

These verses are brimming with information to be unpacked and digested. First of all, notice that in doling out curses, the Lord never uses the word *aror*—*curse*—when referring to Adam or Eve. He curses the serpent and the earth, but not the man or the woman. His words to them are merely descriptions of what mortal life will be like. The same Hebrew word is used in describing the consequences of mortality for *both* Adam and Eve. In sorrow (*itsabon*) will Adam eat the fruit of the ground for the rest of his life. No more random picking of self-springing pomegranates and mangoes. He will have to *labor* and *toil*, the definition of *itsabon*.[4]

Likewise, Eve will have to *labor* to bring forth children, that is a given. Whoever brought forth a child without going through labor? (Excepting the emergency Caesarean section, of course.) Labor is work. It doesn't make you "sorrow"-ful, but you do have to work. That's what God is saying. Earth life takes work. But it will be good for your character. When God tells Eve that he will "multiply" her labor when bearing a child, he does not mean he will increase her pain, but that she will bear multiple children. She will conceive and labor over and over in bringing forth the children of the earth. This is a *good* thing. She *wants* to be the mother of all living. Both Adam and Eve will bring forth life with sweat and tears.

Halevi offers an alternate reading of Genesis 3:18.

Masoretic Reading
Thorns
and thistles
will she (the earth) sprout for you
and you will eat grain
of the plowed field

Alternate Reading
Awake! Arise!
Generation upon generation
will she (Eve) spring for you
and you will enjoy the yield
of her breast.[5]

Halevi defends her translation: "This partnership consists of three parts: two readings of 3:18 and 3:20. Verse 20 is the strongest evidence that a double reading of 3:18 is not only feasible, but indispensable. ... Without the double reading, 3:20 makes no sense whatsoever. ... God informs Adam that he will live a miserable life and then die. Immediately after that grim pronouncement, Adam jumps for joy and calls his wife 'Life' because 'she was Mother to all living.'" Halevi contends that such a reaction on Adam's part would be impossible to understand without the meaning supplied by this alternate translation. It would be a *non sequitur* that would make no sense whatsoever. The reader can easily discern the causal link between Adam's exclamation of praise and the promise made to him that Eve will bear him generations of posterity.[6]

This passage has a familiar feel to it. It brings to mind the Abrahamic Covenant, with its "promise of a multitude of seed and the subsequent renaming of Sarah as the mother of nations," Halevi notes. "Acknowledging the source of a patriarch's greatness, namely his queenly companion, his life-giver, Havah [Eve] and Adam, like Sarah and Abraham, would achieve greatness together as a couple, through the painful toil of mortality and the life-nurturing task of begetting and rearing children."[7]

If we step back and look at the history of the world, God has always depended on a righteous couple to pass along the covenant. He started with Adam and Eve, then again with Noah and his wife. Abraham would not have been the man he was without his righteous Sarah, and passing on the covenantal power follows with their son Isaac and grandson Jacob, who seek wives who understand the covenant and value it. They know that worthy women are essential to the passing along of the covenant.

Sherrie Johnson provides some exciting insights into the naming of Eve. She points out that "Adam called Eve the mother of *all* living (not just the mother of mankind, but the mother of all living) before she ever had children." At the time he names her the mother of all living, the only living beings besides the two of them are animals. "By partaking of the forbidden fruit, Eve initiated the change from an immortal Edenic state to the mortal state we now call life. Perhaps the name 'mother of all living' has reference to this 'birth' process." Johnson notes that we learn much from what Adam names Eve, but what Adam does *not* name Eve is also significant. "He does not name her anything to do with himself. He does not name her 'my help meet' or 'my servant' or 'the mother of my children.' The choice of name indicates that Eve was recognized as a separate individual with a mission and talents and their oneness would come about by adding to each other."[8]

In Genesis 3:16, God says to Eve that her "desire will be to [her] husband," and that he will "rule over [her]." In English this comes across as the description of a master and his slave. She will have to fulfill her lord and master's every desire, and he will rule over her with an iron fist. But the Hebrew does not say this. The word translated as "desire" is from the Hebrew word *teshuqah*, which has the sense of "stretching out after," or "a longing."⁹ This is how a woman feels about a man who treats her like a queen. Her heart "longs" for him, and she "stretches out after" trying to please. It does *not* sound like a woman who is treated as chattel by her husband. God is telling Eve that if she is one with her husband, then he will treat her like royalty.

In the phrase translated "he shall rule over thee," the Hebrew conveys a very different meaning. It says "he shall rule *bak*," which is the preposition *b-* attached to the feminine pronoun for "you." When I learned Hebrew, I was taught that there is a scarcity of prepositions in the Hebrew language. *L-* attached to the beginning of a word meant "to" or "for," *c-* meant "like" or "as," and *b-* meant "in," "with," or "by." There is another preposition—*al*—that stands by itself and means a lot of things, but mostly "upon" or "over." The preposition *b-* in this phrase should read, "and he shall rule *with* you." Other places in the Bible translate *b-* before *rule* as "rule over," but it is clearly talking about a king and his subjects, or one people ruling over another. God has gone out of his way in this chapter and the ones before it to emphasize how the woman is to be an "equal" to the man—a "power" exactly corresponding to him. Together they are to have "dominion" over the earth and populate it. Eve will rule over this newly-created world *with* her husband. She will be his *ezer*—his rescuer, his deliverer, his strength. Elder Bruce Hafen of the Seventy concurs with this interpretation, teaching that the King James translation of Genesis 3:16 ("and he shall rule over thee") is a *mis*translation. In Hafen's words, "*over* in 'rule over' uses the Hebrew *bet*, which means ruling *with*, not ruling over."¹⁰ Elder L. Tom Perry puts the icing on the cake when he tells us, "there is not a president and a vice president in a family. We have co-presidents working together eternally for the good of their family. ... They are on equal footing. They plan and organize the affairs of the family jointly and unanimously as they move forward."¹¹

Carolyn Custis James, writing about the military connotations of the word *ezer* in the Bible (where God acts an *ezer* in coming to the aid of his people in battle) has this to say:

> The military language associated with the word *ezer* ties the same bold imagery to the strong helper (the words used in modern Bible translations for "help meet"). She is a valiant warrior conscripted by God, not to fight against the man but to fight at his

side as his greatest ally in the war to end all wars. Even before the creation, the battle lines were drawn between God and the powers of darkness. In the Garden, God wasn't weaving a great romance. He was building an army, and the enemy was waiting to launch his first assault. Adam and Eve were not simply our first parents. They were God's first recruits, and both of them would soon be in the line of fire. Their mission was overwhelming - more than the two of them could handle together, much less face alone. They would need each other, not just for the sake of company but for strength to fight the battle that lay ahead. ... *Both* were created in the image of God. ... *Both* were commissioned to multiply and fill the earth. As co-regents, *both* were called to subdue and rule the creation. The scope of their joint mission encompassed the whole earth and every sphere of life.[12]

Together, Adam and Eve labored to pass the covenant on to their children. Their call was not just to fill the earth with human beings, but to fill it with people who worshipped God and kept the covenant. That was the purpose of their creation. Eve stands as a lioness in protecting her family from the powers of darkness. But neither Adam nor Eve could fulfill their stewardships without each other. James asserts

> If there is one message in the story of creation, it is that we all need human help. When God raised the problem of Adam's aloneness, he never said, "I am all you need." Instead of giving Adam a lecture on contentment, or a sermon on God's sufficiency, God formed a woman—a tangible, flesh and blood human being—to come alongside and, in her own imperfect way, to enter his struggles. ... But women aren't better suited to cope with aloneness than the man was. Everyone needs an *ezer*. ... It is something all Christians are called to do for one another.[13]

---

[1] Shira Halevi, *The Life Story of Adam and Havah: A New Targum of Genesis 1:26-5:5*, (Northvale, New Jersey: Jason Aronson Inc., 1997), 210.

[2] Halevi (1997), 210–211.

[3] Halevi (1997), 197.

[4] James Strong, *A Concise Dictionary of the Hebrew Bible With Their Renderings in the Authorized English Version*, in *Strong's Exhaustive Concordance of the Bible*, (Peabody, Massachusetts: Hendrickson Publishers, 1881), 90, entry #6093 *itsabon*.

5 Halevi (1997), 232.

6 Halevi (1997), 232–233.

7 Halevi (1997), 233.

8 Sherrie Johnson, *Man, Woman, and Diety*, (Salt Lake City, Utah: Bookcraft, 1991), 18.

9 Strong's Concordance, p.126, entry # 8669 *teshuqah*.

10 Bruce C. Hafen and Marie K. Hafen, "Crossing Thresholds and Becoming Equal Partners," *Ensign*, August 2007, 24–29.

11 L. Tom Perry, *Church News*, 10 April 2004:15.

12 Carolyn Custis James, *When Life and Beliefs Collide: How Knowing God Makes a Difference*, (Grand Rapids, Michigan: Zondervan Publishing House, 2001), 187–188.

13 James (2001), 197.

Chapter 19
Conclusion

We have explored the lives of matriarchs of the Old Testament in detail, gleaning insights from the scriptures and other parabiblical sources. We have reconsidered and expounded the stories of Abraham and Sarah, Isaac and Rebecca, and Jacob and the sister-wives Rachel and Leah. We have focused on their singular mission—to accept and transmit the covenant with God.

I am grateful for the "benefit" (see D&C 91:5) I have received from reading the expanded stories of the matriarchs from these non-canonical sources. I am so grateful for the Spirit that enables me to recognize the truth wherever it may be found.

The bestowal of the covenant and the transmission of that covenant to the next generation is so crucial to the establishment of a holy people that it occupies over half the pages in the book of Genesis. The patriarchs—Abraham, Isaac, and Jacob—received the covenant, but the difficulty of passing it on required the presence of righteous women. Sarah, Rebekah, Rachel, and Leah play major roles in successfully transmitting the indispensable covenant.

Sarah emerges from the pages of Genesis as a noble pillar of strength, not one whit behind Abraham in spreading the doctrine of the one true God and nurturing all who cross her path. She joins her husband in fostering the covenant in Isaac, and in making sure that he is given a righteous companion to advance the cause of transmitting the covenant.

Rebekah is no less pivotal in passing the covenant forward. She has the vision and the resolve to ensure that the birthright passes to worthy Jacob, not to faithless Esau. She takes it upon herself to personally converse with God when she senses something amiss in her pregnancy. She takes action based on her own firsthand revelation to ensure that the son destined by God receives the covenant blessing. She influences Isaac to bless Jacob and send him to a land where he can find a righteous wife who will pass the covenant on to the next generation.

Rachel, too, is obsessed with the concept of succession. Rachel's love story in the book of Genesis is unparalleled in biblical history—indeed in much of world literature. But even possessing the love of an adoring husband cannot fill her emptiness without a child. The focus of her life is evident in the name she chooses for her firstborn son—Joseph, which signifies "he will add." She desires that God will yet "add another" son to her posterity.

We have learned much from the example of Eve, the first woman. She is the primordial example of the meaning and purpose of womanhood. From the narrative surrounding her creation, we learn the purpose and destiny a loving Father has designed for each of his daughters. Sheri Dew notes, "Eve set the pattern. In addition to bearing children, she mothered all of mankind when she made the most courageous decision any woman has ever made and with Adam opened the way for us to progress." She set the example of ideal womanhood, "modeling the characteristics with which we as women have been endowed: heroic faith, a keen sensitivity to the Spirit, an abhorrence of evil, and complete selflessness. Like the Savior, 'who for the joy that was set before him endured the cross,' Eve, for the joy of helping initiate the human family, endured the Fall. She loved us enough to help lead us."[1]

Much like the miner in Boyd K. Packer's poem, collecting nugget after nugget in order to find gold, we have explored many facets in the lives of the matriarchs. I would like to ask a question coined by President Packer. After listening to a person give a presentation or lesson, he would often ask, "Therefore what?" With all this information we have gained, what difference will it make in our lives? When I get up in the morning, how will the choices I make be different? How will my relationships with those around me be different? How has my intimate acquaintance with the matriarchs affected the way I view the world? How will this knowledge make me a better person? How will it help me on my quest for exaltation? Only by emulating the qualities we admire in these women of faith and initiative will our lives be edified. What did these women do that made them indispensable to their husbands? Let us explore a few ideas.

Glen L. Pace perceives, "Men and women can accomplish marvelous things alone. However, they are incomplete until united intellectually, emotionally, physically, and, most important, spiritually. ... Since melding our divine natures is a necessary element in bringing about perfection, we must guard against any deterioration of those natures." Elder Pace warns women to avoid anything that detracts from their divine natures. "You live in a time when you have more opportunities and options available to you than any other women have had throughout the history of mankind. Some of these options will complement your God-given natures. Others will chip away at it. Some things will make you strong. Others will make you hard. Some will increase your spiritual sensitivity. Others will separate you from the Spirit. If the world keeps chipping away at the divine nature of women, it is probable that our relationships in marriage will not bring about the sanctification necessary for exaltation or, as a minimum, the process will be delayed." He elaborates on the fact that women must fulfill their divine design in order to be powerful. He concludes, "I testify that when you stand in front of your heavenly parents in those royal courts on high and look into Her eyes and behold Her countenance, any question you ever had about the role of women in the kingdom will evaporate into the rich celestial air, because at that moment you will see standing directly in front of you, your divine nature and destiny."[2]

According to Elder Pace, "melding our divine natures is a necessary element in bringing about perfection." These natures are complementary to each other and absolutely necessary in creating the perfection worthy of exaltation.

Richard G. Scott has said, "In the Lord's plan, it takes two—a man and a woman—to form a whole. Indeed, a husband and wife are not two identical halves, but a wondrous, divinely determined combination of complementary capacities and characteristics."[3]

Each of these women was the completion of the whole in combination with her husband. Adam could not have been the father of mankind without Eve, nor could she be the "mother of all living" without him. Abraham could not have fulfilled the covenant to bless all the families of the earth without Sarah. Without Rebekah, there would have been no house of Israel. She worked with her husband to ensure that the precious covenant would be passed on to a righteous generation. Rachel and Leah were the matriarchs of the house of Israel. Jacob relied on their righteous support to reinforce his faith in preparing to pass on the precious covenant.

These noble women have taught us many lessons: how to go on when some major piece of our lives is missing or broken, how to put our lives on hold and wait for the Lord to finally come through for us.

While nothing is too hard for the Lord, he's not afraid to keep us waiting. Can we faithfully endure the waiting game? How much of our lives are lived in the interlude, waiting for what we think we want to finally come. We will be happy "as soon as" we graduate, "as soon as" we get married, "as soon as" we have a baby, "as soon as" the baby grows up, "as soon as" we get a house, "as soon as" our career takes off. Carolyn Custis James asks, "What do we do in those long stretches when life comes to a standstill because of God's silence, when day after day you're looking at the same problems, the same unchanged heart, the same unhealed body? It's the hardest thing we ever do."[4]

I ask myself, "Can I live according to the scripture, 'Be still, and know that I am God'"?[5] Can I live in the silence? Can I "walk by faith, and not by sight?"[6] I look to Sarah who waited eighty-nine years before discovering God's purpose for her life.

Sheri Dew provides another insight into our destiny as women. In her discourse titled, "Are We Not All Mothers," she proposes that, as women, we are God's "secret weapon."

> As mothers in Israel, we are the Lord's secret weapon. Our influence comes from a divine endowment that has been in place from the beginning. In the premortal world, when our Father described our role, I wonder if we didn't stand in wide-eyed wonder that He would bless us with a sacred trust so central to His plan and that He would endow us with gifts so vital to the loving and leading of His children. I wonder if we shouted for joy at least in part because of the ennobling stature He gave us in His kingdom. The world won't tell you that, but the Spirit will.[7]

We have received a noble legacy from Eve, Sarah, Rebekah, Rachel, and Leah. We know the purpose for which we were created. The Lord knew that "it is not good for man to be alone." We have learned that men and women require each other in order to become a perfect whole, as "melding our divine natures is a necessary element in bringing about perfection." Women were created to become *ezer*s to their husbands, and by extension, to all those around them. *Ezer* carries the connotation of both "to be strong," and "to save." As women, we can provide strength and "save the day" for those with whom we associate. Men and women are each given divine stewardships to bring the Lord's plan to fruition. Neither can do it without the other. Both are absolutely necessary and indispensable to God. Both are needed to guarantee that God's covenant, as first revealed to Abraham, will be passed on to the next generation. The Lord needs women who know their responsibilities in the house of Israel and who act accordingly.

As Julie Beck stated, "The Lord is depending on millions of Rebekahs to understand their place in carrying on the blessings of the House of Israel." She could have said "millions of Sarahs," or "millions of Rachels," or "millions of Leahs." Each of these women recognized what God's will was for her family and she acted upon it. Having the spirit means knowing God's will and doing it. This is the power of personal revelation. The lioness at the gate of her home or kingdom ensures that the covenant will be carried forth within the walls of that home or kingdom. If that lioness at the gate is aware of the mission of the House of Israel, then that mission will go forward. It is our privilege today to be part of the House of Israel. We need to be lionesses.

---

[1] Sheri L. Dew, "Are We Not All Mothers," *Ensign*, November 2001.

[2] Glen L. Pace, "The Divine Nature and Destiny of Women," *Brigham Young University 2009–2010 Speeches*, given 9 March 2010.

[3] Richard G. Scott, "The Joy of Living the Great Plan of Happiness," *Ensign*, November 1996, 73–74.

[4] Carolyn Custis James, *Lost Women of the Bible*, (Grand Rapids, Michigan: Zondervan, 2005), 78.

[5] See D&C 110:16 and Psalm 46:10.

[6] See 2 Cor. 5:7

[7] Sheri L. Dew, "Are We Not All Mothers," Ensign, November 2001.

Glossary

Alshich Moshe Alshich (1508–1593 AD) was a prominent rabbi, preacher, and biblical commentator in the sixteenth century. He was born in Turkey, but later moved to Safed in northern Israel. His commentaries on the Torah are popular and still studied today, largely because of their powerful influence as practical exhortations to a virtuous life.

Apocrypha That which is "hidden away" or "concealed." *Apocryphon* is the singular noun, and *apocrypha* the plural. These words are used to describe the nature of a certain body of ancient religious writings. *Apocrypha* originally meant "a writing too sacred and secret to be in everyone's hands." It needed to be hidden away and reserved for the spiritually mature. It was a term of dignity and respect. To those who revered the apocryphal books, they were "hidden" because they contained teachings that were too sacred to be revealed except to the initiated.

Abrabanel Isaac ben Judah Abrabanel (1437–1508 AD) was a Portuguese Jewish statesman, biblical commentator, and philosopher. He was well versed in rabbinic literature and Jewish philosophy. He also showed a great mastery of financial matters and was employed by King Afonso V of Portugal as treasurer.

Babylonian captivity This term refers to the deportation and exile of the residents of Judah to Babylon in 587 BC by Nebuchadnezzar II. It coincided with the destruction of the monarchy and the Temple of Solomon. After the overthrow of Babylon by the Persian Empire, the Persian ruler Cyrus the Great gave the Jews permission to return to their homeland and rebuild the temple in 539 BC.

Book of Jubilees Also known as "the Little Genesis" and "The Apocalypse of Moses," this book is attributed to the hand of Moses himself, penned while he was on Mount Sinai as it was dictated by an angel of God. The book is told from the viewpoint of the angel and unfolds heaven's view of history. The text covers the creation of man, Adam's fall from grace, and goes on to fill in many details of Israel's history.

Canon "Canon" comes from the Hebrew word *kanah*, which means "reed." Reeds were originally used as measuring sticks. Thus, *canon* designates the "standard" or the "rule." "Canonical" works are those deemed to be reliable as statements of doctrine and faith. Apocryphal literature is therefore called "non-canonical" or "extracanonical."

Extracanonical Those works that are not found within the accepted scriptures of a religion.

Ibn Ezra Rabbi Abraham Ben Meir Ibn Ezra (1089–1164 AD) was one of the most distinguished Jewish men and writers in the Middle Ages. Ibn Ezra excelled in philosophy, astronomy, poetry, linguistics, and biblical exegesis. He left Spain in 1140 AD to escape persecution of the Jews by the Berber-Muslim dynasty, known as the Almohads. He led a life of restless wandering which took him to Northern Africa, Egypt, the land of Israel, Rome, Verona, France, and England. There is a legend that he died in England from fever and a sickness which came upon him after an encounter with a pack of wild black dogs.

Intertestamental period A term used to refer to a period between the writings of canonical Old and New Testament texts, spanning the ministry of Malachi and John the Baptist. Traditionally, it is considered to be roughly a four hundred year period. During this time, many non-canonical texts were written.

Josephus A first-century Jewish historian who survived and recorded the destruction of Jerusalem in 70 AD. His two most important works are *The Jewish War* (c. 75 AD) and *Antiquities of the Jews* (c. 94 AD). *Antiquities of the Jews* recounts the history of the world from a Jewish perspective. His works give an important insight into first-century Judaism.

Midrash An ancient commentary on part of the Hebrew scriptures that is based on Jewish methods of interpretation and attached to the biblical text.

Midrash Rabbah This term can refer to part of or the collective whole of commentaries on the Hebrew Bible, having "Rabbah"—meaning "great"—as part of their names, i.e. *Genesis Rabbah*, *Exodus Rabbah*, etc.

Mishna The Mishnah is a major work of Rabbinic Judaism, and the first major redaction into written form of Jewish oral traditions, called the Oral Torah.

Netziv Naftali Zvi Yehuda Berlin (1816–1893 AD) was born in Russia and died in Poland. He is also known as Reb Hirsch Leib Berlin, and commonly known by the acronym Netziv. He was an Orthodox rabbi, dean of the Volozhin Yeshiva, and author of several works of rabbinic literature in Lithuania.

Ohr Hachayim Chaim ben Moses ibn Attar (1696–1743 AD), after his popular commentary on the Pentateuch, was a Talmudist and a kabbalist. He was one of the most prominent rabbis in Morocco until he left to settle in Jerusalem. He was received with great honor wherever he traveled because of his extensive knowledge, keen intellect, and extraordinary piety.

Pirke de-Rabbi Eliezer, chap. XII A medieval composition by an anonymous commentator between 600–900 AD, printed in Constantinople in 1514. The author attributed his work to the famous tanna Rabbi Eliezer, son of Hyrkanos (Eliezer the Great) who lived in the latter half of the first century AD.

Pseudepigrapha Falsely attributed works, texts whose claimed authorship is unfounded, whose real author attributed it to a figure from the past. "Pseudepigrapha" is from the Greek *pseudes*, meaning "false," and *epigraph*, meaning "inscription." Thus, a widely accepted but incorrect attribution of authorship may make a perfectly authentic text pseudepigraphical. In religious studies, the Pseudepigrapha are Jewish works written between 200 BC and 200 AD, not all of which are literally pseudepigraphical.

Pseudo-Philo The author of the pseudepigraphical work *Biblical Antiquities*. It a retelling of the stories in the Old Testament that reflects Jewish legend and tradition as they existed in the first century. The author probably lived in Palestine and wrote in Hebrew.

Rabbi Samson Raphael Hirsch German Rabbi Hirsch (1808–1888 AD) was best known as the intellectual founder of the Torah im Derech Eretz school of contemporary Orthodox Judaism. Occasionally termed Neo-Orthodoxy, his philosophy—together with that of Azriel Hildesheimer—has had a considerable influence on the development of Orthodox Judaism. He wrote a number of influential books, and for a number of years published the monthly journal *Jeschurun*, in which he outlined his philosophy of Judaism. He was a vocal opponent of Reform Judaism, and similarly opposed early forms of Conservative Judaism.

Rabbinic literature In its broadest sense, rabbinic literature can refer to the entire spectrum of rabbinic writings throughout Jewish history, but the term often refers to literature from the Talmudic era—the first five centuries—as opposed to medieval or modern rabbinic writing.

Ramban Nahmanides (1194–1270 AD)—also known as Rabbi Moses ben Nahman of Girondi, Spain, and by his acronym Ramban—was a leading medieval Jewish scholar, rabbi, philosopher, physician, kabbalist, and biblical commentator.

Rashi Solomon Isaac (1040–1105 AD), today generally known by the acronym Rashi, was a medieval French rabbi, long highly esteemed as a major contributor to Torah study. He is famed as the author of a comprehensive commentary on the Talmud, as well as a comprehensive commentary on the Tanakh (Hebrew Bible). He is considered the "father" of all commentaries on the Talmud that followed. Acclaimed for his ability to present the basic meaning of the text in a concise, lucid fashion, Rashi appeals to both learned scholars and beginning students, and his works remain a centerpiece of contemporary Jewish study.

The Rav Rabbi Joseph Ber Soloveitchik (1903–1993 AD) was an American Orthodox rabbi, Talmudist, and modern Jewish philosopher. He is widely viewed as having advocated a synthesis between Torah scholarship and Western, secular scholarship as well as positive involvement with the broader community. He served as an advisor, guide, mentor, and role-model for tens of thousands of Jews.

Redaction In the study of literature, "redaction" is a form of editing in which multiple source texts are combined together (redacted) and subjected to minor alteration to make them into a single work. Often this is a method of collecting a series of writings on a similar theme and creating a definitive and coherent work.

Septuagint The oldest Greek version of the Old Testament, or simply "LXX." It is said to have been translated from the Hebrew by Jewish scholars at the request of Ptolemy II. The translation was done in Alexandria, Egypt, and was completed about 250 BC. Because of the Jewish diaspora or "scattering," there were thousands of Jews who could no longer read the Hebrew scriptures. This translation was made to accommodate their needs.

Sforno Obadiah ben Jacob Sforno (1475–1550 AD) was an Italian rabbi, biblical commentator, physician, and philosopher. The characteristic features of his work are respect for the literal meaning of the text and a reluctance to entertain mystical interpretations.

Talmud "Talmud" is from a Hebrew root which means "to teach, to study." The Talmud is a record of rabbinic discussions pertaining to Jewish law, ethics, customs, and history. Over the centuries, the opinions of various rabbis were transmitted orally and later recorded. After the Jewish temple was destroyed in 70 AD, Judaism faced a crisis. The old system of oral scholarship could not be maintained, because the temple no longer existed as a center for learning and discussion. During this period, rabbinic discourse began to be recorded in writing. The Babylonian Talmud was compiled about 500 AD. The Jerusalem Talmud predates its counterpart by two hundred years.

Targum When the Jews returned from the Babylonian captivity to Jerusalem to rebuild their temple, they spoke the *lingua franca* of Babylon, which was Aramaic. Although Aramaic was a cousin to Hebrew, the Jews could no longer understand the Hebrew scriptures when the scribes read them aloud. The scribes had to explain the meaning of the Hebrew words to the people, and their interpretations reflect the way the scriptures were understood at the time. These explanations were called *targums,* and were written down and collected during the following centuries.

Torah "The Law," the first five books of Moses: Genesis, Exodus, Leviticus, Numbers, Deuteronomy.

About the Author

Diana Webb was born and raised in Salt Lake City, Utah. She graduated from the University of Utah in 1972 with a degree in English Education, and earned a MA from BYU in 1994 in Ancient Near Eastern Studies. She has taught Institute at Salt Lake Community College and LDS Business College for twenty years. She is the author of *Forgotten Women of God*. She and her husband currently live in Sandy, Utah.

Made in the USA
San Bernardino, CA
30 November 2015